The New Broadway Song Companion

An Annotated Guide to Musical Theatre Literature by Voice Type and Song Style

David P. DeVenney

THE SCARECROW PRESS, INC.
Lanham • Toronto • Plymouth, UK
2009

Published by Scarecrow Press, Inc.
A wholly owned subsidary of The Rowman & Littlefield Publishing Group, Inc.
4501 Forbes Boulevard, Suite 200, Lanham, Maryland 20706
http://www.scarecrowpress.com

Estover Road, Plymouth PL6 7PY, United Kingdom

British Library Cataloguing in Publication Information Available

Library of Congress Cataloging-in-Publication Data
DeVenney, David P., 1958–
  The new Broadway song companion : an annotated guide to musical theatre literature
by voice type and song style / David P. DeVenney.
    p. cm.
  Rev. ed. of: The Broadway song companion. 1998.
  Includes indexes.
  ISBN 978-0-8108-6943-1 (cloth : alk. paper) — ISBN 978-0-8108-6944-8 (ebook)
  1. Musicals–Bibliography. 2. Popular music–Bibliography. 3. Voice types (Singing)–
Handbooks, manuals, etc. I. DeVenney, David P., 1958– Broadway song companion.
II. Title.
  ML128.M78D48 2009
  016.7821'4–dc22   2009011424

♾™ The paper used in this publication meets the minimum requirements of American
National Standard for Information Sciences—Permanence of Paper for Printed Library
Materials, ANSI/NISO Z39.48-1992. Printed in the United States of America.

The first edition for Bob,
and this one for
Kelly and Johnny

Contents

Preface to the Revised Edition

Since this volume was first published, around thirteen years ago, the Broadway musical has undergone significant change. Shows are now written that are qualitatively different from those penned during Broadway's golden age. Book shows are still common, but they are increasingly joined by shows centering around a concept, shows that have virtually no narrative component, and revues (although there is a long history of the latter on the Great White Way).

These changes and adaptations to the traditional Broadway show have found their way into this revised volume. One of the more notable differences over the past fifteen to twenty years is that the ranges for the singers have become more uniform. Most roles now are written for mezzo sopranos and high baritones, while roles for true sopranos are much rarer. There are still some roles for high tenor voices, but many fewer than there used to be. No longer are characters separated dramatically by their voice ranges, as was once common.

Many shows have also become more realistic in their dramatic approach, and this has resulted in fewer character and comedic roles. Likewise, in their musical construction, many musicals have moved away from set numbers, in favor of longer, through-composed scenes (similar to the change in opera literature from Mozart to Puccini). These scenes change tempo and character throughout. While that makes them more dramatically plausible, it also makes these scenes more difficult to characterize. So I have added the new designation of "scene" to describe these numbers.

As with the previous edition, nearly all of the shows annotated in this volume have been produced on Broadway, although many popular shows were first produced in London, in America's regional theatres, or off-Broadway in New York. I have annotated some non-Broadway musicals when, in my opinion, they have become popular and widely produced. An obvious example of such a show is Disney's *High School Musical*.

I have quoted the vocal ranges for each number in this volume following the same practice I used earlier. However, these ranges may no longer matter. Many shows now come with a notice in the front of the conductor's score that invites the music director to order a number in any key. In this day of computer-generated scores, this is easy to do and quite handy. Thus, the day of having to sing a certain song in a given key in a show may be over—no matter what that may do to the scheme of key relationships a composer has carefully crafted for his or her show!

As before, I have categorized each number according to its song style. The vast majority of these numbers are not given a tempo marking by the composer (an English or Italian word), and almost none are supplied with metronome markings. The style designations, then, are my impressions and as such may be subject to varying interpretation. The Guide to Use gives a brief description of my usage of various terms and indicators. In the indexes, I have included a song in both the "uptempo" and "ballad" categories if I feel that it straddles the line, based on how a singer might possibly interpret it.

A number of people have been helpful to me in compiling this new edition and I wish to thank them here. Jarred Matthes was the catalyst for updating this volume, and Bob Cline, Kelly Martin, Johnny Steiner, and David DeCooman all helped, suggested, pushed, and prodded when I needed it.

Foreword

This book began as a private resource for myself and my students and eventually evolved into the volume that you find in your hands. For twelve years I served on the music faculty at Otterbein College, where many of my principal duties involved teaching our musical theatre students. One of those responsibilities was helping to plan senior cabaret recitals, designed to demonstrate a student's familiarity performing musical theatre selections of all styles and periods, providing a capstone experience to his or her four years of study.

After years of helping them search for appropriate music, I finally became frustrated trying to remember what song came from which musical, what its range was, and whether or not it might be the right type of song for their voices or their cabaret requirements. Thus I began this project: to go through my own collection of scores and categorize the songs by voice type, range, and style. As I discussed the idea with my colleagues, they were uniformly supportive about the project, since all of them had performed similar searches countless times. In sum, this book was born both of frustration and from the idea that there ought to be a practical guide to the great body of musical theatre songs, making them more readily accessible to performers.

The New Broadway Song Companion lists thousands of song titles from over 300 musicals, both early and late, both popular shows and those that were short-lived, from both on- and off-Broadway. The main purposes of this study have been to identify and label solo literature; to identify excerptable duets, trios, quartets, and other ensemble pieces; and finally to provide a listing of other material in these shows, because doing so might be useful to directors, producers, and others who have need for a quick reference to this information.

I have designed this book primarily with the singing actor in mind. A tenor suited to character parts, for example, may need to know whether or not a particular show has a part for him before he takes time out of a busy schedule to audition. A quick glance at one of the shows included here should give him that information. A mezzo looking for a good ballad to fill out a cabaret act she is working on will also find several dozen song choices listed here. A soprano and bass looking for a good trio to perform with a tenor will also find literature suited to their purposes.

Directors and producers will also find this book helpful. A director seeking information while planning an upcoming season, knowing the makeup and nature of the company he or she has hired, can browse at leisure through these pages and find any number of shows that might fit the bill. Similarly, directors who have a good chorus but limited suitable leading players will be able to find shows, both familiar and forgotten, that might fit their casts.

Several caveats need to be mentioned. First, nearly half of these shows were annotated using published piano-vocal scores, available for perusal in public libraries and sometimes for purchase. These published scores may differ in slight ways from materials that are distributed by rental companies. Secondly, "vocal selections" books are notoriously different from both publisher's parts and rental materials. Only full scores have been used to provide the annotations in this volume, and the reader should not be surprised if the version of a song he knows is in a different key or a different arrangement in the vocal selections book he may own. Finally, cast albums of shows may be in yet another key, and frequently contain arrangements of music made to fit the requirements of the recording. While helpful in general, they may differ in significant ways from the actual music of a show, a fact the actor or director should keep in mind.

A note about song titles is in order, also. In this book, I have used the titles found in the conductor's score for each show, since that is the primary source material for this compilation. These may differ slightly (or significantly) from the titles found in the program, on the internet, or on the cast album, which do not always agree either.

While many agents loaned rental materials for annotation here, several shows were not available for reasons of royalty arrangements, part preparation, and so forth, at the time of this compilation. While I have made every effort to be inclusive, certain shows may now be available that were not at the time I wrote this book.

With this said, it is my hope that *The New Broadway Song Companion* will prove useful and valuable to a large number of singers, actors, voice teachers, directors, and producers. My aim has been to provide the user with a complete, accurate, handy compendium of data that will offer access to a body of literature much loved, but often difficult to access. If I have been successful, this great, fascinating music will have been served.

Many people and organizations contributed to this guide, and it is only right to acknowledge them here. Craig Johnson, my colleague from Otterbein College, was very encouraging at the outset of this research, as were my students, especially Bob Cline, Dan Hughes, Johnny Steiner, and Catherine Smart. Dan Yurgaitis and Dick Hansen, the two members of the musical theatre faculty at The University of Arizona, were both helpful in the extreme, and provided scores from their libraries as well as suggestions and encouragement. My friend Josef Knott provided a summer's respite for proofreading on Cape Cod.

Most of the research was undertaken at the Courtwright Memorial Library of Otterbein College, The Ohio State University Music and Dance Library, the Columbus (Ohio) Public Library, The University of Arizona Music Library, and the New York Public Library for the Performing Arts at Lincoln Center. I would like to extend my thanks to the respective staffs of these institutions. I would like to thank the three principal rental agents for the loan of scores and the gentlemen who answered my queries for help with generosity and dispatch: Jim Merrillat of Music Theatre International, Brad Lorenz of Samuel French, Inc., and Peter Hut of Tams-Witmark Music Library, Inc. All provided scores free of charge, without which many of the more recent musicals would not have been included here. Finally, I would like to thank my good friend David DeCooman, who did some research for me, and who, as always, provided unflagging personal support.

Guide to Use

ANNOTATIONS

This *Companion* is designed to provide a quick-reference guide to the solos, duets, trios, and ensemble music of the Broadway musical. Shows appear alphabetically, with the year of their premiere or composition and the names of the composer(s) and lyricist(s). Each song annotated is listed in show order, followed by the name of the character who sings it. When a character's name first appears, it is also identified by voice part (soprano, mezzo, tenor, baritone, or bass; abbreviated as S, M or A, T, Bar, B). The next column lists the exact vocal range according to the following octave method, where middle C is c1:

C to B   c to b   c1 (middle c) to b1   c2 to b2   c3 to b3

Vocal ranges are inclusive, meaning that they include opening recitative sections as well, which in practice might not be excerpted when performed outside the context of a show. When two or more characters sing a given number, their vocal ranges are given in the order in which they sing, separated by a slash (/).

In the third column of each annotation, I have given a style or tempo designation. These fall into three broad categories: ballads, uptempo numbers, and character pieces. A number is often given more than one parameter. An uptempo song might also be a character piece, and will be so labeled. Likewise, a number may be uptempo, but move a bit slower than usual; it would be labeled "mod. [moderate] uptempo." A ballad that moves along somewhat might be defined as a "moving ballad" or a "moderate ballad"; there are also pieces marked "waltz ballad," "blues ballad," "driving ballad," and so on. I am confident the reader will find these designations self-explanatory.

Duets are annotated in the same manner as solos. Most trios, quartets, and larger ensembles are designated only by voice part (a sextet would be listed as SATTBB, for example, without specific voice ranges), and choruses and company numbers are given only a style or tempo label.

Choruses are mixed voicing unless designated otherwise (men's, women's, or children's choruses). Any other pertinent or useful information is given at the end of a show's listings.

DEFINITIONS AND DESIGNATIONS

Only those vocal pieces which are excerptable have been included in this guide; no instrumental numbers have been annotated. A selection is deemed excerptable when it is able to be performed outside the context of a show. A piece where short phrases are passed between several characters without any real expository "aria" portion is therefore not listed as an excerptable solo song.

Musical numbers that are sung by a number of characters without any one character dominating, or that use most or all of the principal characters along with the chorus, are designated by the term "company." "Ensemble" numbers are for several principal characters without chorus. "Incidental" indicates that a character—in some cases the chorus—sings during the song but is not essential to its performance; taken out of context, a song may be performed by excluding these incidental portions, without harm to the musical fabric.

INDEXES

Indexes at the conclusion of the *Companion* are arranged by voice part, and within each voice part by three broad style categories:

Soprano	uptempo songs
	ballads
	character songs
Mezzo	uptempo songs
	ballads
	character songs

and so on, for tenors and then baritones. Duets, trios, and quartets are indexed alphabetically by title, with the voice type following (ST, SSA, TTBB, and so forth). Larger ensemble numbers are similarly listed, while choruses and company numbers are listed by type (women's, children's, men's, mixed) and then alphabetically by title. Within each of the above designations, titles of songs are always given in alphabetical order, followed by a page number referring the reader to the correct show, where the relevant information is located. Finally, there are alphabetical indexes to composers and lyricists.

Catalog of Musicals

Aida (2000)

Music by Elton John   Lyrics by Tim Rice

Song title, Character (Voice)	Range	Song Style
Every story is a love story, Amneris (M)	g-ab1	mod. ballad
Fortune favors the brave, Amneris, Radames (T), male chorus	bb-f2, c-g1	uptempo
The past is another land, Aida (M)	a-b1	mod. ballad
Another pyramid, Zoser (Bar)	f-e1	uptempo
How I know you, Mereb (Bar), Aida	G-a/g-a1	mod. ballad
My strongest suit/Fashion show, Amneris, chorus	gb-f1	uptempo
Enchantment passing through, Radames, Aida	B-f#1/g#-c#1	ballad
Strongest suit reprise, Amneris, Aida	both bb-g1	mod. uptempo
Dance of the robe, Aida, chorus	a-f2	uptempo
Not me, quartet	MTTB	ballad
Elaborate lives, Radames, Aida	Bb-ab1/db1-cb2	mod. ballad
The gods love Nubia, Aida, Nehebka (S), chorus	c1-c2/g-e2	mod. ballad
A step too far, trio	MMT	mod. ballad
Easy as life, Aida	g-c2	ballad
Like father like son, Zoser, Radames, male chorus	f-bb1/g-f1	uptempo
Radames's letter, Radames	c-g1	mod. ballad
How I know you reprise, Mereb	f-g1	ballad
Written in the stars, Aida, Radames	g-c2/c-b1	ballad
I know the truth, Amneris	e-d2	moving ballad
Elaborate lives reprise, Aida, Radames	g-c2/g-a1	mod. ballad
Finale, Amneris; Radames, Aida incidental	g-ab1	uptempo

Ain't Misbehavin' (1978)

Music by Thomas "Fats" Waller, Hoagy Carmichael, and others

Song title, Character (Voice)	Range	Song Style
Ain't misbehavin', company		ballad
'Tain't nobody's biz-ness if I do, company		uptempo
Lookin' good but feelin' bad, company		uptempo
Honeysuckle Rose, Ken (Bar), Nell (M)	d1-eb2	ballad
Squeeze me, Amelia (M)	c1-f2	blues ballad
Handful of keys, Charlaine (S)	eb-bb2	ballad
I've got a feeling I'm falling, Nell	c1-eb2	ballad
How ya baby, Andre (T)	c1-d2	swing uptempo
The jitterbug waltz, company	bb-g2	waltz ballad
The ladies who sing with the band, Andre, Ken	e1-e2	uptempo
Yacht club swing, Charlaine	ab-eb2	swing ballad

When the nylons bloom again, Amelia, women	c1-d2	ballad
(Get some) Cash for your trash, Nell	a-e2	mod. uptempo
Off-time, women, then company		uptempo
The joint is jumpin', company		uptempo
Spreadin' rhythm around, company	d1-e2	ballad
Lounging at the Waldorf, Nell, Ken	c1-b2/c1-e♭2	ballad
The reefer song, Andre	c1-g2	blues ballad
Mean to me, Nell	c1-d2	ballad
Your feet's too big, Ken	c1-e♭2	hard jazz ballad
That ain't right, Amelia, Andre	g-a1	blues ballad
Keeping out of mischief now, Charlaine	a-c2	ballad
Find out what they like and how they like it, Nell	c1-d2	mod. uptempo
Fat and greasy, Andre, Ken	e1-e2	uptempo
(What did I do to be so) Black and blue, company		ballad
I'm gonna sit right down and write myself a letter, Ken	c1-e2	moving ballad
Two sleepy people, Ken, Amelia	c1-e2	ballad
I've got my fingers crossed, Charlaine	d1-f2	uptempo
I can't give you anything but love, Andre	e1-e2	mod. ballad
It's a sin to tell a lie, Andre, Nell	e1-e2	uptempo

Note: Ranges given are for entire songs, both parts included. The company sings backup on nearly every number, which is not indicated here.

All-American (1962)

Music by Charles Strouse   Lyrics by Lee Adams

Song title, Character (Voice)	Range	Song Style
Immigration rag, company		uptempo
What a country!, Fodorski (Bar), chorus	d-e1	mod. uptempo
Our children, Elizabeth (M), Fodorski	a-e2/c-f1	mod. ballad
We speak the same language, Bricker (Bar), Fodorski	A-e1/B-e1	mod. uptempo
I can teach them, Fodorski	B♭-e♭1	mod. uptempo
It's fun to think, company		mod. uptempo
Once upon a time, Fodorski, Elizabeth	B♭-e1/c1-e2	ballad
Football game, chorus		uptempo
Physical fitness, men's chorus		mod. uptempo
Night life, Susan (M), girls' chorus	c1-d2	dirty blues
If I were you, Fodorski, Elizabeth	c-e1/d1-e2	mod. ballad
I couldn't have done it alone, Bricker, girls' chorus	B-d1	mod. uptempo
Once upon a time reprise, Elizabeth	c1-e2	ballad
I've just seen him, Susan, Elizabeth	c1-g2/e1-g2	mod. ballad

The real me, Elizabeth	a-g♭2	mod. ballad
Which way?, Fodorski	c-e1	mod. uptempo
What a country reprise, company		uptempo

Allegro (1947)

Music by Richard Rodgers   Lyrics by Oscar Hammerstein II

Song title, Character (Voice)	Range	Song Style
I know it can't happen again, Grandma (M)	b-b1	ballad
One foot, other foot, chorus		uptempo
A fellow needs a girl, Marjorie (S), Taylor (T) incidental	b♭-f2	ballad
So far, Beulah (M)	c1-d2	ballad
You are never away, Joe (T), chorus incidental	B-g1	uptempo
What a lovely day for a wedding, chorus w/ soli	e♭-f1	uptempo
It may be a good idea, Charlie (T)	d1-d2	uptempo
To have and to hold, company		uptempo
Money isn't everything, five women	SSMMM	waltz ballad
You are never away reprise, Joe	B-g1	uptempo
Ya-ta-ta, company		uptempo
The gentleman is a dope, Emily (M)	a♭-b♭1	mod. ballad
Allegro, company		uptempo
Come home, Marjorie	e♭1-f2	ballad
Ya-ta-ta reprise, company		uptempo

Altar Boyz (2004)

Music and Lyrics by Gary Adler

Song title, Character (Voice)	Range	Song Style
We are the altar boyz, company		uptempo
Rhythm in me, company		funky uptempo
Church rulz, company		uptempo
The calling, Matt (T), Mark (T), boys	e♭-f1/e♭-e♭1	ballad
The miracle song, company		uptempo
Everybody fits, Abe (T), boys	f-c2	mod. uptempo
Confession sessions, company		jazzy uptempo
Something about you, Matt	c-g1	ballad
Body, mind, and soul, Luke (T), boys underscoring	d♭-b2 (one high e3)	funky uptempo
La vida eternal, Juan (T), boys	e-a♭1	salsa uptempo
Epiphany, Mark, boys	d-b1	driving ballad

Number 918, company	uptempo
Finale, company	mod. ballad
We are the altar boyz remix, company	uptempo

Always . . . Patsy Cline (1993)
Music and Lyrics by various artists

Song title, Character (Voice)	Range	Song Style
Honky tonk merry go round, Patsy (M)	g#-a1	mod. uptempo
Back in baby's arms	g-a1	mod. ballad
Anytime	e-b♭1	mod. ballad
Walkin' after midnight	f#-a1	ballad
I fall to pieces	f-a1	mod. ballad
Honky tonk angels	f-g1	shuffle
Come on in	e-b1	mod. uptempo
Your cheatin' heart	f#-b1	rock ballad
Stupid cupid	a-a1	mod. uptempo
You belong to me	f-g1	ballad
I love you honey	a-a1	mod. ballad
Lovesick blues	f-b♭1 (8va higher at last note)	mod. uptempo
Sweetdreams/She's got you	e-b♭1	ballad
Three cigarettes in an ashtray	e-a1	ballad
Crazy	f-b♭1	mod. uptempo
Seven lonely days, Louise (M) incidental	g-a♭1	mod. uptempo
If I could see the world/Closer walk with thee	f#-b1	uptempo
Blue moon of Kentucky, Patsy, Louise	f-d♭1/b♭-f2	uptempo
Gotta lotta rhythm/Shake rattle and roll	g-e2	uptempo
Faded love	e♭-c2	ballad
True love	d♭-a♭1	waltz ballad
Anytime reprise	f-b♭1	mod. ballad
Leaving on your mind	f#-b1	ballad
Bill Bailey	e-c	mod. uptempo

Anne of Green Gables (1969)
Music by Norman Campbell   Lyrics by Don Harron

Song title, Character (Voice)	Range	Song Style
Overture: Anne of Green Gables, chorus		uptempo
Great workers for the cause, women's chorus		uptempo
Gee, I'm glad I'm no one else but me, Anne (S)	d1-f2	mod. uptempo
We certainly requested a boy, trio	SMB	mod. uptempo

The facts, Anne	e♭1-e♭2	uptempo
Where'd Marilla come from?, women's chorus, incidental male solo		jaunty, in 2
Humble pie, Matthew (Bar), Anne	A-d1/a-d2	mod. uptempo
Apology, Anne	d1-g2	mod. uptempo
Back to school, chorus		uptempo
Wond'rin', Gilbert (Bar)	d-f1	mod. ballad
Did you hear?, company		uptempo
Ice cream, Diana (M), Anne incidental, chorus	c1-d2	mod. uptempo
Summer, company		mod. uptempo
Kindred spirits, Anne, Diana	both c1-d2	moving ballad
Open the window, Miss Stacy (M), children's chorus	b♭-d2	mod. uptempo
The words, Matthew	A-e♭1	ballad
When I say my say, Matthew*	d♭-e1	mod. uptempo
I'll show him, Anne, Gilbert	c1-e2/c-e1	uptempo
General store, company		mod. uptempo
Prince Edward Island, trio, children's chorus	SMB	march uptempo
If it hadn't been for me, company		uptempo
Anne of Green Gables reprise, Matthew	B♭-c1	ballad
The words reprise, Marilla (M)	a-d2	ballad
Summer/Ice cream reprise, company		uptempo

*alternate song to *The words*

Annie (1977)

Music by Charles Strouse   Lyrics by Martin Charnin

Song title, **Character (Voice)**	**Range**	**Song Style**
Maybe, Annie (girl S)	b♭-d2	ballad
It's the hard-knock life, Orphan chorus		uptempo
Tomorrow, Annie	b♭-e♭2	ballad
Hooverville, chorus		mod. uptempo
Little girls, Miss Hannigan (M)	a-c2	mod. character
I think I'm gonna like it here, company		uptempo
N. Y.C., Warbucks (Bar), Grace (M), "Star to Be" (M) incidental	c-f1/c1-f2	ballad
Easy street, Rooster (T), Hannigan, Lily (S)	A-g1/a-f #2/a-f#2	mod. uptempo, blues ballad
You won't be an orphan for long, company		uptempo
Fully dressed, Bert (T), backup trio	e-f#1	mod. uptempo
Dressed children, ensemble		mod. uptempo
Cabinet "Tomorrow," Annie, Cabinet (male ensemble)		ballad
Cabinet end, Cabinet		ballad
Something was missing, Warbucks	c-f1	waltz ballad

I don't need anything but you, Annie, Warbucks	c#1-e2/c#-e1	uptempo
Servant's Annie, chorus		uptempo
Same effect on everyone (Maybe), Annie	b♭-d♭2	ballad
A new deal for Christmas, company		uptempo

Note: See also *Annie Warbucks*.

Annie Get Your Gun (1946)
Music and Lyrics by Irving Berlin

Song title, **Character (Voice)**	**Range**	**Song Style**
Col. Buffalo Bill, Charlie (T), chorus	e♭-f1	uptempo
I'm a bad, bad man, Frank (Bar), women's chorus	c-d1	mod. uptempo
Doin' what comes naturally, Annie (M), Kids and Wilson (both incidental)	c1-d2	character ballad
The girl that I marry, Frank	B♭-d1	waltz ballad
You can't get a man with a gun, Annie	b♭-c2	character
There's no business like show business, Annie, Charlie, Buffalo Bill, Frank	b♭-f2/men: B♭-f1	uptempo
They say it's wonderful, Frank, Annie	B♭-d1/b♭-d2	ballad
Moonshine lullaby, Annie, three porters	a♭-c2	blues ballad
I'll share it all with you, Tommy (T), Winnie (S)	d-e♭1/d1-e♭2	uptempo
There's no business like show business reprise, Annie	a-c#2	uptempo
My defences are down, Frank, chorus	c#-g♭1	uptempo
I'm an Indian, too, Annie	b♭-c#2	character
I got lost in his arms, Annie, chorus	b♭-c2	mod. ballad
Why do you love I hope?, Tommy, Winnie	c-d1/c1-d2	mod. uptempo
I've got the sun in the morning, Annie, company	c1-c2	uptempo
The girl that I marry reprise, Frank	B♭-d1	ballad
Anything you can do, Annie, Frank	c1-g2/c-f1	character
There's no business like show business, company		uptempo
They say it's wonderful, company		ballad

Annie Warbucks (1993)
Music by Charles Strouse   Lyrics by Martin Charnin

Song title, **Character (Voice)**	**Range**	**Song Style**
Annie ain't just Annie anymore, company		uptempo
Above the law, Mrs. Doyle (M)	g#-b1	uptempo

Changes, Annie (girl S), Warbucks (Bar)	c1-d2/c-c1	ballad
The other woman, Orphan's chorus		narrative ballad
That's the kind of woman, Drake (Bar), Annie, chorus	c-f1/ab1-eb2	mod. uptempo
A younger man, Warbucks	Ab-e1	ballad
But you go on, Mrs. Kelly (M)	f#-b1	mod. uptempo
Above the law reprise, Mrs. Doyle, Mrs. Kelly	both a-d2	uptempo
I got me, Annie, Orphan's chorus	a-d2	moving ballad
Love, Ella (M)	f#-a1	gospel ballad
Somebody's gotta do somethin', company		uptempo
Leave it to the girls, Mrs. Doyle, Mrs. Kelly	both g-b1	uptempo
All dolled up, company		mostly uptempo
It would have been wonderful, Grace (S)	c1-eb2	moving ballad
When you smile, Warbucks, Annie	Bb-eb1/bb-eb2	mod. uptempo
I always knew, Annie	b-d2	mod. uptempo

Note: See also *Annie*.

Anyone Can Whistle (1964)
Music and Lyrics by Stephen Sondheim

Song title, Character (Voice)	Range	Song Style
Me and my town, Cora (M), chorus	a-eb2	character
Miracle song, Cora, chorus	f#-e2	uptempo
There won't be any trumpets, Fay (M)	g-c2	uptempo
Interrogation scene — Simple, Hapgood (Bar), George (Bar), ensemble	Bb-eb1/eb-eb1	character
A-1 march, chorus		uptempo
Come play wiz me, Fay, Hapgood	a-d2/A-e1	fast character
Anyone can whistle, Fay	g-b1	ballad
There's a parade in town, chorus		uptempo
Everybody says don't, Hapgood	G-e1	uptempo
I've got you to lean on, Cora (M), Schub (T), Magruder (T), Cooley (Bar)	MTTB/then Cora: a-d1	uptempo
See what it gets you, Fay	g-c2	mod. ballad
Anyone can whistle reprise, Fay	a-db2	ballad
Cora's chase, Cora, chorus	a-e2	uptempo
Vocalise (S)	b1-d3	ad lib.
With so little to be sure of, Fay, Hapgood	a-b1/B-e1	ballad

Anything Goes (1934)
Music and Lyrics by Cole Porter

Song title, Character (Voice)	Range	Song Style
I get a kick out of you, Reno (M)	a-d2	mod. ballad
There's no cure like travel, chorus		uptempo
Bon voyage, chorus		uptempo
You're the top, Billy (T), Reno	B-f#/g-d2	mod. uptempo
Easy to love, Billy	c-g1	ballad
The crew song, Whitney (Bar)	c#-d1	mod. waltz
There'll always be a lady fair, quartet	TTBB	uptempo
Friendship, Reno, Moon (Bar)	bb-c#2/Bb-e1	mod. uptempo
It's de-lovely, Billy, Hope (M)	c-g1/c-eb2	flowing ballad
Anything goes, Reno, chorus	ab-d2	uptempo
Public enemy number one, Captain (Bar), Purser (T), chorus	c-f1/c-g1	mod. uptempo
Blow, Gabriel, blow, Reno, chorus	g-d2	uptempo
Goodbye, little dream, goodbye, Hope	a-eb2	ballad
Be like the bluebird, Moon	B#-f#1	mod. character
All through the night, Billy, Hope	c-g1/c1-eb2	flowing ballad
Gypsy in me, Evelyn (T)	c-g1	mod. uptempo
Buddie, beware, Erma (M), sailors	a-c#2	ballad
I get a kick out of you reprise, company		uptempo

Note: Annotated from the 1987 revised score.

Applause (1970)
Music by Charles Strouse   Lyrics by Lee Adams

Song title, Character (Voice)	Range	Song Style
Think how it's gonna be, Bill (T)	B-f1	ballad
But alive, Margo (M), men's chorus, Eve (M) incidental	e-f#1	uptempo
The best night of my life, Eve	g#-c#2	ballad
Who's that girl, Margo	e-a1	uptempo
Applause, Bonnie (M), chorus	g-c2	uptempo
Hurry back, Margo	a-f1	blues ballad
Fasten your seatbelts, company		uptempo
Welcome to the theater, Margo	d-f#1	angry uptempo
Good friends, Buzz (T), Karen (S), Margo	c-g1/eb-g2/c-f1	uptempo
She's no longer a gypsy, Duane (T), Bonnie, chorus		uptempo
One of a kind, Bill, Margo	Bb-g1/cb-a1	waltz uptempo
One Halloween, Eve	ab-bb1	ballad, then fast
Something greater, Margo, Bill incidental	eb1-g2	mod. ballad
Bows: Applause, company		uptempo

The Apple Tree (1966)

Music by Jerry Bock   Lyrics by Sheldon Harnick

Song title, **Character (Voice)**	**Range**	**Song Style**
Part I		
Here in Eden, Eve (M)	a-a1	mod. uptempo
Feelings, Eve	b-e2	moving ballad
Eve, Adam (Bar)	db-db1	ballad
Friends, Eve	bb-e2	ballad
Forbidden fruit, Snake (T)	d-g1	uptempo
Adam's reprise, Adam	d-eb 1	mod. ballad
Fish no. 1 and 2, Adam	db-db1	uptempo
Lullaby, Eve	b-b1	ballad
Fish no. 3, Adam	db-eb1	uptempo
What makes me love him?, Eve	g#-c#2	ballad
Part II		
I'll tell you a truth, opening, Balladeer	c-eb 1	mod. uptempo
Make way, men's chorus		uptempo march
Ai, ai!, chorus		uptempo
Forbidden love, Barbara, Capt. Sanjar	b-eb2/ b-eb1	ballad
Razor teeth, Barbara, Balladeer	g-bb1/d-g1	uptempo
I've got what you want, Barbara	a-c2	ballad
Tiger, tiger, Barbara	f-a1	driving uptempo
Make way—Canon, chorus		processional
Which door?, company		mod. uptempo
I'll tell you a truth, closing, Balladeer	c-f#1	slow, rubato
Part III		
Oh, to be a movie star, Ella	c1-d2	uptempo
Gorgeous, Ella	c1-d2	waltz uptempo
Who is she?, chorus, Ella solo at end		uptempo
I know, Ella, chorus	c1-eb2	uptempo
Wealth, Ella	c1-b	driving uptempo
Real, Flip, chorus	c-eb	mod. uptempo
Oh, to be a movie star reprise, chorus		uptempo
Bows (pastiche of earlier music), company		uptempo

Note: Casting throughout show as follows:
     Eve = Barbara = Ella
     Adam = Capt. Sanjar = Flip
     Snake = Balladeer = Narrator

Aspects of Love (1990)

Music by Andrew Lloyd Webber   Lyrics by Don Black and Charles Hart

Song title, Character (Voice)	Range	Song Style
Love changes everything, Alex (T)	d-g1	ballad
Parlez vous francais?, company		mod. uptempo
Seeing is believing, Alex, Rose (S)	d-ab1/bb-ab2	moving ballad
A memory of a happy moment, George (Bar), Giulietta (M)	G-e1/g-eb2	mod. uptempo
Chanson d'enfance, Rose, Alex	bb-d2/c-f1	scene
Everybody loves a hero, company		uptempo
She'd be better off with you, Alex, George	Bb-g1/Bb-eb1	mod. ballad
Stop, wait, please, George, Giulietta, company	Ab-e1/ab-f2	mod. uptempo
Love changes everything reprise, Alex	c-g1	ballad
Leading lady, Marcel (Bar)	c-e1	mod. uptempo
Other pleasures, George	A#-c#1	ballad
There is more to love, Giulietta	g#-f#2	ballad
Mermaid song, Jenny (S), Alex	bb-eb2/g#-e2	mod. uptempo
What could be sweeter?, George	A#-db1	ballad
The first man you remember, George, Jenny	Bb-d#1/bb-f#2	mod. uptempo
Journey of a lifetime, company		mod. uptempo
Falling, quartet	SMTB	moving ballad
Hand me the wine and the dice, company		uptempo
Anything but lonely, Rose	a-e2	ballad

Assassins (1990)

Music and Lyrics by Stephen Sondheim

Song title, Character (Voice)	Range	Song Style
Opening, Proprietor (Bar), Booth (Bar), Assassins	G-f1/G-f1	character
The ballad of Booth, Balladeer (T), Booth	c#-g#1/F#-e1	narrative ballad
How I saved Roosevelt, Zangara (T), Bystanders	B-a1	uptempo
Gun song, Czolgosz (Bar), Booth, Guiteau (T), Moore (M)	G-c1/c-f#1/c-g1/ab-e2	slow, funny
The ballad of Czolgosz, Balladeer, crowd	d-g1	narrative ballad
Unworthy of your love, Hinckley (T), Fromme (M)	B-d#1/a-d#2	ballad
The ballad of Guiteau, Guiteau	A-gb1	mod. ballad
Another national anthem, Balladeer, Assassins		mod. uptempo
Scene 16, Assassins		slow, dramatic
Everybody's got the right, company		mod. uptempo

Avenue Q (2003)

Music and Lyrics by Robert Lopez and Jeff Marx

Song title, **Character (Voice)**	**Range**	**Song Style**
The Avenue Q theme, company		uptempo
What do you do with a B.A. in English?, Princeton (Bar)	B♭-d1	mod. uptempo
It sucks to be me, company		uptempo
If you were gay, Nicky (T)	c-a1	mod. uptempo
Purpose, Princeton, chorus		mod. uptempo
Everyone's a little bit racist, company		mod. swing
The internet is for porn, company		uptempo
A mix tape, Kate (M), Princeton	f#-d2/B-e1	mod. ballad
I'm not wearing underwear today, Brian (Bar)	B-e1	uptempo
Special, Lucy (M)	g-d♭2	jazzy uptempo
Loud as the hell you want, company		uptempo
Fantasies come true, Rod, Kate, Nicky, Princeton	MTTB	mod. ballad
My girlfriend who lives in Canada, Rod (Bar)	B-g1	uptempo
There's a fine, fine line, Kate	g-d2	mod. uptempo
There is life outside your apartment, company		uptempo
The more you ruv someone, Christmas Eve (M), Kate incidental	b-e♭2	mod. ballad
Schadenfreude, Gary (T), Nicky	d-b♭1/d-g1	uptempo
I wish I could go back to college, Kate, Nicky, Princeton	MTB	mod. ballad
The money song, company		swing uptempo
For now, company		uptempo

Babes in Arms (1937)

Music by Richard Rodgers   Lyrics by Lorenz Hart

Song title, **Character (Voice)**	**Range**	**Song Style**
Babes in arms, Susie (S), chorus	d♭1-f2	uptempo
All at once, Susie, Val (T)	c1-e2/d-f1	ballad
I wish I were in love again, Terry (M), Gus (Bar)	d1-d2/d-d1	mod. ballad
Where or when, Jennifer (S), Val incidental	d1-g2	ballad
Way out West, Bunny (M)	c1-d2	character
Where or when reprise, Jennifer	c-f1	ballad
My funny Valentine, Susie	c#1-e2	ballad
Finale act I, company		mod. uptempo
Imagine, Susie, Terry incidental	c1-e♭2	uptempo

You're nearer, Val, Susie	f-f1/d1-d2	uptempo
The lady is a tramp, Bunny	c#1-e2	fast character
My funny Valentine reprise, Susie	a-b1	ballad
I wish I were in love again reprise, Terry, Gus	c1-d2/c-d1	mod. ballad
Johnny One Note, Bunny	b♭-b♭1 (opt. e♭2)	fast character
Finale act II: Johnny One Note, company		uptempo

Babes in Toyland (1903)

Music by Victor Herbert   Lyrics by Glen MacDonough

Song title, **Character (Voice)**	**Range**	**Song Style**
Lemonade, company		mod. uptempo
Never mind, Bo Peep, company		fast character
Jane, Tom (T), women's chorus	c-e♭1 (opt. f1)	ballad
Before and after, Widow Piper (M), Barnaby (Bar)	b♭ - c2/B♭-c1	character
Floretta, Alan (Bar), women's chorus	G-e1	ballad
Mary, Mary, quite contrary, chorus		mod. uptempo
I'm in a hurry, Mary (S), chorus	d1-g2	character
Barney O'Flynn, chorus		mod. uptempo
Just a whisper away, Mary, Alan	d1-e2/d-e1	ballad
He won't be happy till he gets it, Roderigo (Bar), Gonzorgo (Bar)	both d-d1	character
Go to sleep, slumber deep, Fairy Queen (M), ensemble, Chorus of Fairies	d1-e2	ballad
Hand in hand, Jane (S), Alan	d1-f2/d-f1	ballad
Hail to Toyland, solo voice (S), chorus	d1-a2	uptempo
Toyland, Master Toymaker (Bar), chorus	c-e1	character
Just a toy!, Jill (S), chorus	c1-e2 (opt. a2)	character
Beatrice Barefacts, Mary, Marmaduke (Bar), girls' trio	d1-e2/d-e1	character
March of the toys, Alan; chorus, Jane incidental	b♭-d1	character
Just a whisper away reprise, Mary, Alan	d1-e2/d-e1	ballad
Our castle in Spain, Jane, Tom	c1-d2/c-d1	ballad
Toyland reprise, company		uptempo

Baby (1984)

Music by David Shire   Lyrics by Richard Maltby, Jr.

Song title, Character (Voice)	Range	Song Style
We start today, company		uptempo
What could be better?, Danny (T), Lizzie (M)	f#-a1/a-e2	funny, uptempo
The Plaza song, Alan (Bar), Arlene (M)	c#-e1/d1-f2	mod. uptempo
Baby, baby, baby, Nick (Bar), Pam (M), company	c-f#1/g-f#2	mod. ballad
I want it all, Pam, Lizzie, Arlene	c1-eb2/c1-eb2/ b-eb2	mod. ballad
At night she comes home to me, Nick, Danny	d-f1/d-g1	ballad, then fast
What could be better reprise, Danny, Lizzie	g-f1/c1-c2	uptempo
Fatherhood blues, men	TTBBB	uptempo march
Romance, Pam, Nick incidental	b-c#2	mod. ballad
I chose right, Danny	d-g1	moving ballad
We start today reprise, ensemble		uptempo
The story goes on, Lizzie	g-f2	quick ballad
The ladies singin' their song, women	SSMMM	jazzy uptempo
Patterns, Arlene	bb-eb2	ballad
Romance reprise, Nick, Pam	A-f#1/a1-f#2	ballad, then faster
Easier to love, Alan	c-e1	ballad
Two people in love, Danny, Lizzie	A-f#1 (opt. a1)/a-d2	uptempo
With you, Nick, Pam	A-e1/a-d2	ballad
And what if we had loved like that, Alan, Arlene	d-e1/d1-g2	mod. ballad
We start today reprise, company		uptempo
The story goes on, company		mod. uptempo

The Baker's Wife (1976)

Music and Lyrics by Stephen Schwartz

Song title, Character (Voice)	Range	Song Style
Chanson, Denise (M) (partially in French)	f#-b	waltz ballad
If it wasn't for you, company		mod. uptempo
Merci madame, Aimable (Bar), Genevieve (M)	Ab-e1/ab-c2	mod. uptempo
Bread, company		uptempo
Gifts of love, Genevieve	g-eb2	ballad
Proud lady, Dominique (T)	d-g1	uptempo
Look for the woman, company men		mod., funny
Serenade, Dominique, Denise, Phillippe (Bar), Aimable, Genevieve	MMTBB	mod. ballad
Meadowlark, Genevieve	e-e2	mod., narrative
Finale act I, company		uptempo

Chanson reprise, Denise (partially in French)	a-b1	mod. ballad
If it wasn't for you reprise, company		mod. uptempo
Any day now day, Aimable, company men	c-c1	uptempo
The world's luckiest man, company men		mod. uptempo
Feminine companionship, Marquis (T), company	c-f#1	funny, mod. uptempo
If I have to live alone, Aimable	B-c#1	ballad
Romance, company women		mod. ballad
Where is the warmth?, Genevieve	g#-b1	mod. uptempo
Finale act II, company		mod. uptempo

Barnum (1980)

Music by Cy Coleman   Lyrics by Michael Stewart

Song title, **Character (Voice)**	**Range**	**Song Style**
There is a sucker born ev'ry minute, Barnum (T)	c#-f1	uptempo
Thank God I'm old, Joice Heth (M)	g-c2	ballad
The colors of my life, Chairy (M), Barnum	g-bb1/c-eb1	ballad
One brick at a time, Chairy, chorus	g#-d2	uptempo
Museum song (Egress song), Barnum	d-e1	character
I like your style, Chairy, Barnum	c1-d2/c-d1	waltz ballad
Bigger isn't better, Tom Thumb (T)	d#-g1	fast character
Jenny Lind obbligato, Jenny Lind (S)	g1-c3	vocalise
Love makes such fools of us all, Jenny Lind	a-g2	ballad
Out there, Barnum	Bb-f1	uptempo
Come follow the band, company		uptempo
Love makes such fools . . . reprise, Jenny Lind	bb-f2	ballad
Black and white, Blues Singer (S), Chairy, Barnum, chorus	e-a1/a-a1/eb-f1	blues ballad
The colors of my life reprise, Chairy, Barnum	b-c#2/B-c#1	ballad
The prince of humbug, Barnum	c#-e1	uptempo
Join the circus, Barnum, Bailey (T), company	ab1-f1/e-gb1	uptempo

Beauty and the Beast (1994)

Music by Alan Menken   Lyrics by Howard Ashman and Tim Rice

Song title, **Character (Voice)**	**Range**	**Song Style**
Belle, company		ballad/scene
No matter what, Maurice (Bar), Belle (M)	Bb-db1/bb-f2	mod. uptempo
Me, Gaston (T)	B-f1	mod. ballad
Belle reprise, Belle	d1-d2	uptempo

Home, Belle	g-e2	mod. uptempo
Gaston, Lefou (T), Gaston, company	B-g1/c-e1	uptempo waltz
How long must this go on?, Beast (Bar)	d-c1	mod. uptempo
Be our guest, company		uptempo
If I can't love her, Beast	B-f1	ballad
Something there, Belle, Beast, company	a-e2/A-b1	mod. uptempo
Human again, company		uptempo
Maison des lunes, Gaston, Lefou, M. D'Arque (Bar)	TBB	mod. ballad
Beauty and the Beast, Mrs. Potts (M)	f#-b1	ballad
If I can't love her reprise, Beast	f-eb1	ballad
A change in me, Belle	e-c2	ballad
The mob song, trio, chorus	TBB	uptempo
Home again, Belle	c1-d2	mod. ballad
Transformation/Finale, company		mod. uptempo

Bells Are Ringing (1956)

Music by Jule Styne   Lyrics by Betty Comden and Adolph Green

Song title, Character (Voice)	Range	Song Style
Bells are ringing, women's chorus		uptempo
It's a perfect relationship, Ella (M)	ab-cb2	ballad
Independent, Jeff (T), chorus	d-d1	mod. uptempo
It's a simple little system, Sandor (T), chorus	eb-g1	fast character
Is it a crime, Ella	ab-c2 (much spoken)	ballad
Better than a dream, Ella, Jeff	a-b1/e-d#1	ballad
Hello, hello there, chorus		uptempo
I met a girl, Jeff, chorus	c-gb1	uptempo
Long before I knew you, Jeff, Ella	B-bb1/b-c2	ballad
Mu-cha-cha, company		uptempo
Just in time, Jeff; Ella and chorus incidental	c#-d1	moving ballad
Drop that name, Ella, chorus	f#-b1	fast character
The party's over, Ella, chorus incidental	f#-b1	ballad
Salzburg, Sandor, Sue (S)	f-gb1/e-gb2	uptempo
The Midas touch, chorus		uptempo
Long before I knew you reprise, Jeff	c-c1	ballad
I'm going back, Ella	bb-bb1	ballad, then fast
He met a girl, chorus		uptempo

Best Foot Forward (1941)
Music and Lyrics by Hugh Martin and Ralph Blane

Song title, Character (Voice)	Range	Song Style
Don't sell the night short, chorus		uptempo
Three men on a date, Dutch, Bud, Hunk	all d♭-f1	mod. uptempo
That's how I love the blues, Gale (M), Jack (Bar)	a-d2/A-c#1	blues ballad
The three "B"s, Minerva (M), Blind Date (M), Ethel (M)	b♭-e♭2/a♭-e♭2/b♭-g2	mod. uptempo
Ev'ry time, Helen (S)	c♭1-g♭2	mod. ballad
The guy who brought me can't send me, Gale; Dutch, Bud, Hunk incidental	b♭-c2	mod. uptempo
I know you by heart, Bud (Bar)	B-d#1	ballad
Shady ladybird, Helen	e♭1-f2	mod. uptempo
Buckle down, Winsocki, Greenie (T), chorus	d-g1	mod. march
My first promise at my first prom, Ethel, chorus	e1-a2	waltz ballad
What do you think I am?, Minerva, Hunk (T)	a-e2/e-a1	uptempo
Just a little joint with a jukebox, Blind Date, chorus on encore	a-b1	mod. uptempo
Where do you travel?, Jack, chorus incidental	B♭-c#	mod. uptempo, funny
Ev'ry time reprise, Gale	c1-e♭2	mod. ballad
Buckle down, Winsocki reprise, company		uptempo march

The Best Little Whorehouse in Texas (1977)
Music and Lyrics by Carol Hall

Song title, Character (Voice)	Range	Song Style
20 fans, company		moving ballad
A li'l ole bitty pissant country place, Mona (M), company	f-e2	mod. narrative ballad
Girl you're a woman, Mona, women's chorus	e-g#1	walking ballad
Texas has a whorehouse in it, Melvin (Bar), chorus	B♭-e♭1	fast character
Twenty-four hours of lovin', Jewel (M), chorus	e-g2	uptempo
Doatsey Mae, Doatsey Mae (M)	g-c2	ballad
The Aggie song, men's chorus		uptempo
The bus from Amarillo, Mona	e♭-b♭1	slow ballad
The sidestep, Governor (Bar), company	A-d1	fast character
No lies, Mona, Jewel; girls incidental	g-b1/c1-e2	mod. uptempo

	Range	Song Style
Good old girl, Sheriff (Bar), men's chorus	G-f1	country ballad
Hard candy Christmas, women's chorus		hard blues ballad

Big: The Musical (1996)

Music by David Shire   Lyrics by Richard Maltby, Jr.

Song title, Character (Voice)	Range	Song Style
Can't wait, company		uptempo
Talk to her, Billy (boy), Young Josh (boy)	f#-g1/f#-d2	uptempo
Say goodbye to mom, Mrs. Baskin (M)	a-b♭1	mod. uptempo
You're a big boy now, Billy, Josh (T)	b♭-f1/B♭-a1	mod. uptempo
Time of your life, children's chorus		uptempo
Fun, Macmillan (Bar), Josh, company	c-e1/c-g1	mod. samba
Welcome to Macmillan toys, chorus		uptempo
My secretary's in love, Susan (M)	g-d1	uptempo
Welcome to Macmillan toys reprise, company		mod. uptempo
Let's not move too fast, Susan	a-c2	mod. ballad
Do you want to play games?, Josh	e♭-f1	mod. uptempo
Stars, Josh, Susan	c-e♭1/c1-d2	ballad
Little Susan Lawrence, Susan	a♭-d2	mod. ballad
Cross the line, Josh, company	c#-f1	mod. uptempo
It's time, Billy, children's chorus	a-c2	uptempo
Stop, time, Mrs. Baskin	g-d2	ballad
Dancing all the time, Susan	g#-c#2	mod. ballad
I want to know, Josh	c-f1	mod. ballad
Coffee, black, company		mod. uptempo
The real thing, quartet	SMTB	mod. minuet
The real thing reprise, Susan	a♭-f2	ballad
Big, Josh	e♭-g1	uptempo
We're gonna be fine, Josh, Susan, Zitar incidental	B♭-e♭1/c1-e♭2	ballad

Big River (1985)

Music and Lyrics by Roger Miller

Song title, Character (Voice)	Range	Song Style
Do ya wanna go to heaven, company		uptempo
The boys, male ensemble		uptempo
Waitin' for the light to shine, Huck (T)	d-e1	gospel ballad
Guv'ment, Pap (Bar)	B-f1	character ballad
Hand for the hog, Tom (T)	f-f1 (much spoken)	fast character
I, Huckleberry, me, Huck	c-f1	character ballad

Muddy water, Jim (Bar), Huck	b-f#1/b-a1	uptempo
The crossing, Mezzo solo	c1-c2	gospel ballad
River in the rain, Huck, Jim	A-g1/A-e1	ballad
When the sun goes down in the South,	c-a1/e-a1/e-	dixie ballad
King (T), Duke (Bar), Huck, Jim	a1/Bb-g1	
The royal nonesuch, Duke, chorus	d-f1	fast character
Worlds apart, Jim, Huck	B-g1/B-b1	ballad
	(falsetto)	
Arkansas, Young Fool (T), King	d-e1/b-g1	hillbilly ballad
How blest we are, Daughter (S), chorus	g-c3	gospel ballad
You oughta be here with me, Mary Jane	b-c#2/g-g1/g-g1	country ballad
(M); Joanna (M), Susie (M)		
incidental		
How blest we are reprise, chorus		ballad
Leavin's not the only way to go, Huck,	b-b1/b1-b2/e-e1	ballad
Mary Jane, Jim		
Waitin' for the light to shine, Huck, chorus	a-f#	uptempo
Free at last, Jim, chorus	c-f1	gospel ballad
River in the rain reprise, Jim, Huck	both a-e1	ballad
Bows: Muddy water, Jim, Huck, chorus		uptempo

Billy Elliott (2008)

Music by Elton John   Lyrics by Lee Hall

Song title, **Character (Voice)**	**Range**	**Song Style**
My stars look down, company		ballad
Shine, Mrs. Wilkinson (M), girls' chorus	g-b1	uptempo
Grandma's story, Grandma (M)	f-g1	uptempo waltz
Solidarity, chorus		uptempo
Expressing yourself, Michael (Bar), chorus	g-b1	swing uptempo
The Letter, Billy (T), Mrs. Wilkinson, Dead	g-e2/g-e2/g-d	ballad
Mum (M)		
We were born to boogie, Mrs. Wilkinson	g-a1	uptempo
Merry Christmas Margaret Thatcher, Tony	a-f1	uptempo
(T), chorus		
Deep into the ground, Dad (T), chorus	Bb-eb	ballad
He could be a star, Dad, Tony	both d-g1	mod. uptempo
Electricity, Billy	f-b1	mod. ballad
We once were kings, chorus		mod. ballad
The letter reprise, Billy, Dead Mum	g-d2/c1-d2	ballad
It doesn't matter (Finale), company		uptempo

Note: Annotated from London version of show.

Birds of Paradise (1987)
Music and Lyrics by David Evans

Song title, Character (Voice)	Range	Song Style
So many nights, company	c-f#1	uptempo
Diva, Hope (M); Dave, Andy incidental	b♭-c2	mod. uptempo
Every day is night, Homer (Bar)	B♭-e1	mod. ballad
Somebody, Wood (Bar), company	c-e1	mod. uptempo
Coming true, Homer, Julia (M)	c-a1/b-d2	uptempo
It's only a play, Homer, company	e-f#1	uptempo
She's out there, Andy (Bar)	B♭-b♭	ballad
Birds of paradise, women's quartet	SSMM	mod. uptempo
Imagining you, company		moving ballad
Penguins must sing, Dave (T), Hope, Andy	MTB	slow
You're mine, Marjorie (M)	b♭-e2	ballad
Things I can't forget, Homer, Marjorie incidental	B♭-g1	ballad
After opening night, Marjorie, Homer	b-c#2/B-f#1	uptempo
Chekov, company		mod. uptempo
Something new (Finale), company		slow, then fast

Bittersweet (1929)
Music and Lyrics by Noel Coward

Song title, Character (Voice)	Range	Song Style
That wonderful melody, chorus		ballad
The call of life, Lady Shayne (S), chorus	d1-a2	waltz ballad
If you could only come with me, Carl (T)	f#-g1	ballad
I'll see you again, Sarah (S), Carl	d♭1-a♭2/d♭-a♭1	mod. ballad
What is love, Sarah, chorus	e1-a2	waltz ballad
The last dance, chorus		uptempo
Eeny, meeny, mini, mo, Carl, company	B-g#1	uptempo
Life in the morning, chorus		uptempo
Ladies of the town, women's quartet	all c#1-e2	fast uptempo
If love were all, Manon (M)	b♭-f2 (opt. g2)	ballad
Dear little cafe, Sari (M), Carl	d1-g2/d1-g1	moving ballad
We wish to order wine, chorus		march tempo
Tokay, Capt. Schensi (Bar), chorus	c-e1	ballad
Bonne nuit, merci, Manon (in French)	e♭1-f2	mod. uptempo
Kiss me, Manon	c1-g2	waltz ballad
Ta-ra-ra-boom, chorus		uptempo
Alas, the time is past, women's sextet	SSMMMM	uptempo
Blasé boys are we, male quartet	all c-e1	mod. uptempo
Zigeuner ("Once upon a time"), Sari	c♭1-a♭2	waltz ballad

Added Song:
Evermore and a day, Sari, Carl   e♭1-g2/e♭-g1   ballad

Blood Brothers (1991)
Music and Lyrics by Willy Russell

Song title, Character (Voice)	Range	Song Style
Marilyn Monroe, Mrs. Johnstone (M)	a-a1	mod. uptempo
My child, Mrs. Johnstone, Mrs. Lyons (M)	a-g1/a-a1	mod. ballad
Easy terms, Mrs. Johnstone, chorus	g-a1	ballad
Shoes on the table, Narrator (Bar)	G-g	uptempo
Easy terms reprise, Mrs. Johnstone	g-f1	ballad
Kid's game, company		uptempo
Shoes upon the table reprise, Narrator	G-g	uptempo
Bright new day preview, Mrs. Johnstone	d1-b1	uptempo
Long Sunday afternoon, Mickey (Bar), Eddie (Bar)	d-e1/e-e1	mod. ballad
Bright new day reprise, Mrs. Johnstone, company	d1-b1	uptempo
Marilyn Monroe reprise, Mrs. Johnstone	a-a1	mod. uptempo
The devil's got your number, Narrator	G-g	uptempo
That guy, Mickey, Eddie	both d-e1	mod. uptempo
Shoes upon the table reprise, Narrator	G-f	uptempo
I'm not saying a word, Eddie	E-a	mod. ballad
Miss Jones, Mr. Lyons (Bar), chorus	c-d1	uptempo
Marilyn Monroe reprise, Mrs. Johnstone	a-a1	mod. uptempo
Light romance, Mrs. Johnstone	g-a1	ballad
Shoes upon the table reprise, Narrator	f#-f#1	uptempo
Tell me it's not true, Mrs. Johnstone, company	f-f2	ballad

Bombay Dreams (2004)
Music by A.R. Rahman   Lyrics by Don Black

Song title, Character (Voice)	Range	Song Style
Salaa'm Bombay, company		uptempo
Bollywood, Akaash (T), chorus	a-g#1	uptempo
Love's never easy, Sweetie (S), Priya (M), chorus	g1-g2/b♭-f2	mod. ballad
Lovely, lovely, ladies, Rani (M), chorus	c#1-b1	mod. uptempo
Bhangra, Akaash, chorus	chanted on a	uptempo
Shakalaka baby, company		uptempo
I could live here, Akaash	d#-f#1	ballad
Is this love?, Priya	a-b♭1	ballad

Famous, company		mod. uptempo
Shakalaka baby/Love's never easy reprise, company		scene
Chaiya, chaiya, company		uptempo
How many stars?, Akaash, Priya	c#-g#1/b-d2	mod. ballad
Salaa'm Bombay reprise, Rani, chorus	e♭1-c2	uptempo
Hero, Sweetie, Priya	f1-b♭2/f-d2	ballad
The journey home, Akaash	f-a♭1	mod. ballad
Wedding Qawali, company		mod. uptempo
Salaa'm Bombay bows, company		uptempo

The Boy Friend (1954)
Music and Lyrics by Sandy Wilson

Song title, **Character (Voice)**	**Range**	**Song Style**
Perfect young ladies, unison women's chorus		uptempo
The boy friend, Polly (S), chorus	c1-e2	mod. uptempo
Won't you Charleston?, Bobby (Bar), Maisie (M)	A-e1/a-e2	mod. uptempo
Fancy forgetting, Madame Dubonnet (S), Percival (T)	d1-g2/d-e1	uptempo
I could be happy with you, Tony (T), Polly	c-f1/c1-a2	ballad
The boy friend, ensemble		uptempo
Sur la plage, company		mod. uptempo
A room in Bloomsbury, Tony, Polly	c-g1/c1-g2	uptempo
It's nicer in Nice, Hortense (M), chorus	d1-g2	mod. ballad
The "you don't want to play with me" blues, Madame Dubonnet, Percival, women's chorus	c1-e♭2/c#-d1	uptempo
Safety in numbers, Maisie, men's chorus	b♭-f2	blues ballad
I could be happy with you, Tony, Polly	c-e♭1/c1-e♭2	uptempo
The riviera, chorus with incidental soli		ballad
It's never too late to fall in love, Lord Brockhurst (Bar), Dulcie (M)	d-e♭1/d1-e♭2	uptempo
Poor little Pierrette, Madame Dubonnet, Polly	b♭-f1/g-b♭2	mod. character
I could be happy with you reprise, chorus		uptempo

The Boy from Oz (2003)

Music by Peter Allen
Other music and lyrics by Allen and Adrienne Anderson, Burt Bacharach, Carole
Bayer Sager, David Foster, Tom Keane, Greg Cornell, Michael Caller,
Marsha Malamet, and Dean Pitchford

Song title, Character (Voice)	Range	Song Style
All the lives of me, Peter (Bar)	G-e♭	moving ballad
When I get my name in lights, Young Peter (boy)	a-d2	uptempo
When I get my name . . . reprise, Young Peter	a-d2	uptempo
Love crazy, Chris (T), Peter, ensemble	e-a1/ e-f1	uptempo
All I wanted was the dream, Judy Garland (M)		ballad
Only an older woman, Judy, Peter, Chris, Mark	MTBB	mod. uptempo
Best that you can do, Peter, Liza Minelli (M)	*	mod. uptempo
Don't wish too hard, Judy	*	uptempo
Come save me, Peter, Liza	*	mod. uptempo
Continental American, Peter, company	e♭-f1	mod. uptempo
She loves to hear the music, Liza, ensemble	b♭-e♭2	moving ballad
Quiet please!, Peter, Judy, company	A-f1/e1-f#2	mod. ballad
I'd rather leave while I'm in love, Liza	g-e2	ballad
Not the boy next door, Peter, Marion (Bar) incidental, company	d-g1	dramatic ballad
Bi-coastal, Peter, girls' trio	e-a1	uptempo
If you were wondering, Peter	c-d1	ballad
Sure thing, baby, Dee (M), Greg (T)	a-d2/d-g1	uptempo
Sure thing, baby reprise, Peter, girls	a♭-g1	uptempo
Everything old is new again, Peter, company (version 2:)	c-b1 / c-g1	bouncy uptempo
Everything old . . . reprise, Marion; Dee, Greg incidental	A-d1	uptempo
Love don't need a reason, Peter, Greg at end	c-d1/d-d1	ballad
I honestly love you, Greg	e♭-f1	ballad
You and me, Liza, Peter		moving ballad
I still call Australia home, Peter, ensemble	e-g♭1	mod. ballad
Don't cry out loud, Marion	G-e♭1	ballad
Once before I go, Peter	B-f1	mod. ballad
I go to Rio, Peter, company	f-f#1	driving uptempo

*Missing from score examined.

The Boys from Syracuse (1938)

Music by Richard Rodgers   Lyrics by Oscar Hammerstein II

Song title, Character (Voice)	Range	Song Style
I had twins, company		uptempo
Dear old Syracuse, Antipholus of Syracuse (T)	A-f1	uptempo
What can you do with a man?, Luce (M), Dromio of Ephesus (T)	a-b1/d-e1	fast character
Falling in love with love, Adriana (S)	d1-ab2	ballad
The shortest day of the year, Antipholus of Ephesus (T), Adriana	d-f1/e1-f2	mod. uptempo
This can't be love, Antipholus of S., Luciana (S)	db-f1/db1-f2	mod. uptempo
This can't be love reprise, Luciana	d1-e2	mod. ballad
Ladies of the evening, chorus		uptempo
He and she, Luce, Dromio of S. (B)	ab-eb2/Ab-eb1	ballad
You have cast your shadow on the sea, Antipholus of S., Luciana	eb-e1/c#1-e2	ballad
Come with me, Sergeant (T), men's chorus	c-g1	fast character
Big brother, Dromio of E. (T)	f-f1	ballad
Sing for your supper, Adriana, Luciana, Luce	c1-bb2/bb-g2/bb-eb2	uptempo
Oh, Diogenes, Courtesan (M), chorus	a-c2	uptempo
This can't be love, chorus		uptempo

Brigadoon (1947)

Music by Frederick Loewe   Lyrics by Alan Jay Lerner

Song title, Character (Voice)	Range	Song Style
Opening sequence: Prologue, Brigadoon, Vendor's calls, Down on MacConnachy Square, chorus, many soli		mostly uptempo
Waitin' for my dearie, Fiona (S), women's chorus	c1-a2	ballad
I'll go home with Bonnie Jean, Charlie (T), chorus	d-g1	uptempo
The heather on the hill, Tommy (high Bar)	bb-f1	ballad
Rain scene, chorus		mod. uptempo
The love of my life, Meg (M)	g-c2	mod. ballad
Jeannie's packin' up, women's chorus		mod. uptempo
Come to me, bend to me, Charlie	d-g1	ballad
Almost like being in love, Tommy, Fiona	c-f#1/f1-a2	ballad, then faster
The chase, men's chorus, incidental soli		uptempo
There but for you go I, Tommy, Fiona	c-f1/spoken	ballad

My mother's wedding day, Meg, chorus	c1-f2	character
From this day on/Farewell, Tommy, Fiona, chorus	d-a1/d1-a2	mod. ballad
Finale: Reprises, company		uptempo
Come to me, Heather on the hill,		
I'll go home, From this day on,		
Down on MacConnachy Square		

Bye, Bye, Birdie (1960)

Music by Charles Strouse   Lyrics by Lee Adams

Song title, **Character (Voice)**	**Range**	**Song Style**
An English teacher, Rosie (M)	e#-a#1	uptempo
The telephone hour, chorus		fast character
How lovely to be a woman, Kim (S)	d#1-f#2	ballad
Put on a happy face, Albert (Bar)	B-e1	uptempo
A healthy, normal, American boy, company		moving ballad
Penn Station to Sweet Apple, chorus		ballad
One boy, Kim, Rosie, Two girls incidental	db1-ab2/ab-bb1	ballad
Honestly sincere, Conrad (T), chorus incidental	Ab-f1	swing ballad
Hymn for a Sunday evening, company		character
One last kiss, Conrad, chorus	Ab-f1	uptempo
What did I ever see in him, Rosie, Kim	both g-bb1	ballad
What did I ever see in him reprise, Rosie	g-bb1	ballad
A lot of livin' to do, Conrad, Kim, chorus	db-f1/e1-e2	uptempo
Kids, Mr. and Mrs. Macafee (Bar, M)	f-eb1/f1-eb2	uptempo
Baby, talk to me, Albert, male trio	f#-f#1	ballad
Kids reprise, chorus		uptempo
Spanish Rose, Rosie	g-c#2	uptempo
Rosie, Albert, Rosie	B-d1/a-bb1	ballad

Cabaret (1966)

Music by John Kander   Lyrics by Fred Ebb

Song title, **Character (Voice)**	**Range**	**Song Style**
Wilkommen, M.C. (T), girls	f#-e1	uptempo
Welcome to Berlin, M.C.	f#-e1	uptempo
So what, Fr. Schneider (M)	eb-bb1	character
Don't tell Mama, Sally (M), girls	a-a1	character ballad
Telephone dance, ensemble		mod. uptempo
Perfectly marvelous, Sally, Cliff (Bar)	f#-b1/c#-e1	uptempo
Two ladies, ensemble		mod. uptempo

It couldn't please me more, Fr. Schneider, Herr Schneider (Bar)	f#-a1/f#-g1	ballad
Tomorrow belongs to me, Tenor, chorus	a-a1	uptempo
Why should I wake up?, Cliff	B-e1 (opt. f1)	ballad
Sitting pretty, M.C., girls	e-g1	mod. uptempo
Married, Herr Schneider, Fr. Schneider	d-f1/a-a1	character ballad
Meeskite, Schultz (T), Sally incidental	f#-g1	character
Tomorrow belongs . . . reprise, Fr. Kost (M), company	a- b♭1	ballad
If you could see her, M.C.	d♭-a♭1	mod. ballad
What would you do?, Fr. Schneider	f-a1	ballad
Cabaret, Sally	e-c2	uptempo
Finale: Wilkommen reprise, company		uptempo

Note: 1987 Broadway version is different, including two new songs, "Don't Go" and "I Don't Care Much." Both "Meeskite" and "Why Should I Wake Up?" were dropped from that revised production.

La Cage aux Folles (1983)
Music and Lyrics by Jerry Herman

Song title, **Character (Voice)**	**Range**	**Song Style**
We are what we are, Les Cagelles (men's chorus)		mod. uptempo
A little more mascara, Albin (Bar), chorus incidental	B♭-d1	mod. ballad
With Anne on my arm, Jean-Michel (T)	A-g1	mod. uptempo
The promenade, company		fast waltz
Song on the sand, Georges (Bar)	A♭-e1	ballad
La cage aux folles, Albin, Les Cagelles	B♭-e1	uptempo
I am what I am, Albin	A-f1	hard ballad
Song on the sand reprise, Georges, Albin	both A-e1	ballad
Masculinity, George; Albin and chorus incidental	B-e1	mod. uptempo
Look over there, Georges	B-e1	waltz ballad
Cocktail counterpoint, Georges, Dindon (Bar), Mme. Dindon (M), Jacob (T)	A♭-b♭/B♭-e♭1/g1-a♭2/ B♭-a♭1	uptempo
The best of times, Albin, Jacqueline (M), chorus	c-e♭1/a#-b1	slow uptempo, builds
Look over there reprise, Jean-Michel, Georges incidental	d♭-d♭1	ballad
Grand finale: You on my arm, Georges, chorus	G#-d1	mod. uptempo
La cage aux folles, company		uptempo
The best of times, company		uptempo

Call Me Madam (1950)
Music and Lyrics by Irving Berlin

Song title, **Character (Voice)**	**Range**	**Song Style**
Mrs. Sally Adams, chorus		uptempo
The hostess with the mostes', Sally (M)	a-b1	fast character
The Washington square dance, Sally, chorus	b♭-c2	uptempo
Lichtenburg, Cosmo (T), chorus	B♭-g1	mod. character
Marrying for love, Cosmo, Sally	G-c1/f-b♭1	ballad
The Ocarina, Princess Maria (S), chorus	c1-d2	uptempo
It's a lovely day today, Kenneth (T), Princess Maria, chorus	d-f1/d1-d2	light ballad
The best thing for you, Sally	a-c2	ballad
Something to dance about, Sally, chorus	b♭-c2	uptempo
Once upon a time, today, Kenneth	e-f1	narrative ballad
They like Ike, Wilkins, Brockbank, Gallagher (all T)	g-g1/g-f1/g-f1	fast character
(I wonder why) You're just in love, Kenneth, Sally	d-f#1/d1-c2	mod. ballad
The best thing for you reprise, Sally	b♭-b♭1	mod. uptempo
It's a lovely day today, Kenneth, Maria	c-d1/d1-d2	ballad
Mrs. Sally Adams, chorus		mod. uptempo
You're just in love reprise, Sally, chorus	a♭-c♭2	mod. uptempo

Camelot (1960)
Music by Frederick Loewe   Lyrics by Alan Jay Lerner

Song title, **Character (Voice)**	**Range**	**Song Style**
I wonder what the King is doing tonight, Arthur (Bar)	B♭-c1	uptempo
The simple joys of maidenhood, Guenevere (S)	c#1-d#2	mod. ballad
Camelot, Arthur	c-d1	uptempo
Follow me, women's chorus, incidental soli		mod. uptempo
C'est moi, Lancelot (T)	c-d1	uptempo
The lusty month of May, Guenevere, chorus	d1-a2	uptempo
How to handle a woman, Arthur	A-d1	ballad
The jousts, chorus		uptempo
Before I gaze at you again, Guenevere	c1-e♭2	ballad
Madrigal, Lancelot	c-b1	sprightly ballad
If ever I would leave you, Lancelot	A-d1	ballad
The seven deadly virtues, Modred (B)	c-d1	uptempo
What do the simple folk do? Guenevere, Arthur	c1-e♭2/B♭-e♭1	mod. character
The persuasion, Modred, Morgan (Bar)	spoken	character
I loved you once in silence, Guenevere	d♭-e♭2	ballad

Guenevere, Man (Bar), company	B-d1	mod. ballad
Camelot, company		uptempo

Can-Can (1953)
Music and Lyrics by Cole Porter

Song title, Character (Voice)	Range	Song Style
Maidens typical of France, women's chorus		uptempo
Never give anything away, Pistache (M), women's chorus	a-b1	ballad
C'est magnifique, Pistache, Aristide (T)	a-b♭1/g-e1	mod. ballad
Come along with me, Boris (Bar), Hilaire incidental	d-e1	uptempo
Live and let live, Pistache	g-b1	fast gavotte
I am in love, Aristide	d-f1	uptempo foxtrot
If you loved me truly, ensemble		uptempo
Monmart, chorus		uptempo
Allez-vous-en, Pistache	g-b1	ballad
Never, never be an artist, unison chorus, ensemble	c#-e1	uptempo
It's all right with me, Aristide		uptempo foxtrot
Every man is a stupid man, Pistache	b-a1	mod. ballad
I love Paris, Pistache, chorus	g-b1	ballad
C'est magnifique reprise, Aristide, Pistache	d-f1/d1-d2	ballad
Can-can, Pistache, chorus	b-b♭1	uptempo
Monmart reprise, company		uptempo

Candide (1956)
Music by Leonard Bernstein   Lyrics by Richard Wilbur

Song title, Character (Voice)	Range	Song Style
The best of all possible worlds, company		uptempo
Oh, happy we, Candide (T), Cunegonde (S)	d-a1/d1-a2	uptempo, light
It must be so, Candide	d-e1	recit. folk ballad
Lisbon sequence, company, incidental soli		mod. uptempo
It must be me, Candide	d-e1	recit. ballad
Glitter and be gay, Cunegonde	e♭1-e♭3	fast showpiece
You were dead, you know, Candide, Cunegonde	e-e1/e1-g#2	character ballad
Pilgrim's processions, company		moderate
My love, Governor (T)	d♭-b♭1	character march
I am easily assimilated, Old Lady (M), Cunegonde and chorus incidental	d1-e2	character, tango

Finale act I: Farewell, Cunegonde, Candide, Old Lady, Governor	SMTB	uptempo
Quiet, Cunegonde, Old Lady, Governor incidental	d1-f2/g-f2	mod. ballad
Eldorado, Candide, chorus	d♭-f#1	ballad
Bon voyage, Governor, chorus	c-b♭1	character
Venice gambling scene, Croupie (incidental Bar), company		funny, uptempo
What's the use?, company		character
The Venice gavotte, ensemble		character
Make our garden grow, company		mod. uptempo

Added Song:

Dear boy, Pangloss (Bar)	B-f#1	character ballad

Carnival (1961)
Music and Lyrics by Bob Merrill

Song title, **Character (Voice)**	**Range**	**Song Style**
Direct from Vienna, company		mod. uptempo
Very nice man, Lili (S)	b♭-f#2	ballad
I've got to find a reason, Paul (T)	B♭-f1	mod. ballad
Mira, Lili	c-f1	uptempo
Sword, rose, and cape, Marco (Bar), Roustabouts (male ensemble)	e♭-e♭1	uptempo
Humming, Rosalie (M), Schelgel (Bar)	b♭-c2/B♭-b♭	uptempo
Yes, my heart, Lili, men's chorus	d♭1-f#2	uptempo
Everybody likes you, Paul	B♭-e♭1	mod. ballad
Magic magic, Rosalie, Marco; Lili incidental	d1-d2/d-d1	uptempo
Golden delicious ("Love makes the world go 'round"), Lili; Carrot Top and Horrible Henry incidental	c1-d2	moving ballad
Love makes the world go 'round reprise, Lili, company	b♭-b♭2	mod. waltz
Her face, Paul	B-e♭1	easy ballad
Cirque de Paris, Jacquot (T), Roustabouts	c-c1	uptempo
I hate him, Lili, Paul	c1-b2/A-c1	fast, then mod.
Paris reprise, chorus		uptempo
Always, always you, Marco, Rosalie	A-d1/a-f2	mod. ballad
Always you reprise, Rosalie	g-b♭1	mod. ballad
She's my love, Paul	B♭-e♭1	ballad

Carousel (1945)

Music by Richard Rodgers   Lyrics by Oscar Hammerstein II

Song title, **Character (Voice)**	**Range**	**Song Style**
Mister Snow, Carrie (S), Julie incidental	d1-g2	mod. uptempo
If I loved you, Billy (T), Julie (S)	B♭-g♭1/c1-g♭2	ballad
June is bustin' out all over, chorus		uptempo
Mister Snow reprise, Carrie, Mr. Snow (T)	d1-d1/f#-a1	mod. uptempo
When the children are asleep, Mr. Snow, Carrie	e♭-a1/c#1-f2	ballad
Blow high, blow low, Jigger (Bar), Billy, men's chorus	both d-b	character uptempo
Soliloquy, Billy	B-g1	epic ballad
June is bustin' out all over reprise, chorus		uptempo
A real nice clambake, company		mod. uptempo
Geraniums in the winder/Stonecutters cut it on stone, Mr. Snow, Jigger, chorus	d-f#1/c-b	mod. ballad
What's the use of wond'rin', Julie, girls' chorus	c1-f2	moving ballad
You'll never walk alone, Nettie (M), Julie incidental	c1-g2	ballad
The highest judge of all, Billy	d-g1	mod. uptempo
If I loved you reprise, Billy	d♭-g♭1	ballad
Graduation scene, chorus		mod. ballad

Carrie (1988)

Music by Michael Gore   Lyrics by Dean Pitchford

Song title, **Character (Voice)**	**Range**	**Song Style**
Prologue: In, Ms. Gardener (M), girls' chorus	d♭-d♭2	uptempo
Dear Lord, Carrie (M)	b-b1	mod. ballad
Dream on, girls' ensemble		mod. uptempo
Locker room scene, Ms. Gardener, Sue (M)	both b-b1	slow
Carrie, Carrie	g-d2	moving ballad
Open your heart, Margaret (S), Carrie	b♭-e2/c-d♭2	ballad
Eve was weak, Margaret, Carrie	b♭-e♭2/a-d2	mod. uptempo
Don't waste the moon, company		uptempo
Evening prayers, Carrie, Margaret	g-e♭2/c1-g2	moving ballad
Unsuspecting hearts, Ms. Gardener, Carrie incidental	g♭-c2	moving ballad
Do me a favor, company		uptempo
I remember how those boys could dance, Carrie, Margaret	g-e♭2/b-e♭2	uptempo

Out for blood, Chris (Bar), Billy (T), boys' chorus	A♭-c1/c-g1	uptempo
It hurts to be strong, Sue	g#-c#2	uptempo
I'm not alone, Carrie	f-d2	ballad
Carrie reprise, Margaret, Carrie	g-d2/a-c2	moving ballad
When there's no one, Margaret	f#-c#2	ballad
Wotta night!, chorus		uptempo
Unsuspecting hearts reprise, Ms. Gardener, Carrie	b♭-b1/g♭-e2	mod. ballad
Heaven, Tommy (Bar), septet	B♭-f1	mod. uptempo
Alma mater, chorus		ballad
The destruction, Carrie	g#-d2	uptempo
Carrie (Finale), Margaret	c1-c2	ballad

The Cat and the Fiddle (1932)

Music by Jerome Kern   Lyrics by Otto Harbach

Song title, Character (Voice)	Range	Song Style
La jeune fille, Mme. Abajour (M)	b-c2	ballad
The night was made for love, Pompineau (T)	e♭-a♭1	ballad
She didn't say "yes," Pompineau, Shirley (M)	e-f#1/e1-f#2	moving ballad
La jeune fille reprise, Mme. Abajour	e♭-a♭1	ballad
The love parade, Pompineau, Maizie (M), chorus	e-f1/e1-b1	moving ballad
Victor's studio, Constance (S), Odette (M), Victor (T)	c1-a2/c1-g2/c-g1	ballad
The breeze kissed your hair, Victor, Odette	c-g1/e1-f2	ballad
Try to forget, Shirley	a-e2	ballad
Tableau scene, Commère (M), Coupère (Bar)	b-f#2/G-e1	character
Try to forget, company		uptempo
The crystal candelabra, Pompineau	d-g1	uptempo
She didn't say "yes" reprise, Shirley, Pompineau	e1-g2/c-f1	ballad
A new love is old, Victor	d♭-g♭1	ballad
One moment alone, Shirley, Victor, offstage chorus	a♭1-a♭2/a♭-g♭1	ballad
Phantasy, offstage chorus		mod. uptempo
Ha! Cha! Cha!, Shirley	e♭1-e♭2	mod. uptempo
She didn't say "yes" reprise, company		uptempo

Cats (1982)

Music by Andrew Lloyd Webber   Lyrics by T.S. Eliot and Trevor Nunn

Song title, **Character (Voice)**	**Range**	**Song Style**
Jellicle songs, company		uptempo
The naming of cats, company	mostly spoken	slow
The old gumbie cat, Munkus (T), Gumble (M), girls' trio	d-f#1/g-d♭2	mod. slow
The rum tum tugger, Tugger (Bar), chorus	e-f#1	mod. uptempo
Grizabella the glamour cat, Grizabella (M), Demeter (M), chorus	a-c2/g-c2	slow
Bustopher Jones, company		mod. uptempo
Mungo Jerrie and Rumpleteazer, Mungo (T), Rumple (M)	e-g1/c1-e♭2	mod. uptempo
Old Deuteronomy, company		ballad
Pekes and pollicles, Munkus, male chorus	f#-f1	uptempo
Jellicle ball, company		uptempo
Grizabella the glamour cat reprise, Grizabella	g-e2	ballad
Moments of happiness, Deuteronomy (T), Silabub (M), chorus	e♭-g♭1/b-e2	slow
Gus the theatre cat, Griddlebone (M), Gus (Bar)	g#-e2/A-d1	mod. ballad
Growltiger's last stand, company		mod. uptempo
McCavity the mystery cat, Demeter, Bomba (M)	A-f1	slow
Magical Mister Mistofeles, Tugger, Mistofeles (Bar)	both c-e♭1	mod. uptempo
Journey to the heavyside layer, company		mod. uptempo
The addressing of cats, Deuteronomy, company	B♭-g1	mod. uptempo

Celebration (1969)

Music by Harvey Schmidt   Lyrics by Tom Jones

Song title, **Character (Voice)**	**Range**	**Song Style**
Celebration, Potemkin (Bar), chorus	A♭-d♭1	uptempo
Orphan in the storm, Orphan (boy), chorus	b♭-e♭2	ballad
Survive, Potemkin, incidental chorus	c♭-e♭1	ballad
Somebody, Angel (M), chorus	f-c2	moving ballad
Bored, Rich (Bar)	G-e♭1	mod. fast, funny
My garden, Orphan, chorus	g-f2	moving ballad
Where did it go?, Rich, chorus*	B-e1	jazzy ballad
Love song, company		ballad
I'm glad to see you got what you want, Orphan, Angel	b♭-d2/b♭-f2	ballad

It's you who makes me young, Rich, incidental chorus	G-c1	uptempo, Latin beat
Not my problem, Potemkin, chorus*	B♭-f1	angry ballad
Fifty million years ago, Orphan	e♭-f2	uptempo
Beautician ballet, Rich, women's chorus	G-c1	fast character
Under the tree, Angel, women's chorus	b-e2	ballad
Winter and summer, chorus		driving ballad
Celebration reprise, company		uptempo

*Chorus may be omitted for solo.

Chess (1988)

Music by Benny Andersson and Björn Ulvaeus   Lyrics by Tim Rice

Song title, Character (Voice)	Range	Song Style
Press conference, Florence (M), company	d1-d2	uptempo
Where I want to be, Anatoly (T)	e-f1	driving ballad
How many women, Florence, Freddie (T)	e-c#1/a-g1	uptempo
Merchandiser's song, ensemble		mod. uptempo
U.S. versus U.S.S.R., Molokov (B), chorus	G-c#1	mod. ballad
A model of decorum and tranquility, Molokov, Florence, Arbiter (Bar), Anatoly	c#-d1/f-f2/F-e♭1/F-e	uptempo
You want to lose your only friend?, Florence, Freddie	e-g1/G-a1	driving ballad
Someone else's story, Florence	f-c2	ballad
One night in Bangkok, Freddie, chorus	d-a1 (much spoken)	uptempo
Terrace duet, Florence, Anatoly	a-e2/A-f1	ballad
So you got what you want, Freddie, Florence	e-c♭2/ b-b1	uptempo
Nobody's side, Florence, backup chorus	e-e2	ballad
Anthem, Anatoly	c#-g1	ballad
Hungarian folk song, company		anthem ballad
Heaven help my heart, Florence	a♭-b♭1	ballad
No contest, Freddie, Walter (T)	f-a1/g-a1	mod. uptempo
You and I, Anatoly, Florence, Svetlana (M)	c-g1/g-c2/e#-b1	mod. ballad
A whole new board game, Freddie	e1-a1	driving uptempo
Let's work together, Walter, Molokov	c-d1 (d2 falsetto)/D-d1	recit. like, mod. uptempo
I know him so well, Florence, Svetlana	f-d2/f-c2	ballad
Pity the child, Freddie	B♭-d♭2	slow ballad
Lullaby (Apukad eros kezen), Gregor (B), Florence	A-d1/b-g1	ballad
Endgame, Anatoly, Freddie, company	c-a1/c#-g#1	uptempo
You and I reprise, Anatoly, Florence	A-f1/g-d1	moving ballad
Anthem reprise, Florence	a♭-d♭1	ballad

Chicago (1975)

Music by John Kander   Lyrics by Fred Ebb

Song title, Character (Voice)	Range	Song Style
All that jazz, Velma (M), company	g#-c2	mod., hard jazz
Funny honey, Roxie (M)	f-b♭1	blues ballad
Cell block tango, sextet	SSMMMM	mod. ballad
When you're good to mama, Matron (S)	f#1-a2	uptempo, torch
All I care about, Billy (T), women	c-f#1	mod. ballad
A little bit of good, Mary Sunshine (S)	b♭-b♭2	uptempo
We both reached for the gun, company		uptempo
Roxie, Roxie, men	g♭-d2	mod. fast jazz
I can't do it alone, Velma	f#-c2	mod. uptempo
My own best friend, Roxie, women	g-f2	mod. ballad
I know a girl, Velma	e-a1	mod. uptempo
Me and my baby, Roxie, men incidental	b♭-c2	uptempo
Mister Cellophane, Amos (T)	c#-f#1	ragtime ballad
When Velma takes the stand, Velma, men	spoken	hard, jazz
Razzle dazzle, Billy, company	d-f1	uptempo
Class, Velma, Matron	f#-b♭1/f#-g1	mod. uptempo
Nowadays, Roxie	f#-g1	moving ballad
Nowadays reprise, Velma, Roxie	both f#-a♭1	ballad

Chitty Chitty Bang Bang (2005)
Music and Lyrics by Richard M. and Robert B. Sherman

Song title, Character (Voice)	Range	Song Style
Oh, there never was a car, company		uptempo
You two, Potts (T), two children	d-e1	mod. uptempo
Toot sweets, company		mod. uptempo
Act English, Boris (T), Goran (Bar)	c-g1/B-f#1	character uptempo
Hushabye Mountain, Potts	d#-f1	waltz ballad
Fun fair, chorus		slow, then fast
Me ol' bam-boo, male ensemble, several incidental solos		uptempo
Posh!, Grandpa (Bar), children	c-c1/both c1-c2	uptempo
Chitty chitty bang bang, company		uptempo
Truly scrumptious, Trudy (M), children	d1-c2/both d1-d2	mod. uptempo
Chitty chitty . . . nautical reprise, ensemble		uptempo
Chitty chitty . . . finale reprise, company		uptempo
Vulgarian town square, chorus		moderate
The roses of success, male chorus		mod. ballad
Kiddy-widdy-winkies, Childcatcher (Bar)	d-e1	mod. ballad
Teamwork, Potts, children's chorus		mod. uptempo
Chi-chi face, Baron (Bar), Baroness (M)	c-e♭1/f-g2	mod. ballad
The bombie samba, Baroness, Baron, chorus	g-e♭2/f#-e♭1	mod. uptempo

Doll on a music box, Trudy, Potts	d♭-e♭2/d♭-d♭1	flowing ballad
Teamwork reprise, company		mod. uptempo
Chitty chitty . . . bows, company		uptempo

Chorus Line (1975)

Music by Marvin Hamlisch   Lyrics by Edward Kleban

Song title, **Character (Voice)**	**Range**	**Song Style**
Opening: I hope I get it, company		uptempo
I can do that, Mike (T)	g-a♭1	mod., narrative
". . . and . . . ," company		moderate
At the ballet, Sheila (M), Bebe (M), Maggie (S)	e-d2/a-c2/a-e2	waltz ballad
Sing!, Kristine (M), Al (T)	spoken/g-g#1	character, funny
Hello, twelve, company		uptempo
Nothing, Morales (M)	g-b1	mod., narrative
Mother, company		narrative
Gimme the ball, Richie (T)	c#-g1	uptempo
Dance: ten; looks: three, Val (M)	b♭-d♭2	mod., funny
The music and the mirror, Cassie (M)	b-d2	moving ballad
One, company		mod. uptempo
What I did for love, Morales, company	b♭-b♭1	ballad
One reprise, company		uptempo

Cinderella (1957)*

Music by Richard Rodgers   Lyrics by Oscar Hammerstein II

Song title, **Character (Voice)**	**Range**	**Song Style**
The Prince is giving a ball, chorus, many soli		uptempo
In my own little corner, Cinderella (S)	d1-d2	moving ballad
Your majesties, King (T), Queen (M), others incidental	c-f1/b-b1	character
Boys and girls like you and me, Queen, King	b-e2/B-e1	ballad
In my own little corner reprise, Cinderella	d1-d2	ballad
Impossible, Godmother (M), Cinderella incidental	d1-d2	uptempo
It's possible, Godmother, Cinderella	both d♭1-d♭2	uptempo
Ten minutes ago, Prince (T), Cinderella	c-d1/c#1-d2	waltz ballad
Stepsisters' lament, Joy (M), Portia (M)	both c1-d2	fast character
Waltz for a ball, chorus		waltz ballad
Do I love you because you're beautiful, Prince, Cinderella	e-e1/d1-d2	ballad
When you're driving through the moonlight, Cinderella	b-b1	uptempo

A lovely night, Cinderella, Stepsisters	d1-d2/SS: c1-d2	ballad
Do I love you . . . reprise, Prince, Queen incidental	c-e1	ballad
The wedding, "Do I love you," company		ballad

*Originally written for CBS Television.

City of Angels (1989)

Music by Cy Coleman   Lyrics by David Zippel

Song title, Character (Voice)	Range	Song Style
Prologue, Angel City Four*	SMTB*	uptempo
Double talk, Stine (T)	B#-g#1	mod. uptempo
What you don't know about women, Gabby (M), Oolie (M)	both g-f2	hard, jazzy ballad
Stay with me, Jimmy Powers (T), Angel City Four	g-g1	40s ballad
You gotta look out for yourself, Jimmy, Angel City Four	c-e1	uptempo
The Buddy system, Buddy (Bar)	c-d1	fast, jazzy waltz
With every breath I take, Bobbi (M)	e-db1	blues ballad
The tennis song, Alaura (M), Stone (Bar)	g-e2/G-d1	funny ballad
Everybody's gotta be somewhere, Stone, Angel City Four	c-b1	uptempo
Lost and found, Mallory (M)	g#-c#2	jazz ballad
All you have to do is wait, Muñoz (high Bar), TBB trio incidental	d-f#1	mod. Latin ballad
You're nothing without me, Stine, Stone	d-g1/d-e1	mod. uptempo
Stay with me, nos. 2-3, Jimmy, Angel City Four	c-g1	ballad
You can always count on me, Oolie/Donna	a-db2	mod. funny ballad
It needs work, Gabby	ab-c2	mod. ballad
With every breath I take reprise, Bobbi, Stone	d#-c2/G#-e1	ballad
Funny, Stine	Bb-f1	hard ballad
I'm nothing without you, Stine, Stone, company	d-g1/d-e1	mod. uptempo

*Angel City Four, inclusive ranges for all numbers:
    S = a-a2
    M = a-d2
    T = d#-b1
    B = G-g#1

The following singing roles are double-cast:
    Gabby/Bobbi, Oolie/Donna, Carla/Alaura

A Class Act (2001)
Music and Lyrics by Edward Kleban

Song title, Character (Voice)	Range	Song Style
Light on my feet, Ed (T), company	B-f#1	uptempo
The fountain in the garden, company		moderate
One more beautiful song, Ed, Sophie (M)	A-f1/b♭-e♭2	ballad
Fridays at four, company		uptempo
Charm song, Lehman (Bar), chorus	B♭-e♭1	mod. uptempo
Paris through the window, trio	TBB	mod. ballad
Mona, Mona (M)	f-d♭2	bossa nova
Under separate cover, trio	MMT	mod. ballad
Don't do it again, Felicia (M), Ed	b-e2/c#-e1	jazzy, moderate
Gauguin's shoes, Ed, chorus	B♭-f1	soft shoe
Don't do it again reprise, Lehman	c-e♭1	mod. uptempo
Follow your star, Sophie, Ed, company	g-a1/d-d1	mod. ballad
Better, company		uptempo
Scintillating Sophie, Ed, Sophie incidental	c-f1	ballad
The next best thing to love, Sophie	e♭-a1	uptempo
Broadway boogie woogie, Lucy (M)	f#-b1	uptempo
Better reprise, Ed, company	A-f1	uptempo
Say something funny, company		moderate
When the dawn breaks, Ed	c-f1	uptempo
Self-portrait, Ed, company	g-f1	ballad

Closer Than Ever (1989)
Music by David Shire   Lyrics by Richard Maltby, Jr.

Song title, Character (Voice)	Range	Song Style
Doors, company		uptempo
She loves me not, Woman 1 (S), Man 1 (T), Man 2 (Bar)	b♭-f2/c-a1/c-e2	uptempo
You wanna be my friend, Woman 2 (M), Man 2 incidental	e♭1-d♭2	uptempo
What am I doin', Man 1	c-a2	driving ballad
The bear, the tiger, the hamster, and the mole, Woman 1	a♭-d♭2	mod. uptempo, funny
Like a baby, Man 2, Woman 1, 2	B♭-d1/b♭-e♭2/ b♭-c2	ballad
Miss Byrd, Woman 2	f-d♭2 (with scatted g2)	character
The sound of muzak, company		uptempo
One of the good guys, Man 1	c-f1	ballad
There's nothing like it, company		uptempo
Life story, Woman 1	b♭-c2	ballad

Next time/I wouldn't go back, company + Man 3		mod. uptempo
Three friends, Woman 1, Woman 2, Man 1	a#-f#2/a#-c#2/a#-a1	uptempo
Fandango, Woman 1, Man 2	c1-d2/c-d1	funny, uptempo
There, Woman 2, Man 3 (Bar)	a-c#2/A-f1	whimsical, slow
Patterns, Woman 1	b♭-e♭2	ballad
Another wedding song, Woman 2, Man 2	b♭-c2/b-c1	mod. ballad
If I sing, Man 2	A-e♭1	ballad
Back on base, Woman 2	g-c#2	swing ballad
The march of time, company		uptempo
Fathers of fathers, Man 1, 2, 3	e-g1/others e-f1	moving ballad
It's never that easy/I've been here before, Woman 1, 2	b-g2/g-d1	ballad
Closer than ever, company + Man 3		moving ballad

Added Song:

I'll get up tomorrow morning, Man 2	B♭-e1	uptempo, patter song

The Color Purple (2005)
Music and Lyrics by Brenda Russell, Allee Willis, and Stephen Bray

Song title, **Character (Voice)**	**Range**	**Song Style**
Huckleberry pie/Mysterious ways, company		uptempo
Somebody gonna love you, Celie (M)	f-a1	ballad
Our prayer, company		mod. uptempo
The fine mister, Doris, Darlene, Jarene	MMM (mostly spoken)	uptempo
Big dog, Mister (T), chorus	f-c2	mod. uptempo
Bring my Nettie back, Celie	g-g2	ballad
Dear God/Sofia, Celie	g-g1	mod. ballad
A tree named Sofia, Doris, Darlene, Jarene	spoken	mod. uptempo
Hell no!, Sofia (M), women's ensemble	e-c2	slow funk
Brown Betty, trio and chorus	MMT	uptempo
Shug Avery comin' to town!, company		mod. uptempo
Dear God—Shug, Celie	d-b♭1	mod. ballad
Too beautiful for words, Shug (M)	e-b1	ballad
Push da button, Shug, company	a-e♭2	shuffle uptempo
Uh-oh, company		mod. uptempo
What about love?, Celie, Shug	e-d2/b-d2	ballad
African homeland		
Nettie in Africa, Nettie, company	e♭-d1	mod. uptempo
New Africa 1, chorus		uptempo
Olinka—Exodus, Nettie, company	f#-d♭2	ballad
The color purple, Shug	a#-d♭2	heavy ballad

Gossips Easter, Doris, Darlene, Jarene	MMM	mod. uptempo
Hell no! reprise, women's ensemble		mod. ballad
With these hands, Mister	Ab-f1	ballad
In Miss Celie's pants, women's ensemble		uptempo
Any little thing, Harpo (Bar), Sofia	f#-b/f#-f#2	mod. ballad
The color purple reprise, company		ballad

Company (1970)
Music and Lyrics by Stephen Sondheim

Song title, **Character (Voice)**	**Range**	**Song Style**
Company, Robert (T), ensemble	c-ab1	uptempo
Little things, Joanne (M), chorus	c#-f#1	character
Sorry-Grateful, Harry (Bar), David (Bar), Larry (Bar)	all d-e1	ballad
You could drive a person crazy, April (S), Marta (M), Kathy (M)	e1-a2/e1-e2/e1-e2	uptempo
Have I got a girl for you, ensemble		mod. uptempo
Someone is waiting, Robert	c#-f#1	ballad
Another hundred people, Marta, chorus incidental	c1-eb2	uptempo
Getting married today, Amy (S), chorus with soli	a-a1	uptempo, patter song
Side by side by side/What would we do without you?, company		uptempo
Poor baby, ensemble (various duets)		mod. uptempo
Barcelona, Robert, April	Bb-eb1/bb-eb2	mod. ballad
The ladies who lunch, Joanne	e-a1	character ballad
Being alive, Robert	f-g#1	uptempo
Company reprise, company		uptempo

Note: The 1995 revival added one song, not available for this annotation.

Copacabana (2000)
Music by Barry Manilow   Lyrics by Bruce Sussman and Jack Feldman

Song title, **Character (Voice)**	**Range**	**Song Style**
Copacabana, Stephen (T), company	g-f1	uptempo
Just arrived, Lola (M), women's chorus	g-c#2	uptempo
Dancing fool, Tony (T), men's chorus	c-g#2	swing uptempo
Sweet heaven, Tony, chorus	c-gb1	mod. uptempo
Hoover commercial, trio	MMT	moderate
Changing my tune, Tony	c#-g1	mod. uptempo
Copa girl, Gladys (M)	g-c2	mod. uptempo
Man wanted, Lola	a-c2	ballad

Who needs to dream, Tony, women	A-g1	ballad
I gotta be bad, Lola, women's chorus	f#-e♭2	uptempo
Bolero d'amore, Rico (Bar), chorus	e-f1	mod. ballad
Havana/Caramba, Conchita (M), chorus	g-e♭2	uptempo
Who am I kidding?, company		uptempo
This can't be real, Stephen, Lola	B♭-e1/f-c2	mod. ballad
El bravo, Lola, chorus	g-e♭1	uptempo
Sweet heaven reprise, Tony, Lola incidental, chorus	e♭-g1	mod. ballad
Who needs to dream reprise, Stephen, company	e♭-e♭1	mod. ballad
Copabcabana reprise, company		uptempo

Countess Maritza (1926)

Music by Emmerich Kálmán   Lyrics by Harry B. Smith

Song title, **Character (Voice)**	**Range**	**Song Style**
Dear home of mine, Tassilo (T), Nepomuk (Bar)	c#-g#1/B-e1	ballad
Hola! Follow me, Lazlo (T), chorus	d-a1	uptempo
Live while you live, Manya (S)	d1-g2	uptempo
Call of love, Tassilo, Manya	c-d1/c1-g2	ballad
In the days gone by, Tassilo, Stefan (T)	c#-f#1/e-a1	ballad
Make up your mind, Zingo (T), chorus	d-f#1	fast character
The music thrills me, Maritza (S), chorus	a#-b2	uptempo
Sister mine, Tassilo, Liza (S)	d-f1/g1-b♭2	waltz ballad
Sons of Mars, unison men's chorus		uptempo march
The one I'm looking for, Maritza, Zupan (Bar), chorus	d1-e2/B-f#1	mod. uptempo
Don't tempt me!, Tassilo, Manya	d-b♭1/c1-a2	recit.-like, fast
Love has found my heart, Maritza	e1-b2	waltz ballad
I'll keep on dreaming, Liza, Zupan	c1-g2/c-g1	ballad
Love is just a flash of light, Maritza, Tassilo	d1-a2 (opt. b2)/d-g1	mod. ballad
Play gypsies! Dance gypsies!, company		uptempo
Joy of life, Manya, Zupan, Zingo	mostly unison, d-e1	uptempo

The Cradle Will Rock (1938)

Music and Lyrics by Marc Blitzstein

Song title, **Character (Voice)**	**Range**	**Song Style**
I'm checkin home now, Moll (M), Gent (Bar), Dick (Bar)	f#-d2/B♭-a/c-b	ballad, then faster
Nightcourt scene, company		uptempo

Dear Mrs. Mister, Mrs. Mister (M), Rev. Salvation (Bar)	b♭-e♭2/e-e1	mod. uptempo
Croon, Junior (T), Sister (M)	B-d1/b-d2	mod. ballad
I have called you here, Mr. Mister (Bar), Editor Daily (T)	c-d1/d-a1	uptempo
Let's do something/Honolulu, Mr. Mister, Editor Daily, Junior, Sister	c-c1/c-f1/c-f1/c-d2	uptempo
Drugstore scene, Steve (T), Druggist (Bar), Bugs (Bar)	b-c1/c-d1/ spoken	mod. uptempo
I wonder if anyone could be in love as we, Gus (T), Sadie (M)	B-f#1/b-e♭2	ballad
Don't let me keep you, Dauber (Bar), Yasha (Bar)	both G#-e♭1	mod. uptempo
And we love art for art's sake, Dauber, Yasha	both e-d1	uptempo
Maybe you wonder, Moll	f#-c2	mod. ballad
Makin' a speech, Larry (Bar)	spoken	mod. ballad
The cradle will rock, Larry	A#-d#1	mod. uptempo
Hello doctor, Ella (M)	a-b♭1	mod. character
Listen, here's a story, Ella	f-b♭1	mod. uptempo
The cradle will rock reprise, chorus		mod. uptempo

Crazy for You (1991)
Music and Lyrics by George and Ira Gershwin

Song title, **Character (Voice)**	**Range**	**Song Style**
K-ra-zy for you, Bobby (T)	B♭-e♭1	uptempo
I can't be bothered now, Bobby, girls	d-f1	mod. uptempo
Bidin' my time, Cowboy Trio: Sam (Bar), Mingo (T), Moose (B)	d-d1/d-g1/c-b	mod. ballad
Things are looking up, Bobby	c-d1	mod. uptempo
Could you use me?, Bobby, Polly (M)	A-e♭1/a-d2	uptempo
Shall we dance, Bobby	d♭-f♭1	uptempo
Girls enter Nevada/Bronco busters, chorus		uptempo
Someone to watch over me, Polly	a♭-b♭1	moving ballad
Slap that bass, company		mod. uptempo
Embraceable you, Polly	a-b1	moving ballad
Tonight's the night, chorus		uptempo
I got rhythm, Polly, company	b-d♭	uptempo
The real American folksong, Cowboy Trio, chorus	c-a1/c-f1/A-d1	mod. uptempo, funny
What causes that?, Bobby, Zangler (Bar)	both c-f1	mod. uptempo
Naughty baby, Irene (M), Lank (Bar) incidental, male quartet	a♭-b♭1	mod. uptempo
Stiff upper lip, company		mod. uptempo
They can't take that away from me, Bobby	B♭-e♭1	swing ballad

But not for me, Polly	b♭-c2	ballad
Nice work if you can get it, Bobby, girls	d-d1	swing uptempo
Bidin' my time reprise, Cowboy Trio*	c1-g1/d-d1/c-c1	uptempo
Who could ask for anything more, company		uptempo
Embraceable you, company		ballad

*Sung in French.

Curtains (2007)

Music by John Kander   Lyrics by Fred Ebb and Rupert Holmes

Song title, Character (Voice)	Range	Song Style
Wide open spaces, company		uptempo
What kind of man, quartet	SMTB	mod. swing ballad
Thinking of him, Georgia (M); Bob, Aaron incidental	g-d♭2	ballad
The woman's dead, company		slow
Show people, Carmen (M), Cioffi (Bar), company	g-f2/A-f1	mod. uptempo
Coffee shop nights, Cioffi	A♭-d1	mod. ballad
In the same boat No. 1, trio	SMM	uptempo
I miss the music, Aaron (T)	c-g♭1	ballad
Thataway!, Georgia, chorus	b-e2	uptempo
He did it, company		uptempo
In the same boat No. 2, trio	TBB	uptempo
It's a business, Carmen, chorus	e♭-b♭1	mod. uptempo
Kansasland, company		mod. uptempo
Thinking of him/Missing the music reprise, Aaron, Georgia	A-g♭1/c1-b♭1	ballad
Tough act to follow, Cioffi, Niki incidental, chorus	A♭-e♭1	mod. ballad
In the same boat No. 3, company		uptempo
Wide open spaces reprise, company		uptempo
A tough act to follow reprise, company		uptempo

Dames at Sea (1968)

Music by Jim Wise   Lyrics by George Haimsohn and Robin Miller

Song title, Character (Voice)	Range	Song Style
Wall Street, Mona (M)	b-b1	uptempo
It's you, Ruby (M), Dick (T)	d1-e♭2/d-e♭1	jazzy ballad
Broadway baby, Dick	d-a1	uptempo
That Mister Man of mine, Mona, chorus	g-d#2	mod. uptempo
Choo choo honeymoon, Joan (M), Lucky (Bar)	b♭-e♭2/B♭-e♭1	mod. ballad

The sailor of my dreams, Ruby	a♭-d♭2	mod. ballad
Singapore Sue, company		uptempo
Good times reprise, company		uptempo
Dames at sea, Lucky, Dick, Captain (T), girls trio	all d-f#1 (one to g1)	uptempo
Beguine, Mona, Captain	d1-f#2/e-a♭1	beguine ballad
Raining in my heart, Ruby, chorus	a♭-d#2	mod. ballad
Something about you, Ruby, Dick	d1-d2/d-e1 (opt. f1)	mod. ballad
Echo waltz, Ruby, Joan, Mona, men offstage	women all d♭1-f2	waltz ballad
Star tar, Ruby, chorus	g#-c#2	uptempo march
Simple wedding, company		mod. uptempo

Damn Yankees (1955)
Music and Lyrics by Richard Adler and Jerry Ross

Song title, Character (Voice)	Range	Song Style
Six months out of every year, Meg (M), chorus	g-b1	fast uptempo
Goodbye old girl, Young Joe (T)	d-f1	ballad
Heart, Van Buren (T), ball players (men's chorus)	e♭-f1	uptempo
Heart reprise, ball players		uptempo
Shoeless Joe from Hannibal, Mo., Gloria (M), men	b♭-d♭2	uptempo
A man doesn't know, Joe	B♭-d1	ballad
A little brains, a little talent, Lola (M)	g-a1	fast, character
A man doesn't know reprise, Joe, Meg	c-f1/g-c2	ballad
Whatever Lola wants, Lola gets, Lola	f-c♭2	sleazy character
Heart reprise, ensemble		uptempo
Who's got the pain, Lola, Eddie (Bar)	B♭-b1/b♭-b2	jazz uptempo
The game, ball players		uptempo
Near to you, Joe, Meg	c-f♭1/a-c2	ballad
Those were the good old days, Applegate (Bar)	B-d1	mod. character
Two lost souls, Lola, Joe	both d-d1	ballad
A man doesn't know reprise, Meg, Joe	a♭-f2/f-f1	ballad
Bows: Heart, company		uptempo

Dear World (1973)
Music and Lyrics by Jerry Herman

Song title, Character (Voice)	Range	Song Style
Thru the bottom of the glass, Countess (M)	e-b1	mod. ballad
Just a little bit more, President (Bar),	A♭-e♭1/c♭-	uptempo
Prospector (Bar), Lawyer (T)	f♭1/c-f♭1	
Each tomorrow morning, Countess, chorus	f-b♭1	ballad
I don't want to know, Countess	g#-a♭1	waltz ballad
I've never said I love you, Nina (M)	a-e♭2	mod. ballad
Pretty garbage, Sewerman (Bar), Countess,	A-e/a-e2	moderate
Constance (M), Gabrielle (M)		
Ugly garbage, Sewerman, Constance,	b-e2/a♭-e	moderate
Gabrielle, chorus	men B-e1/b-e2	
One person, Countess, chorus	f-b♭1	mod. uptempo
The spring of next year, President,	G-d1/B♭-e♭1/	waltz ballad
Prospector, Lawyer	B♭-g1	
Memory, Constance	b-e♭2	character ballad
Dickie, Gabrielle, Countess incidental	g-e2	mod. uptempo
Voices, Constance	e1-e2	mod. uptempo
Thought, Countess	g-d1	ballad
Tea party trio, Countess, Constance,	g-d1/e-e1/g-c2	mod. uptempo
Gabrielle		
And I was beautiful, Countess	g-d2	ballad
Dear world, Julian (Bar), company	E-a (half-spoken)	mod. uptempo
Spring of next year reprise, chorus		ballad
Kiss her now, Countess	f#-a1	ballad
Dear world reprise, company		mod. uptempo

The Desert Song (1926)
Music by Sigmund Romberg
Lyrics by Otto Harbach, Oscar Hammerstein II, and Frank Mandel

Song title, Character (Voice)	Range	Song Style
High on a hill, Sid (T), men's chorus	e-a1	anthem ballad
The riff song, Red Shadow (T), Sid, men's chorus	d-g1/f-a1	ballad
Margot, Paul (Bar), men's chorus	e-e1	ballad
Why did we marry soldiers?, women's chorus		character
Oh girls, here are cavaliers, Margot (S), chorus	f1-c3	uptempo
Romance, Margot, women's chorus	d1-b♭2	waltz ballad
incidental		
Then you will know, Margot, Pierre (T), chorus	f-b2/c-e♭1	ballad
I want a kiss, ensemble, chorus		mod. uptempo
It, Susan (M), Bennie (Bar)	d1-d2/d-d1	fast uptempo
The desert song, Margot, Red Shadow	e♭1-b♭2/d♭-g♭1	waltz ballad

Oh, lucky Paul, tell us all, company		uptempo
My little castagnette, Clementina (S), women's chorus	e1-a2	uptempo
Song of the brass key, Clementina, women's chorus, Ali (Bar) incidental	e1-g2	character ballad
One good boy gone wrong, Clementina, Bennie	d1-f#2/d-g1	uptempo
Eastern and western love, ensemble, men's chorus		ballad
The sabre song, Margot, Red Shadow incidental	d1-bb2 (opt. c3)	ballad
All hail to the general, women's chorus		uptempo
It reprise, Bennie	eb-f1	uptempo

Dessa Rose (2005)

Music by Stephen Flaherty   Lyrics by Lynn Ahrens

Song title, Character (Voice)	Range	Song Style
We are descended, company		moderate
Comin' down the quarters, Kaine (T), chorus	f#-f#1	mod. uptempo
Old Banjar, Kaine, Dessa (M)	d#-f#1/f#1-d#2	mod. uptempo
Something of my own, Dessa	a-d2	urgent, in 2
Ink, Nehemiah (Bar)	B-f1	mod. uptempo
The gold band, company		scene
Ladies, Ruth's Mother (M), Dorcas (M)	c#1-d2/a-c2	mod. ballad
Bertie's waltz, Bertie (Bar), Ruth (M)	g-d1/e1-d2	uptempo
At the glen, Ruth	ab-eb2	ballad
Capture the girl, Nehemiah	Bb-db2	moving ballad
Fly away, company		scene
Terrible, company		uptempo/scene
Twelve children, Dessa, ensemble	bb-d2	moving ballad
Noah's dove, company		mod. uptempo
Fly away reprise, company		uptempo
The scheme, Nathan (Bar), Harkes (T), ensemble	A-f1/d-e1	ragtime ballad
In the bend of my arm, Dessa, Kaine, company	ab-db2/A-f1	ballad
Better if I died, Ruth, Dessa, company	d1-c2/d1-d2	moving ballad
Ten petticoats, Ruth's Mother, Dorcas	b-d2/b-e2	uptempo
Just over the line, company		uptempo
A pleasure, Ruth, Mr. Oscar (Bar), Dessa incidental	b-c2/B-d/ a-d2	uptempo waltz
We are descended reprise, company		moderate

Destry Rides Again (1959)
Music and Lyrics by Harold Rome

Song title, Character (Voice)	Range	Song Style
Don't take me back to Bottleneck, chorus		uptempo
Ladies, Frenchy (M), women's chorus	a-db2	uptempo
Hoop-de-dingle, Wash (T), chorus	B-f1	fast character
Tomorrow morning, Destry (Bar)	db-db1 (spoken)	character ballad
Ballad of a gun, Destry, Wash incidental	c-eb1 (spoken)	fast character
I know your mind, Frenchy	e-a1	tango torch song
I hate him, Frenchy	g#-c#2	uptempo, angry
Paradise alley, chorus		mod. uptempo
Anyone would love you, Destry, Frenchy	Bb-c1/g-a1	ballad
Once knew a fella, Destry, men's chorus	B-e1	uptempo
Every once in a while, men's chorus		uptempo
Fair warning, Frenchy	f-c2	uptempo
Ballad of a gun reprise, chorus		uptempo
Are you ready, Gyp Watson?, company		funereal ballad
Not guilty, men's chorus		slow, character
Only time will tell, Destry, chorus	c-d1 (much spoken)	narrative ballad
Respectability, Rose (M), women's chorus	g-bb1	ballad
Ring on the finger, Frenchy, women's chorus	f-bb1	ballad
Once knew a fella reprise, Frenchy, Destry	a-b1/A-d1	uptempo
I say hello, Frenchy	f-a1	ballad
Dirge, chorus		slow
Ballad of a gun reprise, company		uptempo

Dirty Rotten Scoundrels (2005)
Music and Lyrics by David Yazbek

Song title, Character (Voice)	Range	Song Style
What they want, Andre (Bar), Lawrence (Bar), company	c-f1/c-eb1	mod. uptempo
Great big stuff, Freddy (T), chorus	d-f#1	uptempo
Chimp in a suit, Andre	c-e1	mod. uptempo
Oklahoma, Jolene (M)	g-c2	character ballad
All about Ruprecht, Lawrence, Ruprecht incidental	c-e1	mod. swing ballad
What was a woman to do, Muriel (M)	e-b1	mod. uptempo
Here I am, Christine (M)	f-eb2	uptempo
Nothing is too wonderful to be true, Christine, Freddy	a-f2/d-f1	ballad
Finale, Act I, company		uptempo
Ruffhousin' mit shuffhausen, Lawrence, others incidental	c-f1 (yodeled b1)	moderate waltz

Yodel hotel, chorus		uptempo
Like zis, like zat, Andre, Muriel	B♭-e♭1/e-b♭1	ballad
The more we dance, Lawrence, company	c-g1	uptempo
Love is my legs, Freddy, Christine, chorus	d-b♭1/b-d2	pop ballad
Above the waist, Freddy, Christine	f-a♭1/a-c2	uptempo
The reckoning, male trio	TBB	uptempo
Eleven o'clock, Lawrence, Freddy	c-g♭1/f-b♭1	mod. ballad
Dirty rotten crook, trio	MTB	mod. uptempo

Do I Hear a Waltz? (1965)

Music by Richard Rodgers   Lyrics by Stephen Sondheim

Song title, Character (Voice)	Range	Song Style
Someone woke up, Leona (M)	a-b1	uptempo
This week, Americans, Fioria (M)	a-b♭1	character
What do we do? We fly!, ensemble		character
Someone woke up reprise, Leona	a-b1	uptempo
Someone like you, DiRossi (T)	e-f1	ballad
Bargaining, DiRossi	B♭-e3 (falsetto)	fast character
Here we are again, Leona, company	g#-b1	mod. ballad
Thinking, DiRossi, Leona	B-d#1/a-d#2	uptempo
Here we are again reprise, ensemble		ballad
No understand, Eddie (T), Fioria, Giovanna (S)	c#-d1/c#1-d2/a-e2	character
Take the moment, DiRossi	d-a♭1	moving ballad
Moon in my window, Jennifer (M), Fioria, Leona	b-d2/g-a1/g#-a	ballad
We're gonna be all right, Eddie, Jennifer	a-d1/a1-d2	uptempo
Do I hear a waltz?, Leona	a-d♭2	waltz ballad
Stay, DiRossi	a-d♭2	ballad
Perfectly lovely couple, ensemble		uptempo
Take the moment reprise, DiRossi	d-f1	ballad
Last week, Americans, Leona	a-a1	character
Thank you so much, Leona, DiRossi	b♭-d2/d-d1	ballad

Do, Re, Mi (1960)

Music by Jule Styne   Lyrics by Betty Comden and Adolph Green

Song title, Character (Voice)	Range	Song Style
Waiting, Kay (M)	b♭-d♭1	moving ballad
All you need is a quarter, chorus		uptempo
Take a job, Hubie (T), Kay	G-g1/c-e2	moving ballad
All you need is a quarter reprise, chorus		fast–Lindy Hop
It's legitimate, Hubie, Fatso (T), chorus	c#-f#1/e-a2	walking ballad

I know about love, Wheeler (Bar)	B-g1	ballad
Cry like the wind, Tilde (S)	b-b2	ballad
Ambition, Hubie, Tilde incidental	c#-e1/d1-a2	uptempo
Fireworks, Wheeler, Tilde	B-g1/b-g2	uptempo
What's new at the zoo?, Tilde, women's chorus	b-c#2	jazzy ballad
Asking for you, Wheeler	c-f1	ballad
The late, late show, Hubie	c-d1	uptempo
Adventure, Hubie, Kay	c#-c#1/g#-d♭2	uptempo
Make someone happy, Wheeler, Tilde	c-f1/b-f2	ballad
Who is Mr. Big?, ensemble, chorus		mod. uptempo
He's a V.I.P., chorus		mod. uptempo
All of my life, Hubie	c-e1	forceful ballad
Make someone happy reprise, company		uptempo

Dr. Dolittle (1998)
Music and Lyrics by Leslie Bricusse

Song title, Character (Voice)	Range	Song Style
Talk to the animals, Dolittle (T), Polynesia (M), others incidental	B♭-f#1/d♭-d1	mod. uptempo
My friend the doctor, Matthew (Bar), chorus	B♭-e1	uptempo
The vegetarian, Dolittle	c-f1	uptempo
Doctor Dolittle, Matthew, chorus	G-e1	mod. uptempo
I've never seen anything like it, Blossom (M), Dolittle, company	c1-d2/c-d1	jaunty two
When I look in your eyes, Dolittle	d-a♭1	ballad
Like animals, Dolittle	d-e1	uptempo
After today, Matthew	B-f1	fast waltz
Fabulous places, quartet	MTBB	uptempo
Where are the words, Matthew, Dolittle	c-e♭1/B♭-e♭1	ballad
Save the animals, Straight Arrow (B), chorus	F-f1	mod. uptempo
Something in your smile, Dolittle	B♭-e♭1	ballad
My friend the doctor reprise, S. Arrow	B♭-e1	uptempo
The voice of protest, Emma (M), company	b-g#2	militant march
Finale, Blossom, company	d1-d#2	uptempo
Bows: You've never seen anything like it, chorus		uptempo

Dreamgirls (1981)

Music by Henry Krieger   Lyrics by Tom Eyen

Song title, Character (Voice)	Range	Song Style
I'm looking for something, baby, company		uptempo
Tiny Joe Dixon, Tiny Joe (T)	g-g1	blues ballad
Move (you're steppin' on my heart), Effie (M), Lorrell (S), Deena (M) (Dreamettes)	bb-f2/d1-eb2 d1-db2	uptempo
Fake your way to the top, Jimmy (T), Dreamettes, offstage chorus	f-ab1	mod. uptempo
Cadillac car, Curtis (T), ensemble	f-g1	uptempo
Steppin' to the bad side, company		mod. jazz ballad
Party party, ensemble		uptempo
Baby, baby, Jimmy, Dreamettes	f-g1	ballad
Family, ensemble		ballad
Dreamgirls, Deena, Effie, Lorrell	a-e2/c#1-e2/c#1-a2	uptempo
Reporters, ensemble		uptempo
Heavy, Deena, Effie, Lorrell, Curtis incidental	d1-c2/eb1-eb2/e1-bb2	narrative ballad
It's all over, ensemble		uptempo
(And I'm telling you) I'm not going, Effie, ensemble	eb1-f2	uptempo
Opening act II, company		mod. uptempo
You are my dream, Curtis, ensemble	c-e1	mod. ballad
Ain't no party, Jimmy, Lorrell, TTBBB ensemble	g-ab1/bb-gb2	mod. swing ballad
I mean you no harm/Rap, ensemble	SSMMT	slow, then faster
I miss you old friend, ensemble, Les Styles (4 girls)	(mostly spoken)	uptempo
One night only, Effie, chorus	ab-db2	mod. ballad
One night only — disco, company		uptempo
Chicago, ensemble		mod. uptempo
Hard to say goodbye (my love), ensemble		moving ballad

The Drowsy Chaperone (2006)

Music and Lyrics by Lisa Lambert and Greg Morrison

Song title, Character (Voice)	Range	Song Style
Fancy dress, company		uptempo
Cold feets, Robert (T), George (T)	A-a1/A-f1	mod. uptempo
Show off, Janet (M), chorus	g-c2	mod. uptempo
As we stumble along, Drowsy Chap. (M), chorus	f-d2	mod. ballad

Adolpho, Adolpho (B), Drowsy Chap. incidental	E-a1	tango, character
Accident waiting to happen, Robert, Janet	c-ab1/c1-eb2	soft shoe
Toledo surprise, company		uptempo
Message from a nightingale, company		mod. uptempo
Bride's lament, Janet, chorus	ab-e2	mod. uptempo
Love is always lovely, Mrs. Tottendale (M), Underling (Bar)	g-e2/G-a	mod. ballad
Wedding bells, George, Trix (M)	f-g1/ab-cb2	uptempo
I do, I do in the sky, Trix, chorus	ab-eb2	uptempo
As we stumble along reprise, company		uptempo

Elegies: A Song Cycle (2003)
Music and Lyrics by William Finn

Song title, Character (Voice)	Range	Song Style
Looking up/Opening, company		slow
Mister Choi and Madam G, Keith (T), others as chorus	d-a1	driving uptempo
Mark's all-male Thanksgiving, Michael (Bar)	c-f1	mod. uptempo
Joe Papp, Keith, male chorus	c-a1	uptempo
Peggy Hewitt, Christian (Bar), company	B-f#1	mod. uptempo
Passover, Carolee (M)	bb-d2	uptempo
Jack Eric Williams, Michael	A-d1	uptempo
Fred, Christian	A-e1	funny, mod. ballad
Andy, Monica, and Mark, trio	TBB	mod. uptempo
Anytime (I am there), Carolee, men	MTBB	moving ballad
My dogs, Christian	A-c#2	character ballad
Venice, Michael, men	A-f1	mod. uptempo
Dwight Ave., Natick, Massachusetts, Betty (M), Michael or Christian	g#-d2/d-d1	mod. uptempo
When the earth stopped turning, Carolee	c1-d2	ballad
Goodbye, Keith	B-e1	moving ballad
Boom boom, Carolee, men	g#-c#2	mod. ballad
Goodbye reprise, company		mod. uptempo
Looking up, Betty	d-d2	hard ballad
Dear reader, Betty, Carolee	both a-e2	funny, moderate
Only one, Betty	e#-c2	ballad
Infinite joy, Betty	ab-c2	moving ballad

Elegies for Angels, Punks, and Raging Queens (1992)
Music by Janet Hood   Lyrics by Bill Russell

Song title, Character (Voice)	Range	Song Style
Angels, punks, and raging queens, Judith (M)	g♭-d♭2	mod. ballad
I'm holding on to you, company		mod. uptempo
And the rain keeps falling down, Brian (T)	c-g1	moving ballad
I don't do that, Doug (Bar), Brian	f-e♭1/f-f1	blues uptempo
I don't know how to help you, Angela (M)	f-b♭2	ballad
Celebrate, Judith, Angela	c-g2/b♭-e♭2	soul uptempo
We need heroes, quartet	SMTB	ballad
Spend it while you can, company		swing uptempo
My brother lived in San Francisco, Judith	f-d♭2	moving ballad
Learning to let go, Doug, company	c-e1	uptempo

Eubie (1979)
Music by Eubie Blake, arranged by Danny Holgate
Lyrics by Noble Sissle, Andy Razaf, Johnny Brandon,
F.E. Miller, and Jim Europe

Song title, Character (Voice)	Range	Song Style
Shuffle along, company		mod. uptempo
In honeysuckle time, Man 1 (Bar), backup chorus	B-e1	ballad
I'm just wild about Harry, Women 1, 3, 4, 5 (M)	all b♭-d2	mod. uptempo
Daddy, Woman 3	g-e2	blues ballad
I'm a great big baby, Man 5 (T)	d-a1	moderate, jazzy
My handyman ain't handy anymore, Woman 6 (M)	b♭-c2	funny ballad
Low down blues, Man 4 (T)	d-f1	blues ballad
Gee, I wish I had someone to rock me in the cradle of love, Woman 4, Man 4	c1-g2/f-a♭1	moving ballad
I'm just simply full of jazz, company		uptempo
High steppin' days, company		mod. uptempo
Dixie moon, Man 3 (T), chorus	d-f1	mod. uptempo
Weary, Woman 2 (S), chorus	d1-a2	blues ballad
Roll Jordan, company		gospel uptempo
Memories of you, Woman 4	g-e♭2	ballad
If you've never been vamped by a brownskin, you've never been vamped at all, Woman 5, company	b♭-b♭2	funny uptempo
You got to git the gittin' while the gittin's good, Man 2 (Bar)	e-e1	mod. uptempo
Oriental blues, Man 5 (Bar), women	d-e1	blues ballad
I'm craving for that kind of love, Woman 3	b♭-a♭1	ballad

Hot feet, company — uptempo
Goodnight Angeline, company — slow
Finale: I'm just wild about Harry, company — uptempo

Evita (1979)

Music by Andrew Lloyd Webber   Lyrics by Tim Rice

Song title, Character (Voice)	Range	Song Style
Requiem, chorus		ballad
Oh, what a circus, Che (T), Eva (S)	B-a♭1/a♭1-d2	uptempo, angry
On this night of 1000 stars, Magaldi (T), Eva, Che, chorus	d-g1/g-f2/d-a1	Latin ballad
Buenos Aires, Eva	e-f1	jazzy uptempo
Goodnight and thank you, Che, Eva, Magaldi, chorus	g-c2/e1-e♭2/d#-c2	mod. uptempo
The art of the possible, Evita, Generals (male ensemble)	d1-f2	character
Another suitcase, Mistress (M), Eva incidental	a-e1	ballad
Peron's last home, company		narrative mod.
A new Argentina, chorus		mod. dramatic
Balcony/Casa Rosada, Eva, Peron (B)	a♭-e♭2/B♭-g♭1	dramatic ballad
High flying adored, Che, Eva	B-g1/a-e2	moving ballad
Rainbow high, Eva, chorus	e-g2	uptempo
Rainbow tour, company		uptempo
And the money kept rolling in, Che, chorus	A-g1	driving uptempo
Santa Evita, children, chorus		ballad
Waltz for Eva and Che, Eva, Che	a♭-f2/d-g1	character
She's a diamond, Peron, Generals	A-f1	recit., character
Dice are rolling, Peron, Eva	A-f1/a-e♭2	recitative
Eva's final broadcast, Eva, Che incidental	a♭-d♭2	ballad
Montage, ensemble		moderate

Note: Music is continuous with little spoken dialogue.

Falsettoland (1990)

Music and Lyrics by William Finn

Song title, Character (Voice)	Range	Song Style
Falsettoland/It's about time, company		mod. ballad
Year of the child, company		mod. uptempo
Miracle of Judaism, Jason (boy S)	g-b♭1	mod. ballad
The baseball game, company		uptempo, funny
A day in Falsettoland, Mendel (Bar), company	e♭-f♭1	mod. ballad

Song title, Character (Voice)	Range	Song Style
Racquetball I, Whizzer (T), Marvin (T), Jason, company	B#-f#1/B#-g1/d♭-d♭1	uptempo, recit.-like
The argument, Marvin, Trina (M), Jason, Mendel	all mostly e-e1	uptempo, angry
Everyone hates his parents, Mendel, company	B-d2	character ballad
What more can I say, Marvin	d♭-d1	ballad
Something bad is happening, Charlotte (M), Cordelia (M)	b♭-e2/b♭-e♭2	mod. ballad
Racquetball II, Marvin, Whizzer	both B#-f#	uptempo recit.
Trina's song, Trina	g-d2	mod. ballad
Days like this, company		mod. uptempo
Canceling the bar mitzvah, Trina, Marvin, Jason	a-d2/A-d1/d1-c2	mod. ballad
Unlikely lovers, Marvin, Whizzer, Cordelia, Charlotte	B-f1/c#-g1/b-e2/b-c#2	ballad
Miracle reprise, Jason	g-b1	ballad
You gotta die sometime, Whizzer	c-g1	mod., angry
The bar mitzvah, company		uptempo
What would I do, Marvin, Whizzer	A-f#1/e-f#1	ballad

Note: See also *March of the Falsettos*, the second half of *Falsettos* (1992) of which *Falsettoland* is the first half.

Fame (1995)
Music by Steve Margoshes   Lyrics by Jacques Levy

Song title, Character (Voice)	Range	Song Style
Hard work, company		slow, then fast
I want to make magic, Nick (T)	c-g1	mod. uptempo
Can't keep it down, Joe (T), boys	c-g1 (b♭1 at end)	uptempo
Tyrone's rap, Tyrone (T)	b♭1-b♭2 (mostly spoken)	mod. uptempo
There she goes!/Fame, Carmen (M), chorus	a-e♭2	driving uptempo
Let's play a love scene, Serena (M)	g#-d#2	ballad
Bring on tomorrow, Schlomo (T), Carmen	c-f1/d1-d2	ballad
The teacher's argument, Bell (M), Sherman (M)	a-e2/g-e2	moderate
Hard work reprise, company		uptempo
I want to make magic reprise, Nick, chorus	d♭-g♭1	moderate
Think of Meryl Streep, Serena	b-e2	mod. uptempo
Mabel's prayer, Mabel (M), girls incidental	d-d2	character
Dancin' on the sidewalk, Tyrone, chorus	B♭-b♭1	uptempo
These are my children, Sherman	f-c2	gospel ballad
In L.A., Carmen	b♭-e♭2	uptempo
Let's play a love scene reprise, Nick, Serena	A-g1/a-e♭2	driving ballad

Bring on tomorrow reprise, company		uptempo
Fame reprise, company		uptempo

Fanny (1954)
Music and Lyrics by Harold Rome

Song title, Character (Voice)	Range	Song Style
Restless heart, Marius (T), men's chorus	eb-bb1	uptempo
Never too late for love, Panisse (Bar), women's chorus	c#-d1	mostly ballad
Restless heart duet, Marius, Fanny (S)	whistles/e1-e2	uptempo
Why be afraid to dance?, Cesar (Bar), company	d-d1	uptempo
Hakim's cellar, chorus		mod. uptempo
Welcome home, Cesar	A-b	uptempo
I like you, Marius, Cesar	d-gb1/eb-cb1	ballad
I have to tell you, Fanny	e1-a2	uptempo
Fanny, Marius	d-g1	moving ballad
Love motif, chorus		uptempo
The sailing, chorus		ballad
Oysters, cockles and mussels, chorus		mod. uptempo
Panisse and son, Panisse	c#-e1	uptempo
Wedding scene, ensemble		moderate
Finale I: Easter morning, chorus		uptempo
Happy birthday scene, ensemble, chorus		uptempo
To my wife, Panisse	c-d1	ballad
The thought of you, Marius, Fanny	e-a1/a1-f2	uptempo
Love is a very light thing, Cesar	A-bb	waltz ballad
Fanny reprise, Cesar, Marius, Fanny incidental	Bb-eb1/A-bb	ballad
Be kind to your parents, Fanny, Cesar	a-e2/A-c1	fast character
Scene: Front of curtain, chorus		anthem ballad
Welcome home reprise, Panisse, Cesar	both A-a	ballad

The Fantastiks (1960)
Music by Harvey Schmidt   Lyrics by Tom Jones

Song title, Character (Voice)	Range	Song Style
Try to remember, El Gallo (Bar); Luisa, Matt incidental	A-c1	ballad
Much more, Luisa (S)	b-f2	moving ballad
Metaphor, Luisa, Matt (T)	b-g2/d-d1	moving ballad
Never say no, Huck, Bill (both Bar)	both c-e1	fast character

It depends on what you pay, El Gallo, Huck, Bill	A-g1/both d-f#1	character, evil
Soon it's gonna rain, Luisa, Matt	d1-f2/c-f1	ballad
Happy ending, company		uptempo
This plum is too ripe, company		uptempo
I can see it, Matt, El Gallo	B-f1/A-d1	moving ballad
Plant a radish, Bill, Huck	B-f1/d-f1	mod. character
'Round and 'round, Luisa, El Gallo	c#1-bb2/Ab-eb1	waltz ballad
They were you, Matt, Luisa	B-d1/b-d2	ballad
Try to remember reprise, El Gallo, company	A-c1	ballad

Fiddler on the Roof (1964)

Music by Jerry Bock　　　　　　　　　　　　　　Lyrics by Sheldon Harnick

Song title, Character (Voice)	Range	Song Style
Tradition, company		mod. uptempo
Matchmaker, Hodel (M), Chava (M), Tzeitel (S)	b-c2/b-c2/b-d2	uptempo waltz
If I were a rich man, Tevye (B)	c-f1	mod. character
Sabbath prayer, Tevye, Golde (M), chorus	d-c1/d1-c2	anthem ballad
To life, ensemble		uptempo
Tevye's monologue, Tevye	Ab-eb1	ballad, recit.
Miracle of miracles, Motel (T)	e-f#1	uptempo
The dream, chorus		moderate
Sunrise, sunset, Golde, Tevye	c1-ab1/f-db1	ballad
Now I have everything, Perchik (Bar), Hodel	B-e1/b-e2	ballad
Do you love me?, Tevye, Golde	c-d1/c1-d2	mod. ballad
The rumor, chorus		mod. uptempo
Far from the home I love, Hodel	c1-eb2	ballad
Chava sequence, Tevye, company	c-c1	uptempo
Anatevka, company		mod. ballad

Finian's Rainbow (1947)

Music by Burton Lane　　　　　　　　　　　　　Lyrics by E.Y. Harburg

Song title, Character (Voice)	Range	Song Style
This time of the year, company		uptempo
How are things in Glocca Morra?, Sharon (S)	ab-db2	ballad
Woody's entrance, chorus		uptempo
Look to the rainbow, Sharon, chorus incidental	ab-db2	ballad
Old devil moon, Woody (T), Sharon	d-e1/bb-db2	jazzy ballad
How are things . . . reprise, Sharon	bb-db2	ballad

Something sort of grandish, Og (T), Sharon	B-f#1/c1-e2	uptempo
If this isn't love, Woody; Sharon, Finian, chorus incidental	c-f1	uptempo
Something sort of grandish reprise, Og	c#-f#1	uptempo
Necessity, women's chorus		uptempo
That great come-and-get-it day, company		uptempo
When the idle poor become the idle rich, Sharon, chorus	b-a2	uptempo
Old devil moon reprise, Woody, Sharon incidental	d-f1	jazzy ballad
The begat, Senator (T) and TBB trio	TTBB	uptempo
That great come-and-get-it day reprise, company		uptempo

Fiorello! (1959)

Music by Jerry Bock   Lyrics by Sheldon Harnick

Song title, **Character (Voice)**	**Range**	**Song Style**
On the side of the angels, Neil (Bar), then Morris (Bar)	both d♭-e1	uptempo
Angels counter, ensemble		uptempo
Politics and poker, Card Players (male ensemble)	TTTBBBB	uptempo waltz
Unfair no. 1, women's chorus, Dora		uptempo
Unfair, Fiorello version, Fiorello (T), women	d-e1	driving uptempo
Marie's law, Marie (M), Morris	a#-e#2/A#-c#1	mod. ballad
The name's LaGuardia, Fiorello, chorus	c-g1	uptempo
The bum won, Card Players	TTTBBBB	mod. ballad
I love a cop, Dora (M)	c1-e2	fast character
I love a cop reprise, ensemble		uptempo
Till tomorrow, Thea (S), Marie, Morris, chorus	both c1-e2/c-e1	waltz ballad
Home again, chorus		uptempo
When did I fall in love, Thea	d1-g2	fast, then slower
Gentleman Jimmy, Mitzi (M)	g-c2	mod. uptempo
Gentleman Jim reprise, chorus		mod. uptempo
Little tin box, Card Players	TTTBBBB	soft shoe
The very next man, Marie	g#-d1	moving ballad
Politics and poker reprise, men's chorus		uptempo waltz
Very next man reprise, Marie	a-d2	ballad
The name's LaGuardia reprise, company		uptempo
Home again, company		uptempo

The Firefly (1912)

Music by Rudolph Friml   Lyrics by Otto Harbach

Song title, Character (Voice)	Range	Song Style
A trip to Bermuda, company		uptempo
He says yes, she says no, Geraldine (S),	g1-a2/g-c2	uptempo
Jack (T), chorus		
Call me uncle, Thurston (Bar), chorus	A-d1	fast character
Love is like a firefly, Nina (S)	c1-ab2	character ballad
Something, Jenkins (T), Suzette (M)	c#-f#1/f#1-g#2	ballad
Gianna mia, Nina	d#1-b2	ballad
I've found it at last, company		uptempo
In sapphire seas, Sybil (M), ensemble	d1-c3 (opt. g3)	slow ballad
Tommy Atkins, Nina	d1-g2	fast character
Sympathy, Geraldine, Thurston	e1-f#2/e-f#1	character, funny
A woman's smile, Jack	c-a1	ballad
De trop, Jenkins, Suzette, Pietro (T)	c-f1/e1-a2/e-a1	character
We're gonna make a man of you, quintet	STTTB	uptempo, funny
The beautiful ship from Toyland, Franz (Bar),	Bb-f1	mod. character
men's chorus		
When a maid comes knocking at your heart,	c1-a2	mod. ballad
Nina		
Waltz, chorus		waltz ballad
An American Beauty rose, Thurston, chorus	c-f1	ballad
The latest thing from Paris, Pietro, Suzette	d-g1/d1-g2	uptempo
The dawn of love, Nina	d1-bb2	ballad

First Ladies Suite (1995; rev. 2003)

Music and Lyrics by Michael John LaChiusa

Song title, Character (Voice)	Range	Song Style
Opening, company		mod. ballad
Over Texas		
Always something, May (M), Evelyn (M)	a-d2/bb-ab1	mod. uptempo
Ladies . . . tea?, May, Evelyn incidental	g-c#2	moderate
Four more years, May, Evelyn	g#-b#2/b#-f2	uptempo
Caroline, May, Evelyn incidental	ab-a1	uptempo
Kitty cat nap, trio	SMM	uptempo
The smallest thing, First Lady (M)	a-c#2	mod. ballad
What? What?, May, Evelyn	g#-g#1/b-e2	moderate
Where's Mamie?, Mamie (M)	g-d2	uptempo
My husband was an army man, Mamie	g#-a#1	march
Melba gloria, Marion (S)	b-g#2	mod. ballad
In Algiers, Marion, Mamie	c#-f2/a-c2	mod. ballad
Tomorrow I will love you more, trio	SMB	scene
Old rules are old rules, Mamie	g-c2	uptempo

Eleanor sleeps here

This is the beginning of a new era, Eleanor (M), Hick incidental	b♭-e2	uptempo
Eleanor's room, Hick (M)	f-d2	mod. uptempo
Wing walk, Hick, Eleanor incidental	g-b1	scene
Eleanor's hand, Hick	g-c2	mod. uptempo
When Eleanor smiles, Hick	f-d2	uptempo
Eleanor's letter, Eleanor, Hick	f1-f2/b-d2	uptempo
Eleanor sleeps here, Hick, Amelia incidental	g-c2	mod. uptempo
Great ladies, Amelia (M)	b-e2	mod. ballad
First Lady finale, company		mod. uptempo

Note: Songs here are broken down into the titles listed, but in the conductor's score the music is written in continuous scenes.

Five Guys Named Moe (1991)

Music by Louis Jordan, arranged by Clarke Peters

Song title, **Character (Voice)**	**Range**	**Song Style**
Early in the morning (prerecorded Bar)	c#-f1	uptempo
Five guys named Moe, company	TTTBB	swing ballad
Brother, beware, Big Moe (Bar)	a♭-g♭1	uptempo
I like them fat like that, Little Moe (T)	spoken	mod. ballad
Messy Bessy, No Moe (T)	e♭-g1	mod. shuffle
Pettin' and pokin'/Life is so peculiar, company	all e♭-g1	uptempo
I know what I've got/Azure-te, Nomax (Bar), Four-eyed Moe (high Bar)	B♭-g1/e♭-g1	mod. uptempo
Knock me a kiss, company		moderate, jazzy
Safe, sane, and single, company		uptempo
Push ka pi she pie, No Moe (Bar), Eat Moe (T), Four-eyed Moe	all g-d1	uptempo
Saturday night fish fry, Nomax, company	f-b♭1	uptempo
What's the use of gettin' sober/If I had any sense I'd go back home, Big Moe	c-e1	ballad
Dad gum your hide boy, Little Moe, No Moe, company	both g-d1	uptempo
The cabaret, Big Moe, company	b♭-f1	uptempo
There ain't nobody here but us chickens, Four-eyed Moe, No Moe	c-e1/spoken	mod. uptempo
Don't let the sun catch you crying, Eat Moe	B♭-b♭1 (falsetto)	moving ballad
Choo choo ch'boogie, Little Moe, company	f-f1	mod. uptempo
Look out sister, Four-eyed Moe	a♭-f1 (some spoken)	uptempo

Is you is—medley, company   ballad
Five guys named Moe reprise, company   swing ballad

Flora the Red Menace (1965)

Music by John Kander   Lyrics by Fred Ebb

Song title, Character (Voice)	Range	Song Style
Prologue, company		uptempo
Unafraid, Flora (M), company	f#-b1	mod. uptempo
The kid herself, Flora, chorus	g-c2	uptempo
One good break, quartet	MMTB	mod. uptempo
Not every day of the week, Harry (T), Flora	B♭-f1/f-c2	mod. uptempo
Sign here, Harry	c#-g1	uptempo
Mr. Stanley's back, Stanley (Bar)	B-e1	mod. uptempo
A quiet thing, Flora	f#-d♭2	ballad
The flame, Charlotte (M), Harry, chorus	a-d2/g#-f1	slow
Not every day reprise, Harry, Flora	A-g1/a-g2	mod. uptempo
Dear love, Flora, chorus	a-b♭1	mod. uptempo
Keepin' it hot, Kenny (T), Maggie (M)	d-e♭1/b-c2	uptempo
Express yourself, Charlotte	f-c2	mod. uptempo
Where did everybody go?, trio	MMT	mod. slow
You are you, trio	MMT	mod. uptempo
The joke, Harry, company	d♭-g♭1	mod. uptempo
Sing happy, Flora	g-b♭1	ballad

Not in 1987 revival:
Hello waves, Harry, Flora   e-e1/b-d2   mod. uptempo

Florodora (1900)

Music by Leslie Stuart   Lyrics by Owen Hall

Song title, Character (Voice)	Range	Song Style
Opening chorus, chorus		uptempo
The credit's due to me, men's ensemble		mod. character
The silver star of love, Dolores (S)	d♭1-a♭2	ballad
Somebody, Dolores, Abercoed (Bar)	a-a2/c#-e1	lilting ballad
Huzzah the master comes, chorus		uptempo
Come and see our island, company		uptempo
When I leave town, Lady Holyrood (M)	d1-e2	fast character
Galloping, Angela (M), Donegal (T)	c#1-f#2/B-f#1	uptempo
I want to marry a man, I do, Lady Holyrood, Tweedlepunch (Bar), Gilfain (Bar)	b-d2/c-c1/B-c1	fast character
The fellow who might, Angela, chorus incidental	c1-e2	narrative ballad

Phrenology, Gilfain (T), chorus	B-f1	fast character
When an interesting person, Lady Holyrood, Donegal, Angela	f1-f2/d-f1/a-f2	uptempo, funny
The shade of the palm, Abercoed	B♭-e♭1	narrative ballad
Hey, hey, alack aday!, company		mod. ballad
Come lads and lasses, company		uptempo
Tact, Lady Holyrood	c#1-d2	character
The millionaire, Gilfain	c-e1	uptempo
Tell me, pretty maiden, chorus		mod. ballad
I've an inkling, Lady Holyrood	c1-e2	character ballad
And the nations will declare you, company		anthem ballad

Supplementary Numbers:

The queen of the Philippine Islands, Dolores	b-a2	narrative ballad
We get up at 8 a.m., Valleda (S), Leandro (Bar)	e1-e2/e-e1	character
I want to be a military man, Donegal, chorus	d-f1	fast character
He loves, he loves me not, Dolores	b♭-g2	ballad
Willie was a day boy, Angela	c1-d2	narrative ballad
When we are on the stage, Dolores, Tweedlepunch	b-g2/B-g1	ballad
The island of love, Dolores, chorus	b♭-g2	waltz ballad

Flower Drum Song (1958)

Music by Richard Rodgers   Lyrics by Oscar Hammerstein II

Song title, Character (Voice)	Range	Song Style
You are beautiful, Madam Liang (M), Wang Ta (T)	f-c2/e-g1	ballad
A hundred million miracles, ensemble		uptempo
I enjoy being a girl, Linda (M)	a-c#2	uptempo
I am going to like it here, Mei Li (M)	b♭-b♭1	ballad
Like a god, Wang Ta, Mei Li incidental	c#-g1	uptempo
Chop suey, Madam Liang, chorus incidental	g-c2	uptempo
Don't marry me, Sammy Fong (Bar), Mei Li*	d-e1/d1-c2	uptempo
Grant Avenue, Linda, chorus incidental	a-c2	uptempo
Love, look away, Helen (S)	d1-f2	ballad
Fan tan Fanny, Solo S	d1-d2	jazzy uptempo
Gliding through my memoree, Franki (Bar), girls	B-d1	fast character
Love look away reprise, Helen	f1-a♭2	ballad
The other generation, Madam Liang, Wang Ta	both e♭-c♭1	uptempo
You are beautiful reprise, Wang Ta	f-g1	ballad
Sunday, Linda, Sammy	d1-c2/d-e1	mod. ballad
Don't marry me reprise, Sammy	d-e1	ballad

The other generation reprise, company   uptempo
A hundred million miracles reprise, company   uptempo

*Mostly a solo for Sammy.

Floyd Collins (1996)

Music by Adam Guettel   Lyrics by Adam Guettel and Tina Landau

Song title, **Character (Voice)**	**Range**	**Song Style**
The ballad of Floyd Collins, company		mod. uptempo
The call, Floyd (Bar)	B-a1	uptempo
It moves, Floyd	G#-f#1	majestic ballad
Time to go, Floyd	B♭-c2	uptempo
Where a man belongs, company		mod. uptempo
Lucky, Nellie (M), Miss Jane (M)	f#-d#2/f#-c#2	country ballad
Daybreak, Homer (T), Floyd	f#-b1/c-f1	moving ballad
I landed on him, Skeets Miller	spoken	uptempo
Heart an' hand, Miss Jane, Lee (Bar)	a-b1/A-b	moving ballad
The riddle song, Homer, Floyd	A#-c2/c-a1	uptempo
Is that remarkable?, company		swing uptempo
Through the mountain, Nellie	f-g2	mod. uptempo
Git comfortable, Homer	c-g1	mod. ballad
The ballad of Floyd Collins reprise, quartet	MTTB	ballad
The dream, Nellie, Floyd, Homer, chorus	MTT	slow, then faster
How glory goes, Floyd	B♭-g1	moving ballad

Follies (1971)

Music and Lyrics by Stephen Sondheim

Song title, **Character (Voice)**	**Range**	**Song Style**
Beautiful girls, Roscoe (T), company	e-a1	mod. ballad
Don't look at me, Sally (M), Ben (Bar)	a-b1/c#-c#1	ballad
Waiting for the girls upstairs, ensemble		ballad
Rain on the roof, The Whitmans (M, Bar)*	B♭-d1/b♭-d2	ballad
Ah, Paris!, Solange (S)*	c#1-g2	uptempo
Broadway baby, Hattie (M)*	a-b1	jazzy ballad
The road you didn't take, Ben	a-e1	ballad
In Buddy's eyes, Sally	f#-d2	uptempo
Who's that woman, Stella (M), women's chorus	f#-f#2	mostly uptempo
I'm still here, Carlotta (M)	e♭-c2	blues ballad
Too many mornings, Ben, Sally	c-e1/c1-g#2	ballad
The right girl, Buddy (Bar)	c-f1	uptempo
One more kiss, Heidi (S), Young Heidi (girl S)	d-g2/e1-a♭2	waltz ballad

Could I leave you, Phyllis (M)	f#-b1	uptempo waltz

"LOVELAND"

Loveland, company		uptempo
You're gonna love tomorrow, Young Ben (T), Young Phyllis (S)	c#-f#1/c#1-eb2	ballad
Love will see us through, Young Buddy (T), Young Sally (S)	d-f1/eb1-gb2	ballad
The god-why-don't-you-love-me blues, Buddy; Rita (S), Suzanne (M) incidental	d-f1 (opt. a1)	uptempo blues
Losing my mind, Sally	f-b1	ballad
The story of Lucy and Jessie, Phyllis, chorus incidental	g-b1	narrative mod.
Live, laugh, love, Ben, company	c-f1	mod. uptempo

*"Rain on the Roof," "Ah, Paris!," and "Broadway Baby" are combined at end into a trio quodlibet.

Footloose (1999)

Music by Tom Snow   Lyrics by Dean Pitchford
Additional music by Eric Carmen, Sammy Hagan, Kenny Loggins, and Jim Steinman

Song title, **Character (Voice)**	**Range**	**Song Style**
Footloose/On any Sunday, company		uptempo
The girl gets around, Church (T), Ariel (M)	e-b1/c#1-e2	uptempo
I can't stand still, Ren (T)	d-c2	mod. uptempo
Somebody's eyes, company		mod. ballad
Learning to be silent, Vi (M), Ethel (M)	ab-db2/g-c2	ballad
Holding out for a hero, Ariel, company	c1-e2	uptempo
Heaven help me, Shaw (Bar)	G-e1	ballad
I'm free/Heaven help me, Ren, company	d-ab1	mod. uptempo
Let's make believe we're in love, Irene (M), chorus	g-d2	country waltz ballad
Let's hear it for the boy, Rusty (S), girls' chorus	a-f#3	uptempo
Can you find it in your heart?, Vi	a-db2	ballad
Mama says, Willard (T), male trio	Ab-g1	mod. uptempo
Almost paradise, Ren, Ariel	d-a1/g-c2	flowing ballad
Dancing is not a crime, company		uptempo
I confess, Shaw, chorus	A-e1	ballad
Can you find it in your heart reprise, Shaw	A-c1	ballad
Footloose reprise, company		uptempo

Forever Plaid (1993)

Music and Lyrics by various composers and lyricists from 1950s

Song title, **Character (Voice)**	**Song Style**
Three coins in a fountain, Frankie	ballad
Gotta be this or that, Sparky	uptempo
Moments to remember, Jinx	ballad
Crazy 'bout ya baby, Frankie	mod., moving
No not much, Jinx	mod. uptempo
Perfidia, Sparky	mod., funny
Cry, Jinx	mod. ballad
Sixteen tons, Smudge	character ballad
The chain gang, Frankie*	ballad
The catering drill, company	mostly uptempo
The bride cuts the cake	
The tarantella	
Anniversary waltz	
Little town of Bethlehem	
Hava naghelah	
Rock my soul	
She loves you	
A tribute to Mr. C.	
Dream along with me, Jinx	ballad
Sing to me, Mr. C., Sparky	waltz ballad
Catch a falling star, Sparky	moving ballad
The Plaids go calypso	fast, Caribbean
Day-O, Jinx	feel
Kingston market, Jinx	
Jamaica farewell, Smudge, Sparky	
Mathilda, Frankie	
Heart and soul, Frankie	swing ballad
Lady of Spain, Jinx	cafe ballad
Scotland the brave, company	anthem ballad
Shangri-la/Rags to riches, Smudge	mod. uptempo
Love is a many splendored thing, company	ballad

*"Sixteen Tons" and "Chain Gang" then combined in a quodlibet.

Vocal ranges of the singers:
Jinx (T)	B-e2 (falsetto)
Frankie (T)	B-a1
Sparky (Bar)	A-f#1 (g#1 in falsetto)
Smudge (B)	F-f#1 (d2 in falsetto)

The Fortune Teller (1898)

Music by Victor Herbert   Lyrics by Harry B. Smith

Song title, Character (Voice)	Range	Song Style
Introduction, Fresco (Bar), women's chorus	G-e1	uptempo
Always do as people say you should, Irma (S)	e1-b♭2	mod. ballad
Hungaria's hussars, Ladislas (T), men's chorus	e-a1	fast character
Ho! Ye townsmen, Sandor (Bar)	G-d1	slow character
Romany life, Musette (S), ensemble incidental	a-b♭2 (opt. d3)	uptempo
I, a bride, company		uptempo
Chime for the bride so fair, chorus		uptempo
Signor Mons. Muldoni, Fresco (Bar), chorus	B-d1	narrative ballad
Serenades of all nations, company		various
Slumber on my little gypsy sweetheart, Sandor	A-c1	ballad
Only in the play, Pompon (M), Ladislas	d1-g2/d-g1	waltz ballad
Eljen! Eljen! Vivat!, company		uptempo
Gypsy Jan, Sandor, chorus	G-e♭1	narrative ballad
The power of the human eye, Boris (Bar), Count (B)	f-e♭1/E♭-e♭	ballad
The lily and the nightingale, Musette	d1-c3	ballad
Thro' the forest wild and free, company		uptempo

Forty-Second Street (1980)

Music by Harry Warren   Lyrics by Al Dubin

Song title, Character (Voice)	Range	Song Style
Young and healthy, Billy (T), Peggy (M)	B♭-g1/b♭-c#2	mod. uptempo
Shadow waltz, Dorothy (M), women's chorus	g-a1	waltz ballad
Go into your dance, Maggie (M), Andy (Bar), women	b♭-b♭1/d-d♭1	mod. uptempo
You're getting to be a habit with me, Dorothy	a-a1	ballad
Dames, Billy, women's chorus	d-a1	mod. uptempo
I know now, Dorothy, Billy, chorus	e♭-a♭1/d-g1	easy ballad
We're in the money, company		mod. uptempo
Forty-Second Street, Dorothy	b♭-g1	mod. uptempo
There's a sunny side to every situation, company		mod. uptempo
Lullaby of Broadway, company		swing ballad
About a quarter to nine, Dorothy, Peggy	both e♭-b♭1	ballad
Shuffle off to Buffalo, women's chorus		shuffle ballad

Forty-Second Street, Peggy	b-b1	mod. uptempo
Dames/Lullaby of Broadway, company		uptempo

The Frogs (2004)
Music and Lyrics by Stephen Sondheim

Song title, Character (Voice)	Range	Song Style
Invocation and instruction, Actor 1 (Bar), Actor 2 (Bar)	F#-e1/G-e1	mod. uptempo
I love to travel, Dionysos (Bar), Xanthias (Bar)	A♭-d♭1/A#-e1	mod. uptempo
Dress big, Herakles (B), Dionysos, Xanthias incidental	G#-f1/spoken	uptempo
All aboard!, chorus		mod. ballad
Ariadne, Dionysos*	B♭-f1	ballad
The frogs, chorus		uptempo
Hymnos: Evoe!, chorus		slow, then faster
Hades, Pluto (Bar), chorus	A-f1	mod. uptempo
Parabasis: It's only a play, chorus		slow scene
Shaw, Dionysos, chorus	A-f1	uptempo
All aboard! reprise, Charon (Bar)	f-e1	mod. uptempo
Fear no more, Shakespeare (B)*	F#-g#	ballad
Exodus, chorus		slow
Final instructions, Dionysos	A-e1	mod. ballad

*Both songs also included in conductor's score in versions a major third higher.

The Full Monty (2000)
Music and Lyrics by David Yazbeck

Song title, Character (Voice)	Range	Song Style
Scrap, company		mod. uptempo
It's a woman's world, Georgie (M), women	g-c2	uptempo
Man, Jerry (T), Dave (T)	e-a1/e-b1	mod. uptempo
Big ass rock, Jerry, Dave, Malcom (Bar)	TTB	ballad
Life with Harold, Vicki (M), others incidental	g-d2	mambo uptempo
Big black man, Horse (Bar), company	g-g1	uptempo
You rule my world, Dave, Harold (T)	c#-b1/c#-g1	ballad
Michael Jordan's ball, Jerry, company	g-d♭2	shuffle uptempo
Jeanette's showbiz number, Jeanette (S), men	f-b♭2	jazzy, moderate
Breeze off the river, Jerry	c-b1	ballad
The goods, company		uptempo
Man reprise, Jerry	B♭-d♭1	ballad
You walk with me, Malcom, Ethan (T)	g#-a1/b#-g#1	flowing ballad

You rule my world reprise, Georgie, Vicki	both g#-d2	ballad
Let it go, company		uptempo

Funny Girl (1964)

Music by Jule Styne   Lyrics by Bob Merrill

Song title, Character (Voice)	**Range**	**Song Style**
If a girl isn't pretty, company		uptempo
I'm the greatest star, Fanny (M)	g-c2	uptempo
Cornet man, Fanny, chorus	a#-f2	jazz ballad
Who taught her everything?, Mrs. Brice (M), Eddie (T)	a♭-e2/e♭-f1	soft shoe ballad
His love makes me beautiful, Solo T, women	d-b♭1	slow, then faster
I want to be seen with you tonight, Nick (Bar), Fanny	a♭-e♭1/a♭-f2	ballad
Henry Street, chorus		waltz ballad
People, Fanny	a♭-d♭1	ballad
You are woman, I am man, Nick, Fanny	a#-e1/b#-c#2	ballad
Don't rain on my parade, Fanny	e-b1	uptempo
Sadie, Sadie, Fanny, chorus	a-e♭2	ballad
Find yourself a man, Mrs. Brice, Mrs. Strakosh (M), Eddie	women b♭-d2/ B♭-d1	waltz ballad
Rat-tat-tat-tat, Eddie, chorus	d-f#1	uptempo march
Private Schwartz, Fanny, chorus	b-d#2	character
Who are you now?, Fanny	b♭-d♭1	ballad
Don't rain on my parade reprise, Nick	d-d1	uptempo
The music that makes me dance, Fanny	g#-e2	ballad
Don't rain . . . finale, Fanny	e-b1	uptempo

A Funny Thing Happened on the Way to the Forum (1962)

Music and Lyrics by Stephen Sondheim

Song title, Character (Voice)	**Range**	**Song Style**
Comedy tonight, Prologus (Bar), company	A-e♭1	uptempo
Love I hear, Hero (Bar)	B-e1	ballad
Free, Pseudolus (Bar), Prologus	c-f1/c-f1 (opt. a1)	fast character
Lovely, Philia (S), Hero	c#1-f2/d-f1	ballad
Pretty little picture, Pseudolus; Hero, Philia incidental	B-f#1	uptempo
Everybody ought to have a maid, Senex (Bar), Pseudolus incidental, chorus	d-e1	uptempo
I'm calm, Hysterium (T)	d-f1	alt. fast/slow

Song title, Character (Voice)	Range	Song Style
Impossible, Senex, Hero	both B♭-g1	mod. uptempo
Bring me my bride, Miles (T), ensemble, men's chorus	B-f#	uptempo
That dirty old man, Domina (M)	b♭-f#2	uptempo
That'll show him, Philia	c1-f2	mod. uptempo
Lovely reprise, Pseudolus, Hysterium	d-f1/e-g1	ballad
Funeral sequence, Miles; Pseudolus incidental; chorus	c-e1	slow ballad
Comedy tonight reprise, company		uptempo

Gentlemen Prefer Blondes (1949)

Music by Jule Styne   Lyrics by Leo Robin

Song title, Character (Voice)	Range	Song Style
It's high time, Dorothy (M), company	b-c2	uptempo
Bye bye baby, Gus (Bar), Lorelei (M) incidental	B♭-d1	mod. uptempo
I'm just a girl from Little Rock, Lorelei	f-a1	mod. ballad
I love what I'm doing, Dorothy	a♭-c2	mod. uptempo
Just a kiss apart, Henry (T)	d-f#1	waltz ballad
It's delightful down in Chile, Beekman (Bar), Lorelei	B♭-e1/b♭-c2	mod. ballad
Sunshine, Dorothy, Henry	b♭-c2/d-f1	mod. uptempo
Park scene, chorus*		moderate
Sunshine reprise, chorus*		uptempo
I'm atingle, I'm aglow, Gage (T), ensemble incidental	d-f1	mod. uptempo
You say you care, Henry, Dorothy	d♭-f1/g#-b♭1	ballad
Mamie is Mimi, Coles (T), Atkins (T)	both e-g1	uptempo
Coquette, solo T and A from chorus*	A♭-d1/a♭-d2	cafe ballad
Diamonds are a girl's best friend, Lorelei	f-b♭1	ballad
Gentlemen prefer blondes, Lorelei, Gus	a-a1/f-f1	uptempo
Homesick, ensemble		blues ballad
Keeping cool with Coolidge, Dorothy, Mrs. Spofford incidental, chorus	b-b1	Charleston
Button up with Esmond, Lorelei, chorus	g-a♭1	ballad, then fast
Gentlemen prefer blondes/Diamonds are a girl's best friend reprises, company		uptempo

*Much or all in French.

George M! (1968)
Music and Lyrics by George M. Cohan

Song title, Character (Voice)	Range	Song Style
Always leave them laughing, Jerry (T), two girls incidental	g-e♭1	mod. uptempo
Musical moon, Jerry, Nellie (M)	f-e1/c1-b♭1	mod. uptempo
Oh, you wonderful boy, Josie (M)	c1-d2	uptempo
All aboard for Broadway, George (Bar), others incidental	d-e1	uptempo
Musical comedy man, company		mod. uptempo
All aboard for Broadway reprise, company		uptempo
Twentieth century love, company		uptempo
My home town, George	c-f1	ballad
Push me along in my pushcart, Ethel (M), two girls	unison c1-e♭2	waltz ballad
A ring to the name of Rosie, four boys	TTBB	mod. ballad
Give my regards to Broadway, George, company	c#-f1	mod. uptempo
Forty-five minutes from Broadway, George, Rose (M)	A-b1/b-b1	ballad
So long Mary, ensemble	MMTBB	soft shoe ballad
Down by the Erie Canal, chorus		uptempo
Mary's a grand old name, Fay (M)	d-e1	ballad
All our friends, Sam (T), chorus	d-a1	uptempo

Montage

Yankee doodle dandy, George, chorus	c-f1	uptempo
Nellie Kelly, Josie, George, chorus	c1-d2/c-d1	ballad
Harrigan, George, Jerry, two boys	all c-d1	soft shoe ballad
Over there/You're a grand old flag, George, chorus	d-e1	mod. uptempo
The man who owns Broadway, George, chorus	f#-d1	ballad
I'd rather be right, George	B-d1	ballad
Finale: Give my regards/Yankee doodle, George, Agnes (M)	c-c1/c1-c2	uptempo
Bows: I want to hear a Yankee doodle tune/Give my regards, company		march, uptempo

Gigi (1973)
Music by Frederick Loewe   Lyrics by Alan Jay Lerner

Song title, Character (Voice)	Range	Song Style
Thank heaven for little girls, Honoré (Bar)	c#-d1	moving ballad
It's a bore, Gaston (Bar), Honoré	both c-d1	uptempo

The earth and other minor things, Gigi (M)	b♭-d♭2	mod. uptempo
Paris is Paris again, Honoré	c-d♭1	uptempo
She is not thinking of me, Gaston	d-e1 (opt. g1)	waltz ballad
It's a bore reprise, Gaston, Honoré	both c-d1	uptempo
The night they invented champagne, Gigi, Mamita (M), Gaston	b♭-c2/f-f1/d-e1	uptempo
I remember it well, Honoré, Mamita	B♭-c1/b♭-c2	ballad
I never want to go home again, Gigi	b-c2	uptempo
Gigi, Gaston	c-e♭1	uptempo
The contract, Dufresne (Bar), Alicia (M), Mamita	all d♭-d1	uptempo, funny
I'm glad I'm not young anymore, Honoré	d♭-e♭1	mod. uptempo
In this wide, wide world, Gigi	a-d2	moving ballad
Finale: Thank heaven . . . , company		moderate

Girl Crazy (1930)

Music by George Gershwin   Lyrics by Ira Gershwin

Song title, Character (Voice)	**Range**	**Song Style**
Bidin' my time, male quartet	TTBB	easy ballad
But not for me, Kate (M)	g-b♭1	ballad
By Strauss, Zoli (Bar), women's chorus	c-f1	mod. uptempo
Could you use me, Johnny (T), men's chorus	B-a1	uptempo
Bidin' my time reprise, male quartet	TTBB	easy ballad
Bronco busters, chorus		uptempo
Embraceable you, Johnny, Molly (M), chorus	e-g1/d1-e2	ballad
I got rhythm, Kate, chorus	g-c2	uptempo
Strike up the band, Johnny, chorus	d-g2	uptempo
Sam and Delilah, Kate, chorus	g-b♭1	moderate, funny
Gay caballero, chorus		mod. uptempo
Sam and Delilah reprise, Molly, Sam (Bar)	c1-d2/spoken	mod. ballad
That lost barbershop chord, Johnny, male quartet	B♭-g1	mod. ballad
Treat me rough, Kate, Zoli	a-b♭1/c#-f#1	uptempo
But not for me reprise, Molly, Zoli	e♭1-f2/e♭-f1	ballad
Boy! What love has done for me, Kate	g-d♭2	ballad
Finale: I'm bidin' my time, company		uptempo

Godspell (1971)

Music and Lyrics by Stephen Schwartz
Additional Music and Lyrics by Jay Hamburger and Peggy Gordon

Song title, **Character (Voice)**	**Range**	**Song Style**
Prologue: Tower of babble, company		moderate
Prepare ye the way of the Lord, John the Baptist (Bar)	c-d1	ballad
Save the people, Jesus (T), company	g-e1	uptempo
Day by day, Robin (M), women	c1-a1	waltz ballad
Learn your lessons well, Gilmer (Bar)	g-c1	uptempo
Bless the Lord, Joanne (S), company	g-a2	rock ballad
All for the best, Jesus, Judas (Bar)	d-g1/c-d1	uptempo
All good gifts, Lamar (T)	d-a2	ballad
Light of the world, company		uptempo
Learn your lessons well, Lamar	a-c1	uptempo
Turn back, O man, Sonia (M)	g-d2	hard ballad
Alas for you, Jesus	d-f1	uptempo
By my side, Peggy (M), Gilmar	c1-c2/c-c1	ballad
We beseech thee, Jeffrey (T), company	e-f#1 (d2 in falsetto)	uptempo
Day by day reprise, company		slow, then faster
On the willows, company		ballad
Finale, company		slow

The Golden Apple (1954)

Music by Jerome Moross   Lyrics by John Latouche

Song title, **Character (Voice)**	**Range**	**Song Style**
Nothing ever happens in Angel's Roost, Helen (M)	g#-e2	uptempo
It was a grand adventure, Ulysses (Bar)	A-f#1	moving ballad
It's the coming home together, Ulysses, Penelope (S)	d-e1/f1-g2	ballad
It's a lazy afternoon, Helen	a-d2	ballad
Oh, it's grand to see my picture in the papers, Helen, men's chorus	b-f2	uptempo
Don't give up so easy, Ulysses, chorus	d-e1	uptempo
How will we have our revenge on them, Hector (Bar)	c-d1	mod. uptempo
He brought me wildflowers, Penelope	d1-e2	mod. ballad
I've got a storebought suit, Ulysses, men's chorus	c-e1	mod. uptempo
By a goon-a, Lovely Mars (M), Ulysses, chorus	a-d2/d-d1	seductive ballad

Note: Music is continuous throughout the musical. The show includes a number of other solo roles, not identified here, as well as a great deal of ensemble music.

Goldilocks (1958)

Music by Leroy Anderson   Lyrics by Walter and Jean Kerr and Joan Ford

Song title, **Character (Voice)**	**Range**	**Song Style**
Lazy moon, chorus		uptempo
Give the little lady, Maggie (M), chorus	a-c2	uptempo
Save a kiss, George (Bar), Maggie	B-e♭1/a-d2	uptempo
No one'll ever love you, Maggie, Max (Bar)	a-f2/A-f1	mod. uptempo
Who's been sitting in my chair?, Maggie	a♭-d♭2	mod. uptempo
There never was a woman, Max	c-d1	character
The pussy foot, Lois (M), chorus	b♭-f2	uptempo
Lady in waiting, Lois, George	b♭-g2/d-e♭1	ballad
The beast in you, Maggie	a-d2	uptempo
Shall I take my heart?, George	d-e1	mod. uptempo
I can't be in love, Max	c-d1	uptempo
Bad companions, quartet	SMTB	mod. uptempo
I never know when, Maggie	a-c2	ballad
Two years in the making, company		uptempo
Heart of stone, chorus		uptempo

Substitute numbers in conductor's score:

If I can't take it with me, Maggie	f-b3	moving ballad
Little girls should be seen, Maggie	c1-e2	moderate waltz

Good News (1927)

Music by Ray Henderson   Lyrics by B.G. DeSylva and Lew Brown

Song title, **Character (Voice)**	**Range**	**Song Style**
Students are we, chorus		uptempo
Flaming youth, Babe (S), chorus	c1-f2	uptempo
Happy days, Tom (T), boys trio	d-b♭1	mod. uptempo
Just imagine, Connie (S), others incidental	d-f1	mod. ballad
The best things in life are free, Tom	B-e1	mod. ballad
On the campus, quartet	SMTB	mod. uptempo
Varsity drag, quartet	SMTB	uptempo
Baby what, Babe, Bobby (Bar)	d1-d2/d1-g1	moving ballad
Lucky in love, Tom	d-f1	mod. ballad
Tait song, glee club trio	TBB	mod. uptempo
Lucky in love reprise, company		mod. uptempo
The girl of the Pi Beta Phi, Patricia (M), chorus	c1-e2	mod. ballad

Today's the day, girls' chorus		march uptempo
In the meantime, Bobby, Babe	A-e1/a-e2	uptempo
Good news, Flo (M)	d1-d2	mod. ballad
Good news reprise, girls' chorus		mod. ballad
Varsity drag reprise, chorus		uptempo

The Goodbye Girl (1993)

Music by Marvin Hamlisch   Lyrics by David Zippel

Song title, **Character (Voice)**	**Range**	**Song Style**
This is as good as it gets, Paula (M), Lucy (girl S)	both a-d♭2	mod. uptempo
No more, Paula	g♭-c2	ballad
A beat behind, Paula, Billy (T), chorus	f#-c#2/c#-f#1	mod. uptempo
My rules, Elliot (T), Paula	d♭-g♭1/a♭-c2	mod. uptempo
Good news, bad news, Elliot, Paula, Lucy	A♭-f1/a♭-e♭2/b♭-d♭2	mod. ballad
Good news, bad news reprise, Mrs. Crosby (M)	g-d2	mod. ballad
Footsteps, Paula, Lucy	e-c#2/g#-f#1	ballad
How can I win?, Paula	a♭-d♭2	ballad
Richard interred, company		uptempo
Too good to be bad, Paula, Donna (M), Jenna (M)	all a-d♭2	uptempo
2 good 2 B bad, Mrs. Crosby	b♭-e♭2	uptempo
Who would've thought?, quintet	SSSMT	jazzy uptempo
Paula, Elliot, Paula	G-e♭1/a♭-d♭2	mod. ballad
I can play this part, Elliot	g#-c#2	mod. ballad
What a guy, Paula	e-c2	ballad

Grand Hotel (1991)

Music and Lyrics by Robert Wright, George Forrest, and Maury Yeston

Song title, **Character (Voice)**	**Range**	**Song Style**
The grand parade, Doctor (T), Baron (T), company	c-d♭1/e♭-a♭1	mod. uptempo
At the Grand Hotel, Doctor	e♭-a♭1	mod. uptempo
Maybe my baby, Jimmy Nos. 1, 2 (T, Bar)	d-b♭1/G-f1	uptempo, jazzy
Fire and ice, Grushinskaya (M), chorus	b-c2	ballad
Twenty-two years/Villa on a hill, Raffaela (M)	f#-b	ballad
Girl in the mirror, Frieda Flaemme (M)	d-g1	slow, then fast
The crooked path, Preysing (Bar)	B-f#	character ballad

Who couldn't dance with you, Frieda, Kringelein (T)	g-g1/e-e1	uptempo
The merger is on, Zinn (Bar), chorus	e♭-d1	mod. uptempo
Love can't happen, Grushinskaya, Baron	c1-a1/d-a♭1	waltz ballad
What she needs, Doctor	f-b♭1	ballad
Bonjour amour, Grushinskaya, chorus (background)	g-b1	moving ballad
Grand Charleston, company		uptempo
We'll take a glass together, Kringelein, Baron, 2 Jimmys, chorus		uptempo
I waltz alone, Doctor, chorus	c-c1	waltz ballad
Roses at the station, Doctor	B♭-f#1	driving ballad
How can I tell her, Raffaela	b♭-b2	fast, anxious
Finale: Grand Hotel, company		mod. uptempo

Grease (1972)
Music and Lyrics by Jim Jacobs and Warren Casey

Song title, **Character (Voice)**	**Range**	**Song Style**
Rydell alma mater, chorus		anthem ballad
Rydell alma mater parody, chorus		mod. uptempo
Summer nights, Danny (T), Sandy (S), chorus	d-e♭1/d1-e♭2	uptempo
Those magic changes, Doody (T), chorus	e-f1	uptempo
Freddy my love, Marty (M), girls trio	d1-d2	easy rock ballad
Greased lightening, Kenickie (Bar), chorus	c-e♭1	fast character
Rydell's fight song, chorus		uptempo
Mooning, Roger (T), Jan (M)	f-g1/f-b♭1	blues ballad
Look at me, I'm Sandra Dee, Rizzo (M)	a-c1	ballad, character
We go together, company		uptempo
Shakin' at the high school hop, chorus		50s rock
It's raining on prom night, women's chorus		mod. ballad
Born to hand jive, Johnny Casino (Bar)	g-e1	fast uptempo
Beauty school dropout, Teen Angel (T), girls trio	e-f#1	swing ballad
Beauty school dropout reprise	e-b1 (e2 in falsetto)	swing ballad
Alone at the drive-in movie, Danny	f#-g1 (a1-d2 in falsetto)	ballad
Rock and roll party queen, Roger, Doody	both A♭-e♭1	uptempo
There are worse things I could do, Rizzo	d-b♭1	ballad
Look at me, I'm Sandra Dee reprise, Sandy	a-b2	ballad
All choked up, Danny, Sandy	F-f#1/b♭-b♭1	uptempo
We go together reprise, company		uptempo

Grey Gardens (2006)

Music by Scott Frankel   Lyrics by Michael Korie

Song title, **Character (Voice)**	**Range**	**Song Style**
The girl who has everything, Edith (M), Edie (S), ensemble	c1-d♭2/c-e♭2	ballad
On the 5:15, Edith, ensemble	b-b♭1	swing uptempo
Mother, darling, Edie, Edith, ensemble	b-f#2/a-d2	mod. uptempo
Goin' places, Joe (T), Edie	c-f#1/c1-e2	mod. uptempo
Marry well, Major (Bar), ensemble	A#-e1	uptempo
Hominy grits, Edith, ensemble	b-c#2	cowboy ballad
Two peas in a pod, Edie, Edith	d1-e2/d1-c2	mod. uptempo
Drift away, Gould (Bar), Edie incidental	e♭-f1	ballad
Daddy's girl, Edie	c1-e2	uptempo
The telegram, ensemble		scene
Will you?, Edith	c1-e2	ballad
The revolutionary costume, Edie	b♭-c2	uptempo
The cake I had, Edith	e#-c2	mod. ballad
Entering Grey Gardens, company		mod. uptempo
The house we live in, Edie, chorus	a-c2	march uptempo
Jerry likes my corn, Edith, others incidental	g♭-a♭1	mod. uptempo
Around the world, Edie	c1-c#2	uptempo
Choose to be happy, Norman Vincent Peale (Bar), chorus	G-e1	gospel ballad
Around the world reprise, Edie	c#1-b1	mod. ballad
Another winter, Edie, Edith	f#-c#2/g#-e1	ballad
Two peas in a pod reprise, Edith, Edie	c1-b♭1/c1-d2	mod. uptempo

Guys and Dolls (1950)

Music and Lyrics by Frank Loesser

Song title, **Character (Voice)**	**Range**	**Song Style**
Fugue for tinhorns, Nicely (T), Benny (T), Rusty (T)	d-a♭1/d-f1/d-f1	uptempo
Follow the fold, chorus		anthem ballad
The oldest established, men's chorus, ensemble		uptempo, funny
I'll know, Sarah (S)	e♭1-f2 (opt. a♭2)	ballad
A bushel and a peck, Adelaide (M), Hot Box Girls	b-d2	character, mod.
Adelaide's lament, Adelaide	a♭-d2	character ballad
Guys and dolls, Nicely, Benny	both e-g1	uptempo
If I were a bell, Sarah	b♭-e♭2	uptempo
My time of day, Sky (Bar)	c-d1	reflective ballad
I've never been in love before, Sky, Sarah	B♭-e♭1/d1-g2	ballad

Take back your mink, Adelaide, Hot Box Girls	b♭-c2	mod. uptempo
Adelaide's second lament, Adelaide	d-c2	character ballad
More I cannot wish you, Arvide (Bar)	d-d1	ballad
Luck be a lady, Sky, men's chorus	d♭-e♭1	uptempo
Sue me, Nathan (T), Adelaide	d-f1/d1-d2	ballad, funny
Sit down you're rockin' the boat, Nicely, chorus	f-b♭1	fast, narrative
Marry the man today, Adelaide, Sarah	c1-c2/c1-e2	uptempo, funny
Guys and dolls reprise, company		uptempo

Gypsy (1959)

Music by Jule Styne   Lyrics by Stephen Sondheim

Song title, **Character (Voice)**	**Range**	**Song Style**
Some people, Rose (M)	g#-c2	uptempo
Some people reprise, Rose	g#-b1	uptempo
Small world, Rose, Herbie (Bar) incidental	f#-b1	ballad
Let me entertain you, June (girl S)	c#1-e2	mod. uptempo
Mr. Goldstone, Rose, company	f-b♭1	uptempo, funny
You'll never get away from me, Rose, Herbie	f#-c2/B-c#1	mod. ballad
Farm sequence, June (S), boys	c1-f2	mod. ballad
Broadway, June, boys	e#1-d2	uptempo
If Momma was married, Louise (S), June	g-b1/g-c#2	mod. uptempo
All I need is the girl, Tulsa (T)	e-g1	mod. uptempo
Everything's coming up roses, Rose	b♭-c#2	uptempo
Torreadorables, girls' chorus		mod. uptempo
Together wherever we go, Rose, company	a-b1	mod. uptempo
You gotta get a gimmick, Mazeppa (M), Elecktra (M), Tessie (M)	g-d♭2/b♭-d♭2/ b♭-d♭2	character, hard ballad
Let me entertain you, Louise, showgirls incidental	f#-c2	slow strip ballad
Rose's turn, Rose	g-c2	driving uptempo

Hair (1968)

Music by Galt MacDermot   Lyrics by Gerome Ragni and James Rado

Song title, **Character (Voice)**	**Range**	**Song Style**
Aquarius, Ronny (Bar), company	e♭-e♭1	mod. uptempo
Donna, Berger (T), company	f-b♭1	uptempo
Colored spade, Hud (Bar)	B-d1	mod. uptempo
Manchester, England, Claude (T), company	e-f#1	mod. uptempo

Ain't got no, Hud, Woof (Bar), Dionne (M)	men g#-f#1/g#1-f#2	uptempo
Dead end, quartet	all g-c2/G-c1	slow hard rock
I believe in love, Sheila (S), trio backup	g-f2	uptempo
Ain't got no grass, company		march tempo
Air, Jeanie (S); Dionne, Crissy (M) incidental	a1-g2	mod. ballad
I got life, Claude, company	d-g1	uptempo
Going down, Berger, company	c-g1	mod. ballad
Hair, Claude, company	d-g1	mod. ballad
My conviction, Margaret Mead (M)	e-a1	ballad
Easy to be hard, Sheila	c1-c2 (opt. e♭2)	ballad
Don't put it down, Berger, Woof, Steve (T)	e♭-e♭1/g-e♭1/c-a♭1	country ballad
Frank Mills, Crissy	b-c#2	mod. ballad
Be-in, company		uptempo
Where do I go, Claude, company	c-f1	mod. ballad
Electric blues, quartet from chorus	SMTB	mod. ballad
Black boys/White boys, chorus		uptempo
Walking in space, ensemble		rock ballad
Abie, baby, Hud, duo backup	g-b1	uptempo
The war, company		uptempo
Three-five-zero-zero, chorus		mod. uptempo
What a piece of work is man, Ronny, Walter (T)	e-a1/e-g1	ballad
Good morning Starshine, Sheila, chorus	c-b♭1	moving ballad
The bed, chorus		uptempo
The flesh flowers (Let the sun shine in), chorus		mod. uptempo
Eyes look your last, Claude, Sheila, company	f#-f#1/d-f#2	mod. uptempo
Hippie life, Claude, company	c-d1	uptempo

Hairspray (2002)

Music by Marc Shaiman   Lyrics by Scott Wittman and Marc Shaiman

Song title, Character (Voice)	Range	Song Style
Good morning, Baltimore, Tracy (M), company	b♭-c#2	uptempo
The nicest kids in town, Corny (T), chorus	d-f#1	uptempo
Blood on the pavement, trio	MMB	mod. uptempo
Mama, I'm a big girl now, girls' ensemble		mod. uptempo
I can hear the bells, Tracy, chorus	a-e2	ballad
Velma's cha cha, Velma (M), chorus	a♭-e♭2	mod. uptempo
The nicest kids reprise, Corny, chorus	b-f#1	uptempo
The new girl in town, chorus		mod. uptempo

It takes two, Link (T), chorus	e-f#1	mod. ballad
Welcome to the 60s, Tracy, Edna (M), chorus	g-c#2/f-c#2	uptempo
Run and tell that, Seaweed (T), chorus	f-b1	uptempo
Big, blonde, and beautiful, Motormouth (M), company	c1-e2	mod. uptempo
The big doll house, company		uptempo
Good morning, Baltimore reprise, Tracy	a♭-b♭1	moving ballad
You're timeless to me, Wilbur (Bar), Edna	A#-f#1/f#-e2	mod. ballad
Without love, quartet, chorus	SMTT	mod. uptempo
Step on up, company		uptempo
It's hairspray, Corny, chorus	e-g1	mod. uptempo
Cooties, Amber (S), chorus	e1-f2	uptempo
You can't stop the beat, company		uptempo

Added song in score:

Miss Baltimore Crabs, Velma, company	a♭-c♭2	mod. character

Half a Sixpence (1963)
Music and Lyrics by David Heneker

Song title, **Character (Voice)**	**Range**	**Song Style**
Economy, male ensemble, many soli		waltz ballad
Half a sixpence, Kipps (Bar), Ann (M)	c-e♭1/d1-d2	mod. ballad
Money to burn, Kipps, men's chorus	d-g1	uptempo
I don't believe a word of it, Ann, Shopgirls	b-f2	uptempo
A proper gentleman, chorus		mod. uptempo
She's too far above me, Kipps	d-d1	ballad
If the rain's got to fall, Kipps, chorus	d♭-d♭1	mod. ballad
The old military canal, chorus		mod. uptempo
The one who's run away, Kipps, Chitterlow (Bar)	both d-e♭1	mod. uptempo
Long ago, Ann, Kipps	e1-f2/e-f1	ballad
Flash, bang, wallop!, Kipps, chorus	e♭-e1	fast character
I know what I am, Ann	d♭-b♭1	uptempo
The party's on the house, Kipps, chorus	d♭-e♭1	uptempo
Half a sixpence reprise, chorus		mod. ballad
Finale, company*		uptempo

*A pastiche of songs from the show.

Hedwig and the Angry Itch (1998)
Music and Lyrics by Stephen Trask

Song title, **Character (Voice)**	**Range**	**Song Style**
Tear me down, Hedwig (Bar)	g-c2	mod. ballad
The origin of love, and chorus	A-b1	mod. uptempo
Sugar daddy	d#-g#1	mod. shuffle
Angry itch, and chorus	ab-db1	uptempo
Wig in a box	e-d1	various
Wicked little town	d-e1	ballad
The long grift	d-a1	uptempo
Hedwig's lament	e-c1	ballad
Exquisite corpse	g-g1	uptempo
Wicked little town reprise, and chorus	d-e1	ballad
Midnight radio	A-g1	uptempo

Note: Most songs have some backup harmony.

Hello Again (1994)
Music and Lyrics by Michael John LaChiusa

Song title, **Character (Voice)**	**Range**	**Song Style**
Hello again, Whore (M), Soldier (Bar)	f#-d2/G-b	slow waltz
Zei gegent, Soldier, trio	c#-d1	swing uptempo
I gotta little time, Soldier	fb-gb1	mod. uptempo
We kiss, Nurse (S), Soldier	g#-e2/db-f1	mod. uptempo
In some other life, Nurse, College Boy (T)	f-c2/Bb-g1	mod. ballad
Story of my life, College Boy, Young Wife (M), chorus	Bb-f#1/g-eb2	mod. ballad
Ah, mein Zeit, Radio Voice (S)	eb-f2	waltz ballad
Tom, Young Wife, Husband (T)	a-e2/A-f1	mod. uptempo
Listen to the music, Husband, Young Thing (T)	B-f#1/d-e1	mod. uptempo
Montage, Writer (T), Young Thing incidental	f-f#1	uptempo
Safe, Young Thing	c-c2	uptempo
The one I love, Writer, Young Thing	d-g1/c-f#1	mod. uptempo
Silent movie, Actress (M)	d-e2	uptempo
Angel of Mercy, Senator (Bar), Actress	A-c1/c1-e2	mod. uptempo
Mistress of the Senator, Actress, Senator	g-g2/A-c1	uptempo
The bed was not my own, Senator, Whore	db-f#1/f#-c#2	mod. uptempo
Hello again, company		slow waltz

Hello, Dolly (1964)
Music and Lyrics by Jerry Herman

Song title, Character (Voice)	Range	Song Style
Opening, chorus		mod. uptempo
I put my hand in, Dolly (S)	e♭1-g2	uptempo
It takes a woman, Horace (Bar), ensemble	B-c#1	fast, dramatic
Put on your Sunday clothes, Cornelius (T), ensemble	c-g#1	fast uptempo
Ribbons down my back, Mrs. Molloy (M)	a-d2	ballad
Motherhood march, Dolly, Mrs. Molloy	both d1-f2	uptempo
Dancing, Dolly, Mrs. Molloy, Cornelius, Barnaby (Bar)	SMTB	uptempo
Before the parade passes by, Dolly, chorus	d1-f2	uptempo
Elegance, Minnie (S), Mrs. Molloy, Cornelius, Barnaby	SMTB	mod. ballad
Hello, Dolly, Dolly, men's chorus	c1-f2	mod. uptempo
It only takes a moment, Cornelius, chorus	B♭-e♭1	ballad
So long, dearie, Dolly	e♭1-g2	uptempo, angry
Hello, Dolly reprise, company		mod. uptempo

High School Musical (2007)*
Music and Lyrics by various artists

Song title, Character (Voice)	Range	Song Style
Wildcat cheer, chorus		uptempo
Start of something new, company		mod. uptempo
Get'cha head in the game, Troy (T), male chorus	a-b♭1	mod. uptempo
Auditions, company		uptempo
What I've been looking for, Sharpay (M), Ryan (T)	a-a1/f#-f#1	uptempo
What I've been looking for reprise, Troy, Gabriella (M)	f#-g#1/a-c#2	uptempo
Cellular fusion, company		mod. uptempo
Stick to the status quo, company		uptempo
I can't take my eyes off of you, Troy, Gabriella	e♭-b♭1/g-e2	mod. ballad
Wildcat cheer reprise, chorus		uptempo
Counting on you, company		uptempo
When there was me and you, Troy, Gabriella, chorus	B-g#1/f#-c#2	ballad
Start of something new reprise, Troy, Gabriella	e-a1/a-d2	mod. ballad
We're all in this together, company		mod. uptempo
Bop to the top, Sharpay, Ryan, chorus	b♭-a1/g-g1	samba uptempo

Breaking free, Troy, Gabriella, company	B♭-b♭1/b♭-c2	mod. uptempo
We're all in this together reprise, company		mod. uptempo
Megamix, company		various

*Denotes date of national tour.

Hit the Deck (1927)

Music by Vincent Youmans   Lyrics by Clifford Grey and Leo Robin

Song title, Character (Voice)	Range	Song Style
The song of the Marines, men's chorus		uptempo march
Join the Navy, unison men's chorus (some soli)		mod. uptempo
Time on my hands, Bilge (T)	d-f#1	mod. ballad
Join the Navy reprise, men's chorus		mod. uptempo
The song of the Marines reprise, men's chorus		uptempo march
Loo-loo, Looloo (M)	d1-e2	mod. uptempo
Drums in my heart, Gaie (S)	b♭-g2	uptempo
I know that you know, Lavinia (M)	b-e2	mod. ballad
Sometimes I'm happy, Bilge, Looloo	e-e1/e1-e2 (opt. f1, f2)	mod. uptempo
Hallelujah, company		uptempo
Through the years, Bilge	f-f1	ballad
Shore leave, chorus		uptempo waltz
The harbor of my heart, Bilge	c-g1	moving ballad
Sometimes I'm happy reprise, Looloo	f#1-f#2	mod. uptempo
Through the years reprise, Bilge	f-f1	mod. ballad
Finale, company		uptempo

How to Succeed in Business without Really Trying (1961)

Music and Lyrics by Frank Loesser

Song title, Character (Voice)	Range	Song Style
How to succeed . . . , Finch (T)	f-e1	uptempo
Happy to keep his dinner warm, Rosemary (M)	a-c2	moving ballad
Coffee break, chorus		uptempo
The company way, Twimble (Bar), Finch	d♭-e♭/d-g♭1	uptempo
The company way reprise, chorus		uptempo
A secretary is not a toy, Bratt (Bar), chorus	d#-e1	mod. character
Been a long day, Smitty (Bar), Rosemary, Finch	b♭-d♭1/e♭1-b♭1/g-d1	mod. ballad

Grand old Ivy, Biggley (Bar), Finch	c-d1 (opt. g1)/d-g1	uptempo march
Paris original, Rosemary, women's chorus	b♭-b♭1	ballad
Rosemary, Finch, Rosemary	e-e1/b-c2	ballad
Cinderella, darling, Smitty, women's chorus	a-b1	uptempo
Happy to keep his dinner . . . reprise, Rosemary	a-c2	moving ballad
Love from a heart of gold, Biggley, Hedy (M)	c-e♭1/c1-d2	ballad
I believe in you, Finch, men's chorus	f-g1	moving ballad
Brotherhood of man, Finch, Miss Jones (S), men	f-g1/e♭1-a♭2	uptempo
Finale: Company way, company		uptempo

I Can Get It for You Wholesale (1962)
Music and Lyrics by Harold Rome

Song title, Character (Voice)	**Range**	**Song Style**
I'm not a well man, Ms. Marmelstein (S) Pulvermacher (Bar)	c1-d2/c-e♭1	character
The way things are, Harry (Bar)	c-d1	fast character
When Gemini meets Capricorn, Harry, Ruthie (M)	c-e1/c1-d2	mod. uptempo
Momma, momma!, Harry, Mrs. Bogen (M)	B♭-d1/d1-d2	uptempo
The sound of money, Harry, Martha (M)	B-d1/a-d2	ballad, character
The family way, company		uptempo
Too soon, Mrs. Bogen	g-b1	ballad
Who knows, Ruthie	a♭-c2	ballad
Have I told you lately?, Meyer (Bar), Blanche (M)	B♭-e♭1/d1-e♭2	ballad
Ballad of the garment trade, company		uptempo
A gift today, company		waltz ballad
Miss Marmelstein, Ms. Marmelstein	b1-d2	fast character
On my way to love, Ruthie, Harry	c1-d2/c-d1	uptempo
What's in it for me?, Teddy (T), Martha	d-d1	incidental
What are they doing to us now, Ms. Marmelstein, chorus	a-e♭2	uptempo (in 5/4)
Eat a little something, Mrs. Bogen	g-g1	character ballad

I Do! I Do! (1966)

Music by Harvey Schmidt   Lyrics by Tom Jones

Song title, Character (Voice)	Range	Song Style
All the dearly beloved, Michael (Bar), Agnes (M)	B♭-b/a-b1	slow, recit.-like
Together forever, Michael, Agnes	G-c1/g-b♭1	waltz ballad
I do, I do, Michael, Agnes	A-e♭1/a-d2	moving ballad
Goodnight, Agnes, Michael	g-b1/G-c1	ballad
I love my wife, Michael	B♭-e♭1	jazzy ballad
Something has happened, Agnes	g-c2	ballad
My cup runneth over, Michael, Agnes	G-c1/g-c2	ballad
Love isn't everything, Michael, Agnes	G-d1/f-c2	uptempo
Nobody's perfect, Michael, Agnes	F-c1/g-d1	uptempo
It's a well known fact, Michael	a-e♭1	mod. ballad
Flaming Agnes, Agnes	g-c2	torch ballad
The honeymoon is over, Michael, Agnes	A♭-e♭1/ab-e♭2	uptempo
Honeymoon is over/Your eyes shine like lightning, Michael, Agnes	d-d1/g-c2	mixed, mostly uptempo
Where are the snows?, Michael, Agnes	G-c1/f-c2	ballad
When the kids get married, Michael, Agnes	G-e♭1/g-e♭2	mod. uptempo
The father of the bride, Michael, Agnes	G-c1/g-g1	mostly uptempo
What is a woman?, Agnes	a-d♭2	ballad
Someone needs me, Michael, Agnes	A-a/a-c2	waltz uptempo
Roll up the ribbons, Michael, Agnes	B♭-c♭1/g#-a1	ballad
Finale: This house, Agnes, Michael	g-a1/B♭-a1	ballad

I Love My Wife (1977)

Music by Cy Coleman   Lyrics by Michael Stewart

Song title, Character (Voice)	Range	Song Style
We're still friends, chorus		uptempo
Monica, Alvin (Bar), male quartet	e♭-e♭1	mod. ballad
By threes, Wally (Bar), Harvey (Bar), Alan (Bar)	all d-f1	uptempo
A mover's life, Stanley (Bar), Alvin, men's chorus	c-e♭1/c-f1	uptempo
Love revolution, Alvin	a#-d1	hard ballad
Someone wonderful I missed, Monica (M), Cleo (M)	b♭-f1/b♭-d♭1	ballad
Sexually free, company		uptempo, patter
Hey there, good times, men's chorus		uptempo
Lovers on Christmas eve, Monica, Wally	a-c2/a-f#1	ballad
Scream, men's chorus		march uptempo
Everybody today is turnin' on, Wally, Alvin	both d#-g#1	uptempo, patter

Married couple seeks married couple, Wally, Alvin, Cleo, Monica	c-g♭1/c-b♭1/ c1-g♭2/c1-b♭2	ballad
I love my wife, Stanley, company	B♭-g1	jazzy ballad
Bows: Hey there good times, company		uptempo

I'm Getting My Act Together
and Taking It on the Road (1978)

Music by Nancy Ford   Lyrics by Gretchen Cryer

Song title, **Character (Voice)**	**Range**	**Song Style**
Feel the love, Alice (M), Cheryl (M), Jake (T)	g#-c#2/g#- g#1/G#-e1	uptempo
Natural high, Heather (M), others incidental, men's chorus	a-a1	uptempo
Smile, Heather, company	c1-c#2	uptempo waltz
In a simple way I love you, Heather, others incidental	d1-b1	ballad
Miss America, Heather, company	b-d#2	mod. uptempo
Strong woman number, Alice, Heather	a-c2/d♭-c2	uptempo
Dear Tom, Heather	g-c2	ballad
Old friend, Heather	g-b1	ballad
Put in a package, Heather, Alice, Cheryl	b♭-c2/e1-f2/f-d2	uptempo
If only things was different, Jake	g-d1	mod. ballad
Feel the love, company		uptempo
Lonely lady, Heather	f-g1	ballad
Happy birthday, Heather, Alice, Cheryl	all b-d2	mod. uptempo
Natural high reprise, company		uptempo

In Trousers (1979; rev. 1985)

Music and Lyrics by William Finn

Song title, **Character (Voice)**	**Range**	**Song Style**
In trousers, company		uptempo
I can't sleep, Marvin (Bar), three girls	f-e♭1	uptempo
A helluva day, Trina (M)	f#-d♭2	mod. uptempo
I have a family, Marvin	c-f1	slow
How Marvin eats his breakfast, Marvin, girls	A-f#1	funky, moderate
Marvin's giddy seizures, women's ensemble		uptempo
My high school sweetheart, Sweetheart (M), ensemble	d-e♭2	mod. ballad
Set those sails, Miss Goldberg (M), women	a-f3	mod. uptempo
I swear I won't ever again, Marvin	A-f1	ballad

High school ladies at five o'clock, Sweetheart, Marvin, women	c1-d3/c-d1	reggae uptempo
The rape of Miss Goldberg, Marvin, Miss Goldberg; Sweetheart incidental	B-e1/a-e2	mod. uptempo
I swear I won't Part II, Marvin, women	c-f#1	moving ballad
Love me for what I am, Trina, Marvin, company	g-e2/f-e1	ballad
I am wearing a hat, Miss Goldberg, Sweetheart; Trina incidental	a-d2/B-d2	mod. uptempo
Wedding song, company		mod. uptempo
Three seconds, Marvin, company	A-d#1	slow
Wedding song II, company		mod. uptempo
How the body falls apart, women		uptempo
I feel him slipping away, Trina, Sweetheart, Miss Goldberg	a-c#2/c#-e2/ c#-c#2	mod. uptempo
Whizzer going down, Marvin; Sweetheart, Miss Goldberg incidental	B-e1	ragtime uptempo
Marvin's giddy seizures Part II, company		uptempo
I'm breaking down, Trina	a-e2	ragtime
Perking up, Marvin	c-d1	mod. uptempo
Breakfast over sugar, Marvin, Trina	G-d1/g-d2	ballad
How America got its name, company		uptempo
A helluva day reprise, Trina	a-e♭1	ragtime
Another sleepless night, company		mod. uptempo
Goodnight—no hard feelings, Marvin	A♭-e1	mod. ballad
In trousers reprise (The dream), company		mod. uptempo

Note: 1985 version annotated here.

Into the Woods (1987)
Music and Lyrics by Stephen Sondheim

Song title, **Character (Voice)**	**Range**	**Song Style**
Opening: Into the woods, company		mostly uptempo
Cinderella at the grave, Cinderella (S), Cinderella's Mother (M)	c1-e2/f1-f2	uptempo
Hello, little girl, Wolf (Bar), Red Riding Hood incidental	B♭-g♭1	character ballad
I guess this is goodbye, Jack (T)	d#-d#1	ballad
Maybe they're magic, Baker's Wife (M)	g#-e2	uptempo
I know things now, Red (S)	c1-e♭2	narrative ballad
A very nice prince, Cinderella, Baker's Wife	a♭-a♭1/spoken	ballad
First midnight, company		mod. uptempo
Giants in the sky, Jack	c-f#1	mod. narrative
Agony, Cinderella's Prince (Bar), Rapunzel's Prince (Bar)	both c#-e1	ballad, funny
It takes two, Baker's Wife, Baker (Bar)	a-d2/A♭-f1	ballad

Stay with me, Witch (M), Rapunzel incidental	b♭-d♭2/spoken	ballad
On the steps of the palace, Cinderella	a-d2	mod.uptempo
Finale: Into the woods, company		uptempo
Act II opening: Into the woods, company		uptempo
Agony reprise, two princes	both B-e#	ballad, funny
Any moment, Cinderella's Prince, Baker's Wife	B♭-e♭1/c1-d2	ballad
Moments in the woods, Baker's Wife	g-e♭2	uptempo
Your fault, Jack, Baker, Red, Witch, Cinderella	SSMTB	uptempo
Last midnight, Witch	b♭-d♭2	mod. uptempo
No more, Baker, Mysterious Man (Bar)	d-e♭1/G-e♭1	ballad
No one is alone, Cinderella, company	b♭-d♭2	ballad
Finale: Into the woods, company		ballad, then fast

Irene (1919)

Music by Harry Tierney, Charles Gaynor, Wally Harper,
Harry Carroll, Fred Fisher, and Otis Clements
Lyrics by Joe McCarthy, Charles Gaynor, Harry Tierney, and Jack Lloyd

Song title, **Character (Voice)**	**Range**	**Song Style**
What do you want to make those eyes at me for, chorus		mod. uptempo
The world must be bigger than an avenue, Irene (M)	b♭-c2	mod. uptempo
The family tree, Mrs. Marshall (M), women's chorus	e♭1-f2	mod. ballad
Alice blue gown, Irene	a♭-b♭1	ballad
They go wild, simply wild over me, Madame Lucy (M)	d1-d2	uptempo
An Irish girl, Irene, chorus	a-b1	ballad
Mother, angel, darling, Irene, Mrs. O'Dare (M)	f#-b♭1/g-b♭1	mod. uptempo
The last part of ev'ry party, chorus		uptempo
We're getting away with it, Lucy, Ozzie (M), Helen (M), June (M)	all c1-d2	mod. uptempo
I'm always chasing rainbows, Irene	g-a1	ballad
Irene, Donald (Bar), chorus	A-d1	mod. ballad
Greater love tango, Donald, Helen, June	c-d♭1/both c1-f2	uptempo
You made me love you, Donald, Irene	B♭-d1/b♭-c2	ballad
Alice blue gown reprise, company		mod. ballad

Jacques Brel Is Alive and Well
and Living in Paris (1968)

Music by Jacques Brel   Lyrics by Eric Blau and Mort Schuman

Song title, Character (Voice)	Range	Song Style
Marathon, quartet	SMTB	uptempo
Alone, Man 2 (T)	G#-eb1	mod. ballad
Madeleine, quartet	SMTB	uptempo, funny
I loved, Woman 1 (S)	c1-e2	waltz ballad
Mathilde, Man 1 (Bar)	c-d1 (much spoken)	mod. uptempo
Bachelor's dance, Man 2	c-e1 (w/ falsetto c2)	moving ballad
Timid Frieda, Woman 2 (M), men	ab-db2	waltz ballad
My death, Woman 1	c1-c#2	ballad
Girls and dogs, men	both c#-d1	uptempo
Jackie, Man 1	d-d1	mod. ballad
Statue, Man 2	e-f1	march uptempo
The desperate ones, quartet	unison b-b1 (B-b)	ballad
Sons of ——, Woman 1	c#1-e2	waltz ballad
Amsterdam, Man 1, trio	e-f1	uptempo
The bulls, quartet	unison d-c1 (d1-c2)	mod. uptempo
Old folks, Woman 1, trio backup	eb1-db2	ballad
Marieke, Woman 1, trio hum in background	c#1-eb2	mod. ballad
Brussels, quartet	SMTB	uptempo
Fanette, Man 2	c-f1	ballad
Funeral tango, Man 1	d-d1	uptempo tango
Middle class, men	c-e1/c-c#1	mod. uptempo
No love you're not alone, quartet	unison d-c1/d1-c2	mod. ballad
Next, Man 1	db-f1	recit., fast
Carousels, quartet	SMTB	waltz uptempo
If we only have love, quartet	SMTB	ballad

Jane Eyre (2000)

Music and Lyrics by Paul Gordon

Song title, Character (Voice)	Range	Song Style
Prologue, Jane (M), Mr. Brocklehurst (T)	a-c2/d-f1	slow
Children of God, trio, chorus	SMT	uptempo
Forgiveness, Helen (M)	a-c2	ballad
Helen's death, Jane, Helen	g-bb1/ab-db2	ballad
The graveyard, Young Jane (girl), Jane	d1-d2/a-c2	slow
Sweet liberty, Jane, ensemble	a-d2	mod. uptempo

Perfectly nice, Mrs. Fairfax (M), Jane, others incidental	a-c2/a#-c2	uptempo
The icy lane, chorus		mod. uptempo
The master returns, Mrs. Fairfax, Robert (Bar)	b♭-b♭1/B♭-b♭	uptempo
I see a captive bird, Rochester (Bar)	c-d1	moving ballad
As good as you, Rochester	A-e1	ballad
The fire, company		moderate
Secret soul, Jane, Rochester	f#-d2/a-b1	mod. ballad
The aristocrat's arrival, chorus		uptempo
The finer things, Blanche (S)	e♭1-a♭2 (opt. b♭2)	uptempo
Oh, how you look, Blanche, chorus, Rochester incidental	g-b2	waltz uptempo
The pledge, Rochester, Jane	B♭-g♭1/g♭-d♭2	mod. ballad
Sirens, Rochester, Jane; Figure incidental	B♭-f1/g-c2	ballad
Sympathies exist, chorus		slow
Bertha bites Mason, company		mod. uptempo
Painting her portrait, Jane	a♭-d2	uptempo
In the light of the virgin morning, Jane, Blanche	g-d2/b-f2	mod. uptempo
The gypsy, Rochester, ensemble	d-a1	mod. waltz
My hope of heaven, Rochester, Jane incidental	F-g2	mod. uptempo
Slip of a girl, Mrs. Fairfax, Jane incidental	f-b♭1	uptempo
The wedding, company		scene
Behind the door, Rochester	A♭-f1	moving ballad
Farewell good angel, Rochester	G-g1	agitated
Forgiveness reprise, Jane, chorus	g#-b1	mod. ballad
The call, St. John (T), Jane; Rochester incidental	c-g1/a♭-e2	moving ballad
Return to Thornfield, Jane, Mrs. Fairfax	a-b♭1/d-a1	mod. uptempo
Brave enough for love, Jane, Rochester, chorus	e-e♭1/d♭-b♭1	moving ballad

Jekyll & Hyde (1997)
Music by Frank Wildhorn   Lyrics by Leslie Bricusse, Frank Wildhorn, and Steve Cuden

Song title, **Character (Voice)**	**Range**	**Song Style**
Look in the darkness, Jekyll (T)	G#-e1	mod. ballad
I need to know, Jekyll	B-f#1	moving ballad
Facade, company		uptempo
Board of governors, Jekyll, company	B-a1	mod. uptempo
Pursue the truth/Facade reprise, company		slow/uptempo
The engagement party, company		mod. ballad
Take me as I am, Jekyll, Emma (M)	B♭-f#1/b♭-f#2	mod. ballad

Letting go, Emma, Danvere (Bar)	b-d2/d-d1	ballad
Bring on the men, Lucy (M), female ensemble	g#-f#2	uptempo
Lucy and Jekyll at the Dregs, Lucy, Jeykll	b-d2/b-f1	mod. uptempo
This is the moment, Jekyll	B-g#1	moving ballad
The transformation, Jekyll	d-f1	scene
Alive, Hyde, chorus incidental	c-a1	uptempo
His wife and nothing more, quartet	MTBB	mod. ballad
Sympathy, tenderness, Lucy	b-c#2	mod. ballad
Someone like you, Lucy	g-e♭2	ballad
Alive reprise, Hyde	e-a1	uptempo
Murder, murder, chorus		uptempo
Once upon a dream, Emma	b-c#2	ballad
Streak of madness, Jekyll	c-e♭1	mod. ballad
In his eye, Lucy, Emma	b♭-f2/b♭-e♭2	ballad
Dangerous game, Hyde, Lucy	B-a1/b-e♭2	mod. uptempo
Facade reprise no. 2, company		uptempo
The way back, Jekyll	B-g1	mod. ballad
A new life, Lucy	b-d2	moving ballad
Lucy's death (Sympathy, tenderness reprise), Hyde	c#-c#1	ballad
The confrontation, Jekyll/Hyde	B-g1 (opt. a1)	mod. ballad
Facade reprise no. 3, company		uptempo
The wedding, Jeykll, Emma	e-d♭1/f#-c#2	scene

Jerry's Girls (1986)
Music and Lyrics by Jerry Herman

Song title, Character (Voice)	Range	Song Style
Just leave everything/Clothes, Dorothy (M)	e-c2	uptempo
It only takes a moment, Leslie (M)	f1-c2	mod. uptempo
Wherever he ain't, Chita (M)	f-a♭1	uptempo, angry
We need a little Christmas, company		uptempo
Tap your troubles away, Dorothy, company	f#-e2	mod. uptempo
I won't send roses, Leslie	f1-d2	moving ballad
Vaudeville medley		
I was born to play the two-a-day, Dorothy	f-c2	mod. ballad
We'll always be bosom buddies, Chita, Leslie	g♭-d♭2/g♭-b♭1	mod. uptempo
Man in the moon, Dorothy	a-a2	mod. ballad
So long, dearie, Chita	f#-b1	uptempo
Take it all off, company		uptempo
Shalom/Milk and honey, Leslie, company	g-d1	ballad
Before the parade passes by, Chita	f-a♭1	uptempo, brassy
Have a nice day, Dorothy, company	a-d2	recit. ballad

Showtune, Chita, company	e-a1	uptempo
If he walked into my life, Leslie	a♭-c2	ballad
Hello, Dolly, Dorothy, company	d-a1	mod. uptempo
It's today, Leslie	g-e2	mod. uptempo
Mame, company		mod. ballad
I don't want to know, Chita	f#-b♭1 (opt. c2)	waltz ballad
Just go to the movies, company		mod. uptempo
Movies were movies/Look what happened to Mabel, company (could be solo)	(f#-b♭1)	jazzy ballad
Nelson, Dorothy, company	f#-c#2	waltz ballad
Kiss her now, Leslie, Kirsten (M)	g♭-c2/g♭-a1	ballad
Mame reprise, company		mod. ballad
Time heals everything, Dorothy	d-c2	ballad
Gooch's song, Dorothy	f#-e2	character ballad
La cage aux folles, company		mod. uptempo
Song on the sand, Dorothy, company	e♭-b♭1	ballad
I am what I am, Leslie	e♭-b♭1	assertive ballad
The best of times is now, company		uptempo

Note: Premiered off-Broadway in 1981.

Jesus Christ Superstar (1971)

Music by Andrew Lloyd Webber   Lyrics by Tim Rice

Song title, Character (Voice)	**Range**	**Song Style**
Heaven on their minds, Judas (T)	d-d2	rock ballad
What's the buzz, Jesus (T), Mary Mag. (M), Apostles	f-a1/f1-a2	uptempo
Strange thing, mystifying, Judas, Jesus, Apostles	g-g1/f-c2	mod. ballad
Everything's alright, Mary, Jesus, Judas	g-b1/e-b1/B-d1	ballad
This Jesus must die, Annas (T), Caiaphas (B), High Priests	c-f1/f-f1/ TBBBB	recit.-like, ballad
Hosanna, Jesus, Caiphas, chorus	d-f1/F-a♭	mod. uptempo
Simon Zealots, poor Jerusalem, Simon (T), Jesus, chorus	f-a♭1/F-a♭1	uptempo, then quiet
Pilate's dream, Pilate (Bar)	A-b♭	ballad
The temple, Jesus, chorus	B-e2	uptempo
Everything's alright reprise, Mary, Jesus	f#-a1/d-a	ballad
I don't know how to love him, Mary	a-b1	ballad
Damned for all time/Blood money, Judas, Annas, Caiphas, chorus incidental	d-d2/d-d1/G-d1	uptempo
The last supper, Jesus, Judas, Apostles	c-a1/A-c#2	ballad, then fast
Gethsemane, Jesus, Judas incidental	B♭-a♭1	hard ballad
The arrest, company		moderate
Peter's denial, Peter (T), Maid (M), Soldier (T), Old Man (B), Mary	SMTTB	moderate

Pilate and Christ, Pilate, incidental soli	B-g1	ballad
Herod's song, Herod (T)	c#-g1	fast, ragtime
Could we start again please, Mary, Peter, men	a-b1/B-f#1	ballad
Judas's death, Judas, others incidental	d-e2	uptempo
Trial by Pilate, ensemble, chorus		recit., moderate
Superstar, Judas, three "soul girls," chorus	g#-b1	uptempo

John & Jen (1993)

Music by Andrew Lippa   Lyrics by Tom Greenwald

Song title, Character (Voice)	Range	Song Style
Prologue, Jen (M), John (Bar)	c#1-eb2/c#-f1	ballad
Welcome to the world, Jen	c1-d2	uptempo
Christmas No. 1, John, Jen	Ab-gb1/c1-db2	uptempo
Think big, John, Jen	Bb-e1/bb-f2	mod. uptempo
Dear God, John, Jen	c-f1/a-eb2	mod. slow
Hold down the fort, Jen, John incidental	a-d2	rock ballad
Timeline, John, Jen	c-f#1/f-f2	slow
It took me a while, John, Jen incidental	B-f#1	mod. ballad
Out of my sight, John, Jen	c-f1/b-d2	mod. uptempo
Run and hide, Jen, John	a-d2/A-g1	uptempo
Old clothes, Jen	b-d2	mod. ballad
Christmas No. 2, John, Jen	Bb-g1/b-eb2	mod. uptempo
Baseball, John, Jen	B-f#1/g-f2	uptempo
Just like you, Jen	a-f2	mod. uptempo
Bye room, John, Jen	B-g1 (falsetto c2)/a-eb2	uptempo
Talk show, Jen, John	g-eb2/c-f1	uptempo
Smile of your dreams, Jen, John	a#-gb2/spoken	ballad
It took me a while reprise, John	B-f1	ballad
Graduation, Jen, John	bb-d2/e-f1	mod. uptempo
The road ends here, Jen	g-d2	ballad
That was my way, Jen	g-d2	ballad
Every goodbye is hello, John, Jen	c-g1/c1-d2	mod. ballad

Joseph and the Amazing Technicolor Dreamcoat (1969)

Music by Andrew Lloyd Webber   Lyrics by Tim Rice

Song title, Character (Voice)	Range	Song Style
Jacob and sons/Joseph's coat, Narrator (M), company	b-f#2	narrative ballad
Joseph's dreams, ensemble		ballad
Poor, poor Joseph, Narrator, Brothers		uptempo

One more angel in heaven, Brothers	c1-f2	fast, Western
Potiphar, ensemble		uptempo
Close every door, Joseph (T), chorus incidental	c-f1	ballad
Go, go, go Joseph, ensemble		uptempo
Pharaoh story, Narrator, chorus	b-e2	narrative ballad
Poor, poor Pharaoh/Song of the king, Pharaoh (Bar), chorus	B-f#1	uptempo, 60s rock
Pharaoh's dreams explained, Joseph, chorus	B-e1	uptempo
Stone the crows, ensemble		uptempo
Those Canaan days, Reuben (Bar)	c-f1	moving ballad
The brothers come to Egypt/Grovel, grovel, ensemble, chorus		uptempo
Who's the thief?, Joseph, Brothers, chorus		mod. uptempo
Benjamin calypso, Brothers (many solos)		uptempo
Joseph all the time, ensemble		slow
Jacob in Egypt, ensemble		fast
Any dream will do, Joseph	c-g1	mod. ballad

The King and I (1951)

Music by Richard Rodgers   Lyrics by Oscar Hammerstein II

Song title, Character (Voice)	Range	Song Style
Whistle a happy tune, Anna (M), Louis (Bar)	b-d2/B-d1	uptempo
My lord and my master, Tuptim (S)	d#-a#2	mod. uptempo
Hello, young lovers, Anna	c#1-d2	ballad
A puzzlement, King (Bar)	d-d1	mod. ballad
Schoolroom scene, children's/women's choruses		mod. uptempo
Getting to know you, Anna, children's chorus	c#1-c#2	mod. ballad
We kiss in a shadow, Tuptim, Lun Tha (T)	d1-d2/d-d1	ballad
A puzzlement reprise, Prince (Bar), Louis	both G-a	mod. ballad
Shall I tell you what I think of you, Anna	b-c#2	uptempo, angry
Something wonderful, Lady Thiang (S)	c#1-e2	mod. ballad
Something wonderful reprise, Lady Thiang	d1-g2	mod. ballad
Western people funny, Lady Thiang, women's chorus	e1-g2	moderate, funny
I have dreamed, Lun Tha, Tuptim	c-g1/c1-g2	ballad
Hello, young lovers reprise, Anna	c1-d2	ballad
Song of the king, King, Anna incidental	d-d1	mod. ballad
Shall we dance, Anna, King incidental	d1-c2	uptempo waltz
I whistle a happy tune, children's chorus, Anna		uptempo

Kismet (1953)
Music and Lyrics by Robert Wright and George Forrest

Song title, **Character (Voice)**	**Range**	**Song Style**
Sands of time, male quintet	TTBBB	ballad
Rhymes have I, Poet (Hajj) (T), Marsinah (S)	d#-e1/e1-g2	uptempo
Fate, Poet	A-e♭1	uptempo
Fate reprise, Poet	c-e1	uptempo
Bazaar of the caravans, chorus, many soli		uptempo
Not since Nineveh, Lalume (S), chorus	a-b♭2	uptempo
Baubles, bangles and beads, Marsinah, Caliph incidental, chorus	e♭1-e2	moving ballad
Stranger in paradise, Marsinah, Caliph (T)	d1-a♭2/e♭-a♭1	ballad
He's in love, chorus, many soli		uptempo
Gesticulate, Poet, men's chorus	B-f#1	uptempo
Finale act I: Fate reprise, company		uptempo
Night of my nights, Caliph, solo M, chorus	d-b♭1/b♭1-c2	waltz ballad
Stranger in paradise reprise, Marsinah	c#1-e♭2	ballad
Was I Wazir?, Wazir (Bar), two guards	c-f1	character, mod.
Rahadlakum, Poet, Lalume, chorus	A-f1/d1-a2	moving ballad
And this is my beloved, Marsinah, Poet, Caliph, Wazir	STBB	ballad
The olive tree, Poet	c-e♭1	uptempo
Zubbediya, Ayah (M), men's chorus	g-b1	fast character
Finale: Let peacocks and monkeys in purple adornings, company		uptempo

Kiss Me, Kate (1948)
Music and Lyrics by Cole Porter

Song title, **Character (Voice)**	**Range**	**Song Style**
Another op'nin', another show, Hattie (M), chorus	b♭-f1	uptempo
Why can't you behave?, Lois (M)	f#-b♭2	ballad
Wunderbar, Lilli (S), Fred (Bar)	c1-e♭2/a-e♭1	uptempo waltz
So in love, Lilli	c#-f#2	ballad
Padua street scene: We open in Venice, ensemble		uptempo
Tom, Dick, or Harry, ensemble		uptempo
I've come to wive it, wealthily in Padua, Petruchio (T)	B♭-e♭1	character
I hate men, Katherine (S)	d1-e2	moderate, funny
Were thine that special face, Petruchio	c-f1	ballad
I sing of love, chorus, many soli		uptempo
Finale I: So kiss me, Kate, company		uptempo
Too darn hot, Paul (Bar), men's chorus	b-e1	jazzy uptempo

Where is the life that late I led?, Petruchio	B-f1	uptempo
Always true to you in my fashion, Lois	a-c2	uptempo
Bianca, chorus, many soli		mod. ballad
So in love reprise, Fred	c-f1	ballad
Brush up your Shakespeare, two gangsters (Bar)*	both c-e1	fast character
I am ashamed that women are so simple, Katherine	d1-g2	ballad
So kiss me, Kate reprise, company		uptempo
Finale: Brush up your Shakespeare, company		uptempo

*Could be performed as a solo.

Kiss of the Spiderwoman (1993)

Music by John Kander   Lyrics by Fred Ebb

Song title, Character (Voice)	Range	Song Style
Prologue, Spiderwoman (M), male chorus	c#-e1	rhumba uptempo
Aurora, Molina (Bar), Aurora (M), male chorus	c-c1/c#-a2	uptempo
Over the wall, male chorus		freely
Bluebloods, Molina, Valentin (T)	B-c#1/e-e1	mod. uptempo
Dressing them up/I draw the line, Molina, Valentin	c-f#1/e-f1	uptempo
Dear one, quartet	SMTB	mod. ballad
Over the wall 2, male chorus, Valentin, Molina incidental		uptempo
Where you are, Aurora, male chorus; Molina incidental	e-ab1	samba uptempo
Over the wall 3, "Marta," Valentin, male chorus	f-a1	ballad
Interrogation, Spiderwoman	f#-f1	uptempo
I do miracles, Aurora, Marta (M)	f#-ab1/f#-f#2	moderate
Gabriel's letter/My first woman, Gabriel (T), Valentin	d#-g1/c-g1	uptempo/habanera
Morphine tango, male chorus		uptempo
You could never shame me, Molina's mother (M)	f-d2	ballad
A visit, Spiderwoman, Molina	c-g1/eb-eb1	ballad
Morphine tango 2, male chorus		uptempo
She's a woman, Molina	c-a1	ballad
Let's make love, Aurora, male chorus	d-a1	uptempo
Good times, Aurora, male chorus	e-a1	scene
The day after that, Valentin	d-a1	driving ballad
Mama, it's me, Molina	c-e1	moving ballad
Anything for him, trio	MTB	ballad

Kiss of the Spiderwoman, Spiderwoman	c#-a1	mod. uptempo
Over the wall 4, Warden (Bar), male chorus	d-e♭1	uptempo
Only in the movies, Molina, company	B-f	uptempo

Note: Spiderwoman/Aurora often notated an octave higher than intended to be sung in order to avoid numerous ledger lines.

Knickerbocker Holiday (1938)

Music by Kurt Weill   Lyrics by Maxwell Anderson

Song title, Character (Voice)	Range	Song Style
Washington Irving song, Irving (Bar)	c-d1 (much spoken)	narrative ballad
Clickety-clack, women's chorus		mod. uptempo
Hush, hush, Roosevelt (T), men's chorus	d-e1	narrative ballad
There's nowhere to go but up!, Brom (Bar), Tienhoven (Bar)	both B♭-e♭1	uptempo
It never was anywhere you, Brom, Tina (S)	B♭-e♭1/c1-a2	moving ballad
How can you tell an American?, Irving, Brom	both B-e1	uptempo
Will you remember me?, Tina, Brom incidental, chorus	a-g2	ballad
One touch of alchemy, Stuyvesant (Bar), chorus	d-f1	mod. uptempo
The one indispensable man, Stuyvesant, Tienhoven	B-d1/a♭-e1	fast character
Young people think about love, Tina, company	d1-d2	waltz ballad
September song, Stuyvesant	c-e♭1	ballad
All hail, the political honeymoon, company		uptempo
Ballad of the robbers, Irving	A-e1	narrative, quick
Sitting in jail, Stuyvesant	c-d1	habanera ballad
We are cut in twain, Brom, Tina	A♭-d♭1/f1-f2	quick, rhumba
There's nowhere to go ... reprise, Irving	B♭-e♭1	mod. uptempo
To war!, men's chorus		march uptempo
Our ancient liberties, Councillors (male ensemble)		waltz ballad
May and January, chorus		ballad
The scars, Stuyvesant, chorus	G-e1	uptempo
Dirge for a soldier, chorus		anthem ballad
No, ve vouldn't gonto do it, Councillors, chorus		ballad, character
Finale: How can you tell an American?, company		uptempo

Lady in the Dark (1941)

Music by Kurt Weill   Lyrics by Ira Gershwin

Song title, **Character (Voice)**	**Range**	**Song Style**
I. Glamour dream		
Oh fabulous one, chorus		uptempo
Huxley, Sutton (Bar), Liza (M)	c#-e1/d1-d2	uptempo
One life to live, Liza	b♭-e♭2	uptempo
Girl of the moment, company		mostly uptempo
II. Wedding dream		
Mapleton High choral, chorus		anthem ballad
This is new, Randy (Bar)	B♭-e♭1	ballad
The princess of pure delight, Liza, company	c1-e2	narrative ballad
III. Circus dream		
The greatest show on earth, Ringmaster (T), chorus	d-e1	uptempo
The best years of his life, Ringmaster, Randy Liza, chorus	c-e1/B♭-d1/b♭-e♭2	waltz ballad
Tschaikowsky, Ringmaster, chorus incidental	d-g1	uptempo
The saga of Jenny, Liza, unison chorus	c1-e♭2	moving ballad
IV. Childhood dream		
My ship, Liza	c1-f2	ballad

The Last Five Years (2002)

Music and Lyrics by Jason Robert Brown

Song title, **Character (Voice)**	**Range**	**Song Style**
Still hurting, Cathy (M)	a-d2	ballad
Shiksa goddess, Jamie (T)	A-g#1	Latin uptempo
See, I'm smiling, Cathy	e-c#2	mod. uptempo
Moving too fast, Jamie	c#-a1	funky uptempo
I'm a part of that, Cathy	b♭-e♭2	uptempo
The schmuck song, Jamie	c#-a♭1	mod. ballad
A summer in Ohio, Cathy	f-e♭2	mod. uptempo
The next ten minutes, Jamie, Cathy	c#-a1/g#-e2	ballad
A miracle would happen, Cathy, Jamie	a-d2/e-a1	uptempo
Audition sequence, Cathy	g-d2	uptempo
If I didn't believe in you, Jamie	B♭-g1	moving ballad
I can do better than that, Cathy	a-d2	mod. uptempo
Nobody needs to know, Jamie	e♭-g1	mod. uptempo
Goodbye until tomorrow, Cathy	f#-d♭2	uptempo
I could never rescue you, Jamie	c-f1	mod. ballad

The Life (1997)

Music by Cy Coleman   Lyrics by Ira Gasman

Song title, Character (Voice)	Range	Song Style
Check it out, company		mod. uptempo
Use what you got, Jojo (T), chorus	c#-b♭1	uptempo
Spent all night, Queen (M)	c1-c2	recitative
A lovely day to be outta jail, Queen, Sonja (M)	a-d2/a-e♭2	mod. uptempo
Oh daddy, Queen, Fleetwood (T)	d1-f2/d-f#1	recitative
Ok, ok, you got me, Queen, Queen, Fleetwood	d1-d2/e#-d1	recitative
Piece of the action, Fleetwood	c-b♭1	funky uptempo
The oldest profession, Sonja	a-e♭2	waltz ballad
Don't take much, Memphis (T)	B-g1	mod. uptempo
Go home, Queen, May (M)	a-b1/a-a1	recitative
You can't get to heaven, company		mod. uptempo
My body, company		uptempo
Why don't they leave us alone, Jojo, chorus	c-f1	jazz march
Easy money, quartet	MTTT	uptempo
He's no good, Queen	b-e2	mod. ballad
I'm leaving you, Queen	c1-f2	mod. ballad
Hooker's ball, Lacy (M), Jojo incidental, company	b-e2	uptempo
Step right up, quartet	TTBB	uptempo
Mister Greed, Jojo, male ensemble	e♭-b♭1	swing uptempo
My way or the highway, Memphis, Queen incidental	b-e1	hard ballad
People magazine, Lou (T), May	d-a1/d#1-e2	uptempo
We had a dream, Queen	b♭-c2	ballad
Someday is for suckers, Sonja, girls ensemble	b♭-c2	slow, recit.-like
My friend, Queen, Sonja	a-e2/f-c2	ballad
We gotta go, Queen, Fleetwood	d1-g2/d-e1	driving uptempo
Check it out reprise, company		uptempo

The Light in the Piazza (2005)

Music and Lyrics by Adam Guettel

Song title, Character (Voice)	Range	Song Style
Statues and stones 1, Margaret (S), Clara (S)	a-g2/b-a2	uptempo
Statues and stones 2, Margaret, Clara	b-a2/d1-a2	uptempo
The beauty is, Clara	c♭-g2	mod. uptempo
Il mondo era vuoto 1, Fabrizio (T)	B♭-g♭1	ballad
Il mondo era vuoto 2, Fabrizio	d#-a♭1	ballad
Passegiata 1, Fabrizio	B-g#1	moderate waltz
Passegiata 2, Fabrizio, Clara	c#-e♭1/1-c#2	moderate waltz

Passegiata 3, Fabrizio	c-g♭1	moderate waltz
The joy you feel, Franca (S)	b♭-g♭2	ballad
Dividing day, Margaret	g-e2	mod. uptempo
Hysteria/Lullaby, Clara, Margaret, company	d-a♭2/c-e2	mod./ballad
Say it somehow, Clara, Fabrizio	c1-a2/c-a1	moving ballad
Aiutami, company		uptempo
The light in the piazza, Clara	a-f#2	moving ballad
Octet 1, company		moving ballad
Clara's tirade, Clara	b-g2	uptempo
Octet 2, company		moving ballad
The beauty is reprise, Margaret	b#-g#2	ballad
Let's walk, Margaret, Signor N. (Bar)	g-c2/B♭-e♭1	ballad
Love to me, Fabrizio	d-f#1	ballad
Fable, Margaret	c#1-f#2	ballad

Li'l Abner (1956)

Music by Gene de Paul   Lyrics by Johnny Mercer

Song title, **Character (Voice)**	**Range**	**Song Style**
A typical day, chorus		mod. uptempo
If I had my druthers, Abner (T), men's chorus	e-c1	bouncy ballad
If I had my druthers reprise, Daisy (M)	e1-c2	bouncy ballad
Jubilation T. Cornpone, Marryin' Sam (T), chorus	d-g1	uptempo
Rag off'n the bush, chorus		uptempo
Namely you, Daisy, Li'l Abner	c1-e♭2/e♭-g1	ballad
Unnecessary town, company		uptempo
What's good for General Bullmoose, Secretaries (women's chorus)		mod. uptempo
The country's in the very best of hands, Li'l Abner, Marryin' Sam, chorus	e-e1/d-g1	uptempo
Oh happy day, Scientists (men's trio)	all d-e1	uptempo
Past my prime, Daisy, Marryin' Sam	d1-c2/d-e♭1	moving ballad
Love in a home, Li'l Abner, Daisy	c-f1/b♭-f2	ballad
Progress is the root of all evil, Gen. Bullmoose (Bar)	e-d1	mod. uptempo
Progress . . . reprise, Gen. Bullmoose	d#-d1	mod. uptempo
Put 'em back, Wives (women's chorus)		fast character
Stomp, Marryin' Sam, chorus	f-f1	uptempo
Cornpone, company		uptempo

The Lion King (1997)

Music by Elton John   Lyrics by Tim Rice and others

Song title, **Character (Voice)**	**Range**	**Song Style**
Circle of life, company		uptempo
Grasslands, chorus		uptempo
Circle of life reprise, chorus		slow
The morning report, ZaZu (Bar), Mufasa (T), Simba incidental	e♭-f1/f-f♭1	uptempo
Lioness chant, chorus		mod. uptempo
I just can't wait to be king, Simba (boy), company	c1-d2	mod. uptempo
Chow down, trio	MTB	uptempo
They live in you, Mufasa, chorus	c#-f#1	mod. ballad
Be prepared, Scar (Bar), chorus	A-a	uptempo
Stampede, chorus		mod. uptempo
Eulogy, Rafiki (Bar), Scar incidental, chorus	G-e♭1	mod. uptempo
Hakuna matata, company		uptempo
One by one, company		uptempo
The madness of King Scar, Scar, company	e♭-f1	scene
Shadowland, Nala (M), Rafiki, chorus	e-d2/c-c1	ballad
Endless night, Simba, chorus	e1-a2	ballad
Can you feel the love tonight?, company		mod. ballad
He lives in you, Rafiki, chorus	c#-e1	mod. uptempo
Circle of life finale, company		uptempo

Little Fish (2003)

Music and Lyrics by Michael John LaChiusa

Song title, **Character (Voice)**	**Range**	**Song Style**
Days, Charlotte (M), company	b♭-e2	uptempo
Robert, Charlotte	a-d2	mod. uptempo
It's a sign, Cinder (M)	g-c2	mod. uptempo
The pool, Part 1, Charlotte, company	c1-c2	mod. ballad
Locker room, Part 1, women's ensemble		mod. uptempo
Winter is here/The pool, Part 2, Charlotte	a-e2	moderate
Short story, company		swing uptempo
Perfect, Kathy (M); Charlotte, Cinder incidental	f-e2	mod. ballad
John Paul/Disco, Charlotte, Kathy	b1-d2/g-c2	bossa nova
He, Robert (T), company	A-a1	uptempo
Cigarette dream, Charlotte, chorus	a♭-c♭2	mod. uptempo
Flotsam, Young girl (M)	c1-b1	mod. ballad
Marco/I ran, Marco (T)	c-g1	uptempo
Mr. Bunder/By the way, Bunder (Bar)	G#-d1	mod. swing

Remember me, Kathy	g-d2	ballad
Anne, Young Girl	a-c2	uptempo
Little fish, Marco	d-e1	mod. ballad
Poor Charlotte, Cinder	f-d♭2	uptempo
Flotsam reprise, Charlotte	b♭-b1	ballad
Simple creature, Charlotte	g-e2	mod. uptempo
Galley/Perfect reprise, Charlotte, Kathy	g#-e2	mod. ballad
incidental		
In twos and threes, company		uptempo

Little Johnny Jones (1904)
Music and Lyrics by George M. Cohan

Song title, **Character (Voice)**	**Range**	**Song Style**
The Cecil in London Town, company		mod. uptempo
Then I'd be satisfied with life, Anstey (Bar)	c-e♭1	mod. ballad
Yankee doodle boy, Johnny (T), chorus	e-g1	uptempo
Oh, you wonderful boy, Goldie (M), Flo (M), girls	d1-e2/e1-c2	mod. uptempo
The voice in my heart, Mrs. Kenworth (S), girls	d-c♭3	waltz ballad
Yankee doodle reprise, Wilson (Bar), McGee (T)	both f-d1	uptempo
Finale act I: Good luck, Johnny, company		uptempo
Captain of a ten day boat, Captain (Bar), chorus	B♭-d1	fast character
Goodbye Flo, Flo, men's chorus	a-d♭2	mod. ballad
Funny proposition, Johnny	d#-e1	mod. uptempo
Let's you and I just say goodbye, Goldie	d1-g2	ballad
Give my regards to Broadway, Johnny, chorus	d-f1	mod. uptempo
American ragtime, McGee, Flo, chorus	d-g1/f1-e2	mod. ragtime
Voice in my heart reprise, Captain, Mrs. Kenworth	c-d1/d1-b♭2	ballad
Finale act II, company		mod. uptempo

Note: Substantially revised in 1980.

Little Mary Sunshine (1959)
Music and Lyrics by Rick Besoyan

Song title, **Character (Voice)**	**Range**	**Song Style**
The forest ranger, Capt. Jim (Bar), men's chorus	g-d1	uptempo march
Little Mary Sunshine, Mary (S), solo S, ch.	d1-d2/d1-c2	mod. ballad

Look for a sky of blue, Mary, men's chorus	c1-e♭2	mod. ballad
You're the fairest flower, Capt. Jim	G-d1	mod. ballad
In Izzen Schnooken, Madame Ernestine (M)	b♭-c2	character ballad
Playing croquet, unison women's chorus		mod. waltz ballad
Swinging, chorus, many soli		mod. waltz
Tell a handsome stranger, chorus		mod. uptempo
Once in a blue moon, Billy (Bar), Nancy (M)	B♭-e♭1/spoken	mod. uptempo
Colorado love call, Capt. Jim, Mary	A-f1/a-e2	mod. ballad
Every little nothing, Mme. Ernestine, Mary	g-a1/b-d2	mod. uptempo
What has happened, company		uptempo
Such a merry party, chorus		uptempo
Say uncle, Oscar (Bar), women's chorus	c#-d1	mod. character
Heap big Injun, Chief (Bar)	B♭-d♭1	fast character
Naughty, naughty Nancy, Mary, women's chorus	c1-f2	mod. uptempo
Mata Hari, Nancy, Oscar	b-c2/B-d1	waltz ballad
Do you ever dream of Vienna?, Mme. Ernestine, chorus	b-c2	mod. ballad
Coo-coo, Mary, chorus	d1-a1	character ballad
Colorado love call reprise, Capt. Jim, company	B♭-f1	mod. ballad
Forest rangers reprise, men's chorus		uptempo march
Finale: When e'er a cloud appears, company		uptempo

Little Me (1962)
Music and Lyrics by Carolyn Leigh and Cy Coleman

Song title, Character (Voice)	Range	Song Style
The truth, Patrick (Bar), Belle (M), men's chorus	A-d1/a-c2	uptempo
I love you, Noble (T), Young Belle (M), chorus	d♭-f1/d♭1-e2	mod. ballad
Their side of the tracks, Young Belle	a-d2	uptempo
Deep down inside, Young Belle, Pinchley (T), Junior (T), chorus	b♭-f#2/B♭-f#1/d-f#1	mostly uptempo
To be a performer, Bernie (T), Bennie (T), Belle	d-g1/d-g1/d-f	uptempo
Oh! Dem dimples!, Belle, men's chorus	b♭-d2	soft shoe ballad
Boom boom, Val (S), women's chorus	c#1-g2	fast character
I've got your number, George (Bar)	e♭-f♭1	mod. uptempo
Real live girl, Fred (Bar), chorus	d-c1	waltz ballad
I love sinking you, Noble, Young Belle	c-f1/c1-f2	ballad
Poor little Hollywood star, Young Belle	g-e2	mod. ballad
Be a performer reprise, Bennie, Bernie	both e-e1	mod. uptempo
Little me, Belle, Young Belle	a-c#2/a-c#2	mod. ballad

Goodbye, Prince (T), chorus	B-f#1	character ballad
Here's to us, Belle, men's chorus	f-b♭1	mod. uptempo

A Little Night Music (1973)
Music and Lyrics by Stephen Sondheim

Song title, **Character (Voice)**	**Range**	**Song Style**
Overture, Liebeslieders	SSMTB	mod. uptempo
Night waltz, Liebeslieders	SSMTB	mod. ballad
Now, Frederick (Bar), Anne (S)	B♭-e1/spoken	uptempo, patter
Later, Henrick (T)	b#-b1	uptempo
Soon, Anne, Henrik, Frederick	c#1-g#2/g-a1/ b-d	mod. ballad
The glamorous life, Frederika (girl S), Desiree (S), Madame Arnfeldt (M), Liebeslieders	d1-e♭2/e1-a2/c-e♭1	uptempo
Remember, Liebeslieders	SSMTB	waltz ballad
You must meet my wife, Frederick, Desiree	c-e♭1/c1-e2	mod. waltz
Liaisons, Mme. Arnfeldt	d-f1*	slow, inward
In praise of women, Carl Magnus (Bar)	c#-f1	uptempo
Every day a little death, Charlotte (M), Anne	both g#-b1	ballad
A weekend in the country, company		uptempo
Night waltz reprise, Liebeslieders	SSMTB	mod. ballad
It would have been wonderful, Frederick, Carl Magnus	both c-e1	ballad, funny
Perpetual anticipation, Liebeslieder women	SSM	uptempo
Send in the clowns, Desiree	g♭-a♭1	ballad
The miller's son, Petra (M)	f#-b1	ballad, with faster parts

*Notated an octave higher.

Little Shop of Horrors (1982)
Music by Alan Menken   Lyrics by Howard Ashman

Song title, **Character (Voice)**	**Range**	**Song Style**
Little shop of horrors, Chiffon (S), Crystal (M), Ronnette (M)	e1-d2/e1-d2/b-g1	mod. ballad
Skid row (Downtown), company		mod. uptempo
Grow for me, Seymour (T)	B♭-f1	50s rock ballad
Don't it go to show ya never know, ensemble		jazzy uptempo
Somewhere that's green, Audrey (M)	b-c2	ballad
Closed for renovations, Seymour, Audrey, Mushnik (Bar)	B♭-g1/b♭-c2/ B♭-f1	uptempo

Dentist!, Orin (Bar), women's trio	G-e1	uptempo
Mushnik and son, Mushnik, Seymour	G-e♭1/e-g1	mod. uptempo
Feed me (Git it), Seymour, Audrey II (T)	g-g1/B♭-g1	driving uptempo
Now (It's just the gas), Seymour, Orin	B♭-g♭1/f#-e♭1	uptempo, patter
Call back in the morning, Seymour, Audrey	B#-d#1/b-c#2	mod. uptempo
Suddenly, Seymour, Seymour, Audrey	A-c#1/a-c#2	mod. ballad
Suppertime, Audrey II, women's trio	g-f1	uptempo
The meek shall inherit, company		mod. uptempo
Finale: Don't feed the plants, company		uptempo

Little Women (2005)

Music by Jason Howland · · · · · · · · · · · · · · · · Lyrics by Mindi Dickstein

Song title, **Character (Voice)**	**Range**	**Song Style**
An operatic tragedy, company		uptempo
Better, Jo (M)	b-b1	uptempo
Our finest dreams, Jo, girls' trio at end	f#-b1	uptempo
Here alone, Marmee (M)	g-e♭1	mod. ballad
Could you, Aunt March (M), Jo	d-f#2/e-a2	mod. uptempo
Delighted, sisters	SMMM	uptempo
Take a chance on me, Laurie (T)	B-b♭1	ballad
Off to Massachusetts, Beth (S), Mr. Laurence (Bar)	c#1-f2/c#-d1	mod. uptempo
Five forever, company		uptempo
More than I am, Mr. Brooke (T), Meg (S)	e-f#1/e1-f#2	moving ballad
Astonishing, Jo	g-d2*	uptempo
The weekly volcano press, Jo, company	g#-d2	mod. uptempo
How I am, Bhaer (Bar)	A-f#1	mod. ballad
Some things are meant to be, Beth, Jo	b-e2/c#1-c2	mod. ballad
The most amazing thing, Amy (M), Laurie	c1-e2/B♭-g1	mod. uptempo
Days of plenty, Marmee	e♭-d♭2	ballad
The fire within me, Jo	f#-d2	ballad
Small umbrella in the rain, Bhaer, Jo	G-f1/b-e2	moving ballad

*Also included in score a half-step higher.

Lost in the Stars (1949)

Music by Kurt Weill · · · · · · · · · · · · · · · · Lyrics by Maxwell Anderson

Song title, **Character (Voice)**	**Range**	**Song Style**
The hills of Ixopo, Leader (T), chorus	d-e1	narrative ballad
Thousands of miles, Stephen (Bar)	A-c1	ballad
Train to Johannesburg, Leader, chorus	d-g1	uptempo
The search, men's chorus, many soli		mod. uptempo
The little gray house, Stephen, chorus	A♭-d♭1	narrative ballad

Who'll buy?, Linda (M), chorus	b♭-d♭2	character
Trouble man, Irina (S)	c1-f2	ballad
Murder in Parkwold, double chorus		uptempo
Fear!, chorus, many soli		driving uptempo
Lost in the stars, Stephen, chorus	A♭-c1 (opt. f1)	ballad
The wild justice, Leader, chorus	d-a♭1	mod. ballad
O Tixo, Tixo help me!, Stephen	d-f1	soliloquy
Stay well, Irina	c1-f2	ballad
Cry the beloved country, Leader, M solo, chorus	a-e1/a1-e2	moving ballad
Big mole, Alex (Bar)	B♭-c1	character
A bird of passage, Bar solo, chorus	e♭-e♭1	mod. ballad
Finale: Each lives in a world of dark, company		mod. uptempo

Lucky Stiff (1988)

Music by Stephen Flaherty   Lyrics by Lynn Ahrens

Song title, Character (Voice)	Range	Song Style
Something funny's going on, company		uptempo
Mr. Witherspoon's Friday night, Harry (Bar), ensemble	d-e1	uptempo
Rita's confession, Rita (M), others incidental	f#-d2	mod. uptempo
Good to be alive, Harry, ensemble	c#-f#1	uptempo
Lucky, Harry	B♭-d#1	mod. uptempo
Annabel's pursuit, Harry	d-d1	moderate
Dogs versus you, Annabel (M), Harry	a-e2/c-e1	uptempo
The phone call, Vinnie (T)	d-f#1	character uptempo
Speaking French, Dominique (M), others incidental	g-c2	uptempo
Times like this, Annabel	g-d2	mod. ballad
Fancy meeting you here, Rita, offstage chorus	a♭-d♭2	mod. uptempo
Good to be alive reprise, company		uptempo
Something funny's going on reprise, company		uptempo
Him, them, it, her, company		mod. uptempo
Nice, Annabel, Harry	f#-c#2/B♭-d1	mod. ballad
Harry's nightmare, company		uptempo
A woman in my bedroom, Harry	B-e♭1	mod. uptempo
Confession No. 2, quartet	MMTB	mod. uptempo
Good to be alive finale, Harry, Annabel	B-e1/b-d2	ballad

Mack and Mabel (1974)
Music and Lyrics by Jerry Herman

Song title, Character (Voice)	Range	Song Style
Movies were movies, Mack (Bar)	A-d1	mod. uptempo
Look what happened to Mabel, company		uptempo
Big time, Lottie (M), chorus	e-b1	uptempo
I won't send roses, Mack, Mabel (M)	G-c1/g-d1	ballad
I want to make the world laugh, Mack, chorus	A-e1	ballad
Wherever he ain't, Mabel	a-d2	mod. uptempo
Hundreds of girls, Mack, women's chorus	A-f#1	uptempo
When Mabel comes in the room, company		mod. uptempo
Hit 'em on the head, Mack, Kleinman (T), Fox (T), men's chorus	all B-f1	mod. uptempo
Time heals everything, Mabel	f#-d2	ballad
Tap your troubles away, Lottie, women's chorus	f-b♭1	mod. uptempo shuffle
Happy ending, Mack	G-d1	mod. ballad

Mama Mia! (2001)
Music and Lyrics by Björn Ulvaeus and Benny Andersson

Song title, Character (Voice)	Range	Song Style
Honey, honey, Sophie (M); Cali (M); Lisa (M) incidental, chorus	c1-c2	uptempo
Money, money, money, Donna (M), chorus	g-b1	mod. uptempo
Thank you for the music, trio	MTB	mod. ballad
Mama mia!, Donna, company	f#-a1	uptempo
Chiquita, Rosie (M), Tanya (M), women's chorus	g-c2/a♭-c2	ballad
Dancing queen, trio, chorus	MMM	uptempo
Lay all your love, Sky (T), Sophie, company	e♭-a♭1/b♭-e♭2	mod. uptempo
Super trouper, trio, women's chorus	MMM	uptempo
Gimme, gimme, gimme, company		uptempo
The name of the game, Sophie, chorus; Bill incidental	f#-c#2	ballad
Vouler vous, company		mod. uptempo
Under attack, Sophie, chorus	b-c#2	mod. uptempo
One of us, Donna, chorus	a-c2	ballad
S.O.S., Sam (T), Donna, chorus	a♭-a♭1/d1-a1	uptempo
Does your mother know?, Tanya, Pepper (M), chorus	a-b♭1/a-f1	uptempo
Knowing me, knowing you, Sam, chorus	f#-f#1	mod. ballad
Our last summer, Harry (Bar), Donna, chorus	f#-e1/f#-f#1	mod. ballad

Slipping through my fingers, Donna, women's chorus; Sophie incidental	a-c2	ballad
The winner takes it all, Donna	g-c2	ballad
Take a chance, Rosie, Bill (Bar), chorus	f-b♭1/B♭-d1	mod. uptempo
I do, I do, I do, Sam, Donna, company	g-f1/c1-b1	mod. uptempo
I have a dream, Sophie, company	a♭-d♭1	mod. ballad
Mama mia! reprise, company		uptempo

Mame (1966)
Music and Lyrics by Jerry Herman

Song title, **Character (Voice)**	**Range**	**Song Style**
St. Bridget, Agnes (M), Patrick (boy S) incidental	b-f2	slow, quasi-character
It's today, Mame (M), chorus	a-f2	uptempo
Open a new window, Mame, Patrick, chorus	f1-c2/c1-c2	mod. uptempo
The moon song, Vera (M), women's chorus	g-a1	character ballad
My best girl, Patrick, Mame	a♭-c2/g-c2	ballad
We need a little Christmas, Mame; Agnes, Ito, Patrick at end	f-b♭1	uptempo
The fox hunt, chorus		uptempo
Mame, Beau (Bar), chorus	d-c#1	mod. ballad
Opening act II: Letters, Patrick (boy), Patrick (T)	d-b♭1/g-d1	slow, epistolary ballad
My best girl reprise, Patrick	c-e1	mod. ballad
Bosom buddies, Mame, Vera	both e♭-b♭1	moderate, funny
Gooch's song, Agnes	g-c2	ballad, funny
That's how young I feel, Mame, ensemble	g-b♭1	uptempo
If he walked into my life, Mame	f#-b♭1	ballad
It's today reprise, Mame, chorus	a-b♭1	uptempo
Finale: Open a new window/Today, company		uptempo

Man of La Mancha (1965)
Music by Mitch Leigh · Lyrics by Joe Darion

Song title, **Character (Voice)**	**Range**	**Song Style**
Man of la Mancha (I, Don Quixote), Don Quixote (Bar), Sancho (T)	c-e1/d-g1	uptempo, driving
It's all the same, Aldonza (M), Muleteers incidental	e♭-a♭2	angry uptempo
Dulcinea, Don Q., Muleteers	B-e1	ballad
I'm only thinking of him, Antonia (M), Padre (T), Housekeeper (M)	c1-f2/g-g1/f-e♭2	moving ballad

We're only thinking of him, as before w/ Dr. Carracco (Bar)	MMTB	moving ballad
I really like him, Sancho	g-g1	character ballad
What does he want of me?, Aldonza	d1-f2	moving ballad
Little bird, little bird, Muleteers (male ensemble)		ballad
Barber's song, Barber (T)	f-g1	character
Golden helmet of Mambrino, Don Q., Barber; Sancho incidental, chorus	B-d1/d-e1	uptempo
To each his Dulcinea, Padre	c-f1	ballad
The impossible dream, Don Q.	c-eb1	ballad
Knight of the woeful countenance, Innkeeper (Bar), chorus	B-c#1	uptempo
Man of la Mancha reprise, Don Q.	c-d1	uptempo
Aldonza, Aldonza	ab1-e2	angry uptempo
A little gossip, Sancho	c-f1	mod. funny
Dulcinea reprise, Aldonza	g1-f2	ballad
Man of la Mancha reprise, Don Q., Sancho, Aldonza	men: c-c1/her: c1-c2	uptempo
The psalm, Padre	f-f1	anthem ballad
Finale: The impossible dream, company		ballad

A Man of No Importance (2002)

Music by Stephen Flaherty   Lyrics by Lynn Ahrens

Song title, Character (Voice)	Range	Song Style
Opening sequence, company		scene
A man of no importance, company		mod. uptempo
The burden of life, Lily (M)	e-c#2	uptempo
Going up!, Carney (Bar), chorus	A#-f#1	moderate swing
Princess, Adele (M), Alfie incidental	c1-e2	mod. uptempo
First rehearsal, Alfie (Bar), company	Bb-d1	uptempo
The streets of Dublin, Robbie (T), chorus	e-a1	uptempo
Love's never lost, Alfie	A-e1	ballad
Books, Carney, Lily	A-b/a-b1	mod. uptempo
Man in the mirror, Alfie, Oscar incidental	Ab-f1	moving ballad
The burden of life reprise, Lily	ab-ab1	mod. uptempo
Love who you love, Alfie	B-e1	ballad
Our father, Mrs. Patrick (M), chorus	d1-e2	uptempo
Confession, Alfie, Robbie; Fr. Kenny incidental	B-d#1/db-f#1	mod. uptempo
The cuddles Mary gave, Baldy (Bar)	eb-f1	moving ballad
Art, Ernie (Bar), Mrs. Grave (M), company	A-b1/c#1-b1	uptempo
Confusing times, Carney	A-a	slow
Man in the mirror reprise, company		scene
Tell me why, Lily	f-bb1	ballad

A man of no importance reprise, chorus		mod. uptempo
Love who you love reprise, Adele	a♭-d♭2	moving ballad
Welcome to the world, Alfie	c-c1	mod. uptempo

March of the Falsettos (1981)
Music and Lyrics by William Finn

Song title, Character (Voice)	Range	Song Style
Four Jews in a room bitching, Marvin (Bar), Mendel (Bar), Jason (boy S), Whizzer (T)		uptempo
Tight-knit family, Marvin	c#-e1	moving ballad
Love is kind, Mendel, company	G#-e1	moving ballad
Thrill of first love, Whizzer, Marvin	G#-f#1/g#-d#1	mod. uptempo
Marvin at the psychiatrist's, Jason, Marvin, Mendel	a-c2/B-f1/d-f1	recit. ballad
My father's a homo, Jason, Trina (M), Marvin; Whizzer incidental	a-b1/b-d2/d-d1	mod. uptempo
I'm breaking down, Trina	g#-c2	moving ballad
Please come to our house, Jason, Trina, Mendel	b-c#2/b-e2/B-c#1	uptempo
Breakfast over sugar, Marvin, Trina	G-c1/g-c2	ballad
Jason's therapy (Feel alright), company		mod. ballad
Marriage proposal, Mendel	c-e2	mod. ballad
Tight-knit family reprise, Marvin, Mendel	c#-d1/c#-e1	mod. ballad
Trina's song, Trina	a-d#2	ballad
The chess game, Marvin, Whizzer	A-d#1/A-f1	waltz ballad
Making a home, Trina, Mendel, Whizzer incidental	c1-e♭2/e-e♭1	moving ballad
The games I play, Whizzer	B-g1	driving ballad
Marvin hits Trina, company		uptempo
I never wanted to love you, company		mod. uptempo
Father to son, Jason, Marvin; Mendel incidental	g-b♭1/A-c1	ballad

Note: See also *Falsettoland*, the second half of the musical *Falsettos* (1992) of which this show is the first half.

Marie Christine (1999)
Music and Lyrics by Michael John LaChiusa

Song title, Character (Voice)	Range	Song Style
Before the morning, company		uptempo
Mamzell' Marie, M.C. (M), Mother (M), chorus	a-f2/b-f2	mod. uptempo

Your grandfather is the sun, Mother, M.C.	d-e2/g#-e2	moving ballad
Beautiful, M.C.	f-d2	ballad
In an instant, company		slow
The map of your heart, trio	MMT	uptempo
Way back to paradise, M.C., Lisette (S)	d1-g2/d1-b2	moderate
C'est l'amour, ensemble		uptempo
To find a lover, M.C., chorus	a-g2	uptempo
Dante's sequence, Dante (Bar)		
The adventure never ends	B♭-f1	mod. uptempo
Nothing beats Chicago	B-e1	mod. uptempo
Ocean is different	c-a1	moving ballad
Danced with a girl	B-e1	mod. uptempo
Miracles and mysteries, Mother, chorus	e-f2	moderate
I don't hear the ocean, Dante, M.C.	e♭-f1/c1-e2	moving ballad
Bird inside the house, quartet	SMTB	uptempo
All eyes look upon you, Jean (M)	a-e2	mod. uptempo
A month ago he comes here, 2 maids (M)	c1-c#2/b-e2	uptempo
We're gonna go to Chicago, Dante, M.C.	c♭-f1/e♭1-g♭2	moving ballad
Never fall under the spell/Danse y calinda, Lisette, trio	e-c3/SMM	uptempo
And would you lie, trio	SMM	slow
I will give you my money, M.C., chorus	b♭-f♭2	slow
Act I finale, company		scene
Five years up and down the coast, Dante, M.C., women's trio	d♭-f1/a♭-g♭2	ballad
Cincinnati, Magdalena (S), company	g-f#2	mod. uptempo
You're looking at the man, company		uptempo
The scorpion, Dante, M.C. incidental	c-f1	mod. uptempo
Love bring me summer, M.C., daughters	SMM	moderate
Tell me, M.C.	g-f2	ballad
Billy was sweet, Magdalena	f#-g1	slow
There's a rumor, Magdalena	g♭-c#2	moderate swing
Paradise is burning down, Magdalena, women's chorus	e♭-e♭2	moderate
Prison is a prison, M.C., women's chorus	g-d2	mod. ballad
Better and best, McMahon (T), Leary (T)	c-c2/a♭-g1	mod. uptempo
Good looking woman, Gates (Bar)	g-e1	moderate
No turning back, Paris (M)	g1-e2	mod. ballad
Silver mimosa/Before the morning reprise, company		slow
Wedding, company		uptempo
I will love you, M.C.	g-f2	ballad
Helena's death, Dante	G#-a1	moving ballad
Innocence dies, company		mod. slow

Martin Guerre (1997)

Music by Claude-Michel Schönberg   Lyrics by Alain Boublil and Stephen Clark

Song title, Character (Voice)	Range	Song Style
Prologue, Arnaud (T), Martin (T)	f#-d1/c-e♭1	scene
Without you as a friend, Arnaud, Martin	f#-f#1/f#-g1	ballad
Your wedding day, company		uptempo
The deluge, company		mod. uptempo
I'm Martin Guerre, Martin	d-a1	uptempo
Live with somebody you love, Arnaud, Martin	both d-a1	ballad
Back in Artigat, company		scene
The conversion, company		ballad
God's anger, company		slow
How many tears?, Bertrande (M)	a-c2	moving ballad
Welcome to the land, company		mod. uptempo
Without you as a friend reprise, Arnaud, Bertrande incidental	a♭-f1	ballad
The seasons turn, company		slow scene
Don't, Arnaud, Bertrande	d-f1/b-c2	uptempo
The holy fight, chorus		hymn
The dinner, company		mod. uptempo
The revelation, Guillaume (T), company	d-a1	mod. uptempo
Alone, Bertrande, Arnaud, company	c♭1-e2	mod. uptempo
If you still love me, Martin, Arnaud	c-a♭1/d♭-g♭1	flowing ballad
The courtroom, company		mod. uptempo
Who/Martin Guerre reprise, company		uptempo
All that I love, trio	MTB	ballad
The imposter is here, company		mod. uptempo
The final witness, company		scene
The verdict, company		ballad
Justice will be done, company		uptempo
Why?, trio	MTT	ballad
You will be mine, trio	TTB	mod. uptempo
How many tears? reprise, Bertrande, Arnaud	c1-d♭2/d♭-f1	flowing ballad
Live with somebody you love reprise, Martin, Bertrande	B-a♭1/b-e2	ballad

Note: Annotated from the London production. This annotation was also taken from a score with several pages missing.

Mary Poppins (2006)

Music by Robert B. Sherman and Anthony Drewe
Lyrics by Robert B. and Richard M. Sherman and George Stiles

Song title, Character (Voice)	Range	Song Style
Chim chim cher-ee, Bert (Bar)	c-d1	mod. uptempo
Cherry Tree Lane, company		uptempo

Perfect nanny, Jane, Michael (children)	a-b1/d1-b1	mod. ballad
Cherry Tree Lane No. 2, company		uptempo
Practically perfect, Mary (S), kids	a-g2	mod. uptempo
All me own work, Bert	c#-d#1	mod. uptempo
Jolly holiday, company		uptempo
Let's hope she will stay, George (Bar), Winnifred (M), kids	A-ab/g#-a1	uptempo
Spoonful of sugar, Mary, company	db1-ab2	uptempo
Precision and order, chorus, many incidental soli		march uptempo
A man has dreams, George	Bb-eb1	ballad
Feed the birds, Mary, Birdwoman (M), chorus	both gb-db2	mod. ballad
Supercalifragilisticexpialidocious, company		uptempo
The wind may blow, Bert	B-c1	mod. ballad
Temper temper, company		mod. uptempo
Chim chiminey, Bert, Mary	c-d1/c#1-a1	mod. ballad
Cherry Tree Lane reprise, company		mod. uptempo
Brimstone and treacle, Miss Andrew (M)	g#-f1	moderate waltz
Let's go fly a kite, Bert, company	Bb-d1	flowing ballad
Good for nothing/Being Mrs. Banks, George, Winnifred	Bb-d1/g#-db2	ballad
Brimstone and treacle Part 2, Mary, Miss Andrews	bb-c3/3-ab2	slow, then faster
Practically perfect reprise, Mary, kids	a-d2	mod. uptempo
Step in time, Bert, company	B-f1	uptempo
A man has dreams/Spoonful of sugar reprises, George, Bert	Bb-c1/Bb-c#1	mod. ballad
Anything can happen, company		mod. uptempo
Anything can happen bows, company		mod. ballad
Supercalif . . . reprise, company		uptempo

Maytime (1917)

Music by Sigmund Romberg   Lyrics by Rida Johnson Young and Cyrus Wood

Song title, Character (Voice)	Range	Song Style
Tap, fellows, tap, men's chorus		uptempo
In our little home, sweet home, Ottillie (S), Richard (T)	d1-b2/d-g1	uptempo
It's a windy day on the battery, Matthew (T), women's chorus incidental	d-g1	uptempo waltz
Gypsy song, Rudolpho (T)	d-a1	waltz ballad
Sweetheart, will you remember?, Ottillie, Richard	eb1-bb2/e-ab1	ballad
Jump, Jim Crow, Matthew	e-f#1	mod. uptempo
The road to paradise, Ottillie, Richard	eb1-ab2/eb-gb1	ballad

Old things, old things, unison chorus		uptempo
Will you remember reprise, Ottillie	c1-g2 (opt. b♭2)	ballad
Since the war in Europe, unison women's chorus*		uptempo
Dancing will keep you young, Ermintrude (M), Matthew	e♭1-g2/f-g1	uptempo waltz
Go away, girls, Richard	e-f1	mod. ballad
Sweetheart, will you remember reprise, Richard	b♭-g2 (opt. b♭2)	ballad

*In several languages: Spanish, French, and English.

Me and Juliet (1953)

Music by Richard Rodgers   Lyrics by Oscar Hammerstein II

Song title, **Character (Voice)**	**Range**	**Song Style**
A very special day, Jeanie (M)	c1-e2	ballad
That's the way it happens, Jeanie, Larry (T)	b-c#2/e♭-f1	uptempo
Marriage type love, Charlie (Bar); Juliet (S), chorus incidental	d-e1	ballad
Marriage type love reprise, Juliet, Charlie	e♭1-g2/e♭-e♭1	ballad
Keep it gay, Bob (T), women's chorus; then chorus	d-e1	fast, calypso
Keep it gay reprise, Betty (M)	b♭-c1	uptempo
The big black giant, Larry	d♭-e♭1	uptempo
No other love, Jeanie, Larry	d1-a♭2/d-a♭1	tango ballad
The big black giant reprise, Ruby (M)	c1-c2	uptempo
It's me, Betty, Jeanie	both c1-d♭2	uptempo, funny
No other love reprise, Juliet	e♭1-a♭2	tango ballad
Intermission, chorus, many soli		uptempo
It feels good, Bob	c-f1	uptempo
We deserve each other, Carmen (M)	b♭-c2	uptempo
I'm your girl, Jeanie, Larry	d♭1-f2/e♭-f1	ballad
Marriage type love reprise, Betty, chorus	e♭1-f2	ballad

Me and My Girl (1986)

Music by Noel Gay   Lyrics by L. Arthur Rose and Douglas Furber

Song title, **Character (Voice)**	**Range**	**Song Style**
A weekend in Hareford, company		uptempo
Thinking of no one but me, Jacquie (S), Gerald (T)	b♭-c2/f-f#1	mod. ballad
The family solicitor, Parchester (T), ensemble	d-g1	fast character
Me and my girl, Bill (Bar), Sally (M)	B♭-c1/f-d2	mod. uptempo
An English gentleman, Staff (ensemble)		mod., funny

You would if you could, Jacquie, Bill	c-e2/spoken	mod. ballad
Hold my hand, Bill, Sally	c-d1/c1-c2	moving ballad
Once you lose your heart, Sally	ab-db1	ballad
The fugue, company		uptempo
The Lambeth walk, Bill, company	c-e1	swing uptempo
The sun has got his hat on, Gerald, company	e-g1	uptempo
Take it on the chin, Sally	a-c2	mod. uptempo
Once you lose your heart reprise, Sally	ab-db1	ballad
Song of Hareford, Duchess (M), Ancestors (TTBB)	a-f2	narrative ballad
Love makes the world go round, Bill, Sir John (Bar), Ancestors	both c#-f1	uptempo
Leaning on a lamppost, Bill	Bb-e1	swing ballad
The world keeps on turning, company		uptempo
Bows: Me and my girl/Lambeth walk, company		mod. uptempo

Meet Me in St. Louis (1989)
Music and Lyrics by Hugh Martin and Ralph Blane

Song title, **Character (Voice)**	**Range**	**Song Style**
Meet me in St. Louis, company		uptempo
The boy next door, Esther (M)	ab-bb1	easy waltz
Whenever I'm with you, company		uptempo
You'll hear a bell, Mrs. Smith (M)	bb-d2	mod. ballad
A raving beauty, Warren (Bar), Rose (M)	c-eb1/bb-db2	uptempo
Skip to my Lou, trio, chorus	MTB	uptempo
Under the bamboo tree, trio	SMM	mod. ballad
Over the bannister, John (Bar)	Bb-eb1	ballad
The trolley song, Esther, chorus	a-bb1	uptempo
A touch of the Irish, Katie (M); Esther, Rose incidental	f-bb1	character uptempo
The boy next door reprise, John, Esther	d-e1/c1-a1	ballad
A day in New York, company		mod. uptempo
You'll hear a bell reprise, Mrs. Smith	bb-bb1	ballad
Wasn't it fun?, Mr. Smith (Bar), Mrs. Smith	Ab-db1/f-b1	easy waltz
The banjo, Lon (T), chorus		mod. uptempo
You are for loving, John, Esther	db-f1/bb-c2	uptempo
Have yourself a merry little Christmas, Esther	g-c2	ballad
The trolley song reprise, chorus		uptempo
Meet me in St. Louis reprise, company		uptempo

Merrily We Roll Along (1981)
Music and Lyrics by Stephen Sondheim

Song title, **Character (Voice)**	**Range**	**Song Style**
The hills of tomorrow, chorus		anthem ballad
Merrily we roll along, company		uptempo
Rich and happy, Frank (T), Mary (M), company	c-e1/c1-c2	moderate
Old friends/Like it was, Mary	f-c2	jazzy ballad
Franklin Shepard, Inc., Charley (T)	db-gb1	fast character
Old friends, Frank, Charley, Mary	men: Bb-eb1/ab-f#2	jazzy ballad
Not a day goes by, Beth (S)	d1-f#2	ballad
Now you know, Mary, company	ab-d2	uptempo
It's a hit, Frank, Mary, Charley, Joe (T)	SMTB (all need g1/g2)	uptempo
The blob, Gussie (Bar)	B-d1	uptempo
Good thing going, Charley	B-d1	ballad
The blob reprise, company*		alt. slow/fast
Bobby and Jackie and Jack, Frank, Mary, Charley, Piano Player incidental	STBB	uptempo
Not a day goes by reprise, Frank, Mary	e-e1/f#-e2	ballad
Opening doors, company		uptempo
Our time I, Frank	db-gb1	ballad
Our time II, Frank, Charley	db-gb1/Bb-gb1	ballad
Our time III, company		ballad
The hills of tomorrow reprise, company		uptempo

*Combines "The Blob" with "Good Thing Going."

The Merry Widow (1907)
Music by Franz Lehar   Lyrics by Adrian Ross

Song title, **Character (Voice)**	**Range**	**Song Style**
Now, ladies and gentlemen, chorus		uptempo
A dutiful wife, Natalie (S), Camille (T)	d1-g2/d-bb1	uptempo
In Marsovia, Sonia (S), chorus	b-b2	uptempo
Maxim's, Danilo (T)	A-g1	uptempo
Home, Camille	e-a1	mod. uptempo
Ladies, choice!, company		uptempo waltz
I bid you wait, chorus		mod. uptempo
Vilia, Sonia	d1-b2	mod. uptempo
The cavalier, Sonia, Danilo incidental	e1-a2	uptempo
Women, male sextet	TTTBBB	march uptempo
Love in my heart, Camille	f-a1 (opt. c2)	ballad
Ha! Ha! Ha!, company		uptempo

The girls at Maxim's, Zozo (M), female sextet, chorus	b-e2	saucy uptempo
Quite Parisian, Nisch (Bar), chorus	c-e1	character ballad
I love you so, Sonia, Danilo	d1-a2/d-f#1	ballad
You may study her ways, company		march uptempo

Milk and Honey (1961)
Music and Lyrics by Jerry Herman

Song title, Character (Voice)	Range	Song Style
Sheep song, chorus, many soli		mod. uptempo
Shalom, Phil (T), Ruth (S)	A-e1/b♭-a♭2	mod. uptempo
Hora I, chorus		uptempo
Hora II, Phil, chorus	e-f#1	uptempo
Milk and honey, David (T), chorus	A-g#1	mod. ballad
There's no reason in the world, Phil	c#-f#1	ballad
Chin up, ladies, Mrs. Perlman (M), Mrs. Weiss (M), Mrs. Segal (M)	all e-c2	mod. character
That was yesterday, Ruth, company	b♭-d2	ballad
Let's not waste a moment, Phil	A-f1	uptempo
The wedding, company		uptempo
Like a young man, Phil, men's chorus	A-f#1	ballad
I will follow you, David	d-b♭1	mod. ballad
Hymn to Hymie, Mrs. Weiss	a♭-c2	mod. character
There's no reason . . . reprise, Ruth	a-g2	ballad
Milk and honey reprise, Adi (S), chorus	e1-g2	mod. ballad
As simple as that, Phil, Ruth	c-d1/c1-e2	ballad
There's a short forever, Phil; Ruth incidental	A-f1	uptempo

Minnie's Boys (1970)
Music by Larry Grossman | Lyrics by Hal Hackady

Song title, Character (Voice)	Range	Song Style
Five growing boys, Minnie (M)	g-b1	uptempo
Rich is, ensemble		mod. uptempo
More precious far than gold, Julie (S), Herbie (T)	f1-b♭2/f-b♭1	mod. uptempo
The four nightingales, trio	STT	mod. uptempo
Underneath is all, Maxie (T), girls' chorus; Julie incidental	d-f#1	moving ballad
Mama, a rainbow, Adolph (T)	d♭-g1	ballad
You don't have to do it for me, Minnie, boys incidental	g#-d♭2	mod. uptempo
If you wind me up, company		mod. uptempo

Where was I?, ensemble		mod. uptempo
You remind me of you, Groucho (T), Minnie	B♭-a1/f#-f#1	moving ballad
Minnie's boys, company		uptempo
Be happy, Minnie, company	a-b1	ballad
They give me love, Minnie	f#-b1	ballad
The act, company		uptempo

Miss Saigon (1991)

Music by Claude-Michel Schönberg   Lyrics by Alain Boublil and Richard Maltby, Jr.

Song title, Character (Voice)	Range	Song Style
Backstage dreamland, Engineer (Bar), company	c-f1	uptempo
The heat is on in Saigon, company		uptempo
The movie in my mind, Gigi (M), Kim (M), girls' chorus	both a♭-e♭1	ballad
Bartending for Kim, company		scene
Why God, why?, Chris (T)	g-g1	moving ballad
The money's yours, Chris, Kim	e♭-e1/a♭-d♭2	mod. ballad
Sun and moon, Kim, Chris	f#-d2/A-f#1	flowing ballad
Telephone song, Chris, John (T)	d♭-e1/d-g1	mod. uptempo
The deal, Engineer, Chris	f#-f1/g-f#1	uptempo
The wedding, Kim, chorus	c1-d2	mod. uptempo
Thuy's intervention, trio	MTB	scene
Last night of the world, Chris, Kim	e-g#1/a-c#2	mod. ballad
The morning of the dragon (The fall of Saigon), company		uptempo
I still believe, Kim, Ellen (M)	g-d2/a-e♭2	ballad
Coo-coo princess, trio, male chorus	MTB	uptempo
Thuy's death, Thuy (T), Kim incidental	f-f1	uptempo
You will not touch him, Kim, Thuy, chorus	c1-e♭2/c1-b♭1	ballad
If you want to die in bed, Engineer	A-g♭1	uptempo
Kim and Engineer, Kim, Engineer	a-d2/d-g♭1	uptempo
I'd give my life for you, Kim, chorus	g-e2	mod. ballad
Bui doi, John, chorus	A♭-b♭1	hard ballad
The revelation, John, Chris	d-f1/c#-f#1	scene
Bangkok, trio, company	MTB	uptempo
Please, John, Kim	g#-e1/e-d2	mod. ballad
Chris is here, quartet	MTBB	uptempo
Kim's nightmare, Thuy	c-e1	uptempo
Fall of Saigon, company		uptempo
Sun and moon reprise, Kim	e-d2	ballad
Kim and Ellen, Kim, Ellen	a-d2/a♭-d2	scene
Now that I've seen her, Ellen	f#-e2	ballad
Ellen and Chris, quartet	MMTB	mod. uptempo
Paper dragons, Engineer, Kim	c1-g1/b-e1	scene

The American dream, Engineer	A-ab1	mod. ballad
Finale: This is the hour, Kim, Chris incidental	a-d2	mod. ballad

M'lle Modiste (1905)

Music by Victor Herbert   Lyrics by Henry Blossom

Song title, Character (Voice)	Range	Song Style
Furs and feathers, Nanette (M), Fanchette (S), women's chorus	d1-f#2/f#1-b2	sprightly uptempo
When the cat's away the mice will play, Fanchette, Nanette, Madame Cecile (A)	d1-a2/c1-g2/f-c2	ballad
The time and the place and the girl, Etienne (T), chorus	e1-a2	march uptempo
If I were on the stage (Kiss me again), Fifi (S)	b-c3	uptempo
Love me, love my dog, Gaston (T)	e-g1	character ballad
Hats make the woman, Fifi, women's chorus	c#1-g2	character ballad
No she shall not go alone, company		uptempo
Footmen's chorus, men's chorus		march uptempo
I want what I want when I want it, Count (Bar), chorus	B-e1	moving ballad
Gladly we respond, chorus		march uptempo
Ze English language, Gaston	eb-f1	character ballad
The mascot of the troop, Fifi, men's chorus	d1-a2	march uptempo
The dear little girl who is good, René (Bar)	G-c1	ballad
The Keokuk culture club, Mrs. Bent (M), chorus	b-e2	character
The nightingale and the star, Fifi	c#1-a2 (opt. b2)	uptempo waltz
Hark the drum, Fifi, chorus	d1-b2	uptempo

The Most Happy Fella (1956)

Music and Lyrics by Frank Loesser

Song title, Character (Voice)	Range	Song Style
Ooh! My feet, Cleo (M)	bb-bb1	character
Somebody, somewhere, Rosabella (S)	e1-g2	moving ballad
The most happy fella, Postman (Bar), Tony (Bar), chorus	e-e1/e-g1	uptempo
Standing on the corner, Barbershop quartet	TTBB	ballad
Joey, Joey, Joey, Joe (Bar)	db-f1	mod. ballad
Rosabella, Tony	d-f1	waltz ballad
Abbondanza, trio*	TTB	fast character

Sposalizio, chorus		uptempo
Benvenuta, trio	TTB	uptempo
Don't cry, Joe	c-e♭1	ballad
Fresno beauties, company		uptempo
Love and kindness, Doc (T)	e♭-a♭1	waltz ballad
Happy to make your acquaintance, Rosa, Tony	d1-e2/c#-e1	ballad
I don't like this dame, Marie (M), Cleo	e♭1-d2/b♭-c2	uptempo
Big D, Cleo, Herman (Bar)	c1-a2/d-a♭1	fast character
How beautiful the days, Rosa, Marie, Tony, Joe	SMBB	ballad
Young people, Marie	c1-e2	uptempo
Warm all over, Rosa	c#1-f#2	ballad
I like everybody, Herman, Cleo incidental	g-g1	uptempo
My heart is so full of you, Tony, Rosa	d♭-f1/f1-g♭2	moving ballad
Mamma, mamma, Tony	c#-g1	ballad
Abbondanza reprise, trio	TTB	uptempo
Goodbye, darlin', Cleo, Herman	g#-b1/f-f1	mod. uptempo
Song of a summer night, Doc, chorus	f#-f#1	ballad
Please let me tell you, Rosa	e1-e2	ballad
Nobody's ever gonna love you, Marie, Tony, Cleo	MMB	uptempo
I made a fist!, Cleo, Herman	d1-b♭1/f-a♭1	character
My heart is so full of you, company		mod. uptempo

*In Italian.

Music in the Air (1932)

Music by Jerome Kern   Lyrics by Oscar Hammerstein II

Song title, Character (Voice)	Range	Song Style
Melodies of May, chorus*		slow
I've told every little star, Karl (Bar)	c-e♭1	mod. ballad
Prayer, Sieglinde (M), chorus	b-e1	ballad
There's a hill beyond a hill, chorus		madrigal-like
At Stony Brook, Cornelius (T), chorus	B♭-f1	mod. ballad
I am so eager, Frieda (S)	d1-b♭2	uptempo waltz
I've told every little star, Sieglinde, Karl	c1-f2/c-e♭1	ballad
Tingle-tangle, Bruno (T), Frieda, chorus incidental	d-f1/b♭-g2	uptempo
In Egern on the Tegern See, Marthe (M)	g-f2	ballad
One more dance, Bruno	c#-f#1	waltz ballad
Episode of the swing, company		uptempo
Night flies by, Frieda, Bruno	c#1-a2/c-f#1	ballad
I'm alone, Frieda	b♭-d2	ballad
When spring is in the air, Sieglinde, chorus	d1-g2	uptempo
In Egern on the Tegern See reprise, Lilli (M)	a-e♭2	ballad

The song is you, Bruno	c-f1	moving ballad
The song is you reprise, Frieda, Bruno	d1-g2/e-g1	ballad
The village of Edendorf, company		uptempo

*Beethoven's Op. 2, No. 3, arranged by Kern.

The Music Man (1961)
Music and Lyrics by Meredith Willson

Song title, Character (Voice)	Range	Song Style
Rock Island, male ensemble	spoken	uptempo, patter
Iowa stubborn, chorus, many soli		mod. uptempo
Ya got trouble, Harold (Bar), chorus	Ab-eb1	uptempo
Piano lesson/If you don't mind my saying so, Marian (S), Mrs. Paroo (M)	ab-d2/d1-eb2	ballad, character
Goodnight my someone, Marian	b-e2	ballad
Seventy-six trombones, Harold, chorus	B-f1	uptempo march
Sincere, Barbershop quartet	TTBB	ballad
The sadder but wiser girl, Harold, Marcellus (T) incidental	d-e1 (much spoken)	character
Pick-a-little, talk-a-little, Townsladies, Barbershop quartet		uptempo
Marian the librarian, Harold	Bb-f1	moving ballad
My white knight, Marian	c1-f#2	ballad
The Wells Fargo wagon, chorus, many soli		uptempo
It's you, Barbershop quartet	TTBB	ballad
Shipoopi, Marcellus	g-a1	uptempo
Pick-a-little reprise, Townsladies		uptempo
Lida Rose/Will I ever tell you, Marian, barbershop quartet	d1-f#2	ballad
Gary, Indiana, Winthrop (boy S); Marian, Mrs. Paroo incidental	c1-eb2	character ballad
Lida Rose reprise, Barbershop quartet	TTBB	ballad
Till there was you, Marian, Harold	d1-g2/eb-c1	ballad
Goodnight my someone/76 trombones, company		uptempo

My Fair Lady (1956)
Music by Frederick Loewe · Lyrics by Alan Jay Lerner

Song title, Character (Voice)	Range	Song Style
Why can't the English?, Higgins (Bar)	B-d1	uptempo
Wouldn't it be loverly?, Eliza (S), chorus	c1-eb2	ballad
With a little bit of luck, Doolittle (Bar), Jamie (T), Harry (Bar)	G-d1/c-e1/e-g	fast character

I'm an ordinary man, Higgins	B♭-b♭	uptempo
With a little bit . . . reprise, Doolittle, chorus	G-e1	fast character
Just you wait, Eliza	c1-e♭2	uptempo, angry
The servant's chorus, ensemble	SMTTBB	mod. uptempo
The rain in Spain, Eliza, Higgins, Pickering (Bar)	c1-f2/men: c-f1	uptempo
I could have danced all night, Eliza	b-g2	uptempo
Ascot gavotte, chorus		stately ballad
On the street where you live, Freddy (T)	c-e1	ballad
You did it, Pickering, Higgins, servants	c-e1/c-f1	uptempo
On the street . . . reprise, Freddy	c-e1	ballad
Show me, Eliza	d1-g2	uptempo
The flower market, chorus		ballad
Get me to the church on time, Doolittle, chorus	B-d1	uptempo
A hymn to him, Higgins	B-d1	uptempo
Without you, Eliza	b-e♭2	uptempo
I've grown accustomed to her face, Higgins	A-b♭1	ballad/ends fast

My Favorite Year (1993)

Music by Stephen Flaherty   Lyrics by Lynn Ahrens

Song title, Character (Voice)	**Range**	**Song Style**
20 million people, company		mod. uptempo
Larger than life, Benjy (T)	e♭-f1	uptempo
Musketeer sketch, company		mod. uptempo
Rookie in the ring, Belle (M)	g-b♭1	mod. uptempo
Manhattan, Swann (Bar), chorus	G-e♭1	uptempo
The gospel according to King, King (Bar)	B-c#1	uptempo
Funny/The joke, KC (M), Alice (M)	a-e#2/f#-b1	uptempo, funny
Welcome to Brooklyn, company		uptempo
If the world were like the movies, Swann	G#-e1	mod. ballad
Exits, Swann	G-d♭1	ballad
Shut up and dance, KC, Benjy, chorus incidental	a-c#2/g\f#-d1	mod. uptempo
Professional showbizness comedy, King, Alice, chorus (clowns)	B♭-d1/b-b1	mod. uptempo
Comedy cavalcade theme, chorus		mod. uptempo
The lights came up, Swan, Benjy	A♭-d1/B♭-e1	moderate
Maxford house song, girls' trio	SMM	moderate, jaunty
My favorite year, Benjy, company	d♭-g♭1	easy ballad

My One and Only (1983)

Music by George Gershwin   Lyrics by Ira Gershwin and B.G. DeSylva

Song title, Character (Voice)	Range	Song Style
I can't be bothered now, company		uptempo
Boy wanted/Soon, Edythe (M), Billy (Bar)	g-d2/c-e1	moving ballad
High hat, Billy, Mr. Magix (Bar), men's chorus	d-d1/c-e♭1	mod. ballad
He loves and she loves, Billy, Edythe, men's chorus on reprise	A-b/a-c2	moving ballad
Flying, male ensemble ("New Rhythm Boys")		uptempo
'S wonderful, Billy, Edythe	c-c#1/c1-c2	mod. ballad
Finale: Strike up the band, Billy	c-d1	ballad, then fast
In the swim/What are we here for, female sextet	SSSMMM	uptempo
Nice work if you can get it, Edythe	g#-b1	mod. ballad
My one and only, Billy, Mr. Magix	both d-e♭1	uptempo
Funny face, Mickey (Bar), Nikki (M)	B♭-b♭/b♭-d2	moving ballad
My one and only reprise, Billy	d-d1	uptempo
Kickin' the clouds away, Montgomery (Bar)	d-d1	uptempo
How long has this been going on?, Edythe, Billy incidental	a-b1	ballad

The Mystery of Edwin Drood (1987)

Music and Lyrics by Rupert Holmes

Song title, Character (Voice)	Range	Song Style
There you are, company		mod. uptempo
Two kinsmen, Drood (M), Jasper (T)	b-d2/e-f1	uptempo
Moonfall, Rosa (S)	b-g2	ballad
The wages of sin, Puffer (M)	g♭-c2	moving ballad
A British subject, ensemble		tango ballad
Both sides of the coin, Jasper, Chairman (Bar)	d#-e2/d-f#1	mod. uptempo
Perfect strangers, Drood, Rosa	c#1-d#2/c#1-f2	mod. ballad
No good can come from bad, ensemble		mod., patter
Never the luck, Bazzard (T)	c-b♭	waltz ballad
Off to the races, Chairman, Durdles (Bar), Deputy (T), company	c-f1/c-d1/c-f1	mod. uptempo
England reigns, Chairman	c-c1	anthem ballad
A private investigation, Datchery (M or Bar), Puffer	A♭-d♭1/a♭-d♭2	mysterious, narrative ballad
The name of love/Moonfall reprise, Rosa, Jasper, company	d1-b2/d-g1	uptempo/ballad
Don't quit while you're ahead, company		soft shoe ballad

The garden path to hell, Puffer	g-a1	mod. ballad
Puffer's revelation, Puffer	a-b♭1	quick, agitated
Out on a limerick, Datchery, company	a-c#2 if woman, c-e1 if man	mod. ballad or uptempo
Jasper's confession, Jasper	b-a1	hard ballad
*Murderer's confession**		mod. uptempo
Helena	g-b1	
Bazzard	a-b♭1	
Neville	e-f1	
Crisparkle	d-f1	
Rosa	a-a♭2	
Puffer	f-c2	
Durdles	c-e1	
*Perfect strangers reprise**		moving ballad
Rosa or Helena or Puffer, with	c#1-e2	
Durdles or Sapsea or Jasper; company	c#-e1	
The writing on the wall, Drood, company	g-e2	uptempo

*Only one character or duo sings these numbers depending upon who is named by the audience as the murderer.

Myths and Hymns (1998)
Music and Lyrics by Adam Guettel

Song title, Character (Voice)	Range	Song Style
Saturn returns	a-b♭2	mod. uptempo
Icarus, Icarus, Daedalus, backup singers	d-c2/e♭-b♭1	funky uptempo
Migratory V	b-e2	ballad
Pegasus, trio	MTT	mod. uptempo
Jesus, the mighty conqueror, solo and chorus	b-c3	uptempo
Children of the heavenly king	g-a1	hymn
At the sounding, company or chorus		march uptempo
Build a bridge	b-b♭2	gospel ballad
Sisyphus, Sisyphus, chorus	c1-g2	character uptempo
Life is but a dream	g-d2	ballad
Hero and Leander	c1-d3	moving ballad
Come to Jesus, Emily (S), Matthew (T)	b♭-a2/c-b♭1	ballad
How can I love you?	d-f#2	fast waltz
The great highway, company		moving
There is a land, quartet	SMTB	mod. uptempo
There's a shout, solo and chorus	f#-d2	uptempo
Awaiting you	a-d3	ballad

Note: All ranges given as notated in the conductor's score. If sung by men, then the range would be an octave lower, except where characters are noted, above.

Naughty Marietta (1910)

Music by Victor Herbert   Lyrics by Rida Johnson Young

Song title, **Character (Voice)**	**Range**	**Song Style**
Come, for the morn is breaking, chorus		uptempo
Tramp, tramp, tramp, Capt. Dick (T), men's chorus	g-c2	character march
Taisez vous, chorus		uptempo
Naughty Marietta, Marietta (S)	b-a2	uptempo
It never, never can be love, Marietta, Capt. Dick	e1-g#2/e-f#1	ballad
If I were anybody else but me, Lizette (S), Simon (Bar)	c1-f2/Bb-f1	ballad, funny
'Neath the Southern moon, Adah (M)	g#-f2	mod. ballad
Italian street song, Marietta, chorus	e1-c3	character
Oh, la, papa!, company		uptempo
You marry a marionette, Etienne (Bar)	F-d1	character, mod.
New Orleans jeunesse doreé, men's chorus		uptempo
Lovers of New Orleans, chorus		uptempo
The sweet by and by, Lizette	c1-c2	ballad
Live for today, Marietta, Adah, Capt. Dick, Etienne	SMTB	moving ballad
I'm falling in love with someone, Capt. Dick	eb-bb1	waltz ballad
It's pretty soft for Simon, Simon	e-g#1	mod. character
Ah, sweet mystery of life, Marietta, Capt. Dick, company	c#1-a2/e-a1	uptempo

A New Brain (1998)

Music and Lyrics by William Finn

Song title, **Character (Voice)**	**Range**	**Song Style**
Prologue, Gordon (Bar)	B-e1	mod. uptempo
Specials, ensemble	SMTTB	uptempo
911 Emergency, company		uptempo scene
Heart and music, company		mod. uptempo
Trouble in his brain, trio	SMB	scene
Mother's gonna make things fine, Mother (M), Gordon	a-a1/c-f1	ballad
Be polite to everybody, Bungee (Bar), ensemble	db-eb1	funny uptempo
Sailing, Gordon, Roger (Bar)	g-g1/A-g1	mod. uptempo
Family history, quartet	SMTT	uptempo
Gordo's law of genetics, company		mod. uptempo
And they're off, Gordon, ensemble	c-g1	mod. uptempo
Roger arrives, ensemble		uptempo
Just you, Gordon, Roger	c-d1/e-e1	mod. uptempo

Poor, unsuccessful and fat, trio	TTB	funny uptempo
Sitting becalmed in the lee of Cuttyhunk, company		slow
Craniotomy, Doctor, Nang, Minister	MTB	uptempo
An invitation to sleep in my arms, quartet	MMTT	mod. uptempo
Change, Lisa (M)	f-d2	mod. ballad
Yes, Gordon, Bungee, company		mod. uptempo
In the middle of the room, Gordon, Mother, Richard incidental	G-e1/g-b♭	ballad
Throw it out, Minnie (M)	g-a1	character uptempo
In the middle of the room reprise, Gordon	A-e1	slow
A really lovely day in the universe, Lisa, Roger	a-c#2/A-d1	ballad
Brain dead, Gordon, Roger	d#-d1	mod. uptempo
Whenever I dream, Rhonda (M), Gordon	a-b♭1-A-d1	mod. uptempo
Eating myself up alive, ensemble		disco uptempo
The music still plays on, Mother	f-e1	ballad
Don't give in, Bungee, ensemble	B-d1	moderate swing
You boys are gonna get me in such trouble, Gordon, Richard (B)	B♭-g♭1/g#-d2	swing uptempo
On the street, Lisa, Gordon, Roger	g#-d2/B-f1/B-e1	mod. uptempo
Time, Gordon, Roger	c-c1/c-f1	ballad
Time and music, company		moving ballad

New Girl in Town (1957)
Music and Lyrics by Robert Merrill

Song title, Character (Voice)	Range	Song Style
Roll your socks up, company		uptempo
Anna Lilla, Chris (Bar)	c-c1	folksy ballad
Sunshine girl, Larry (Bar), Oscar (T), Pete (T)*	d#-c1/d#-f1/d#-a1	mod. uptempo
On the town, Anna (M)	e-a2	angry uptempo
Flings, Marthy (S), Lily (S), Pearl (S)	g1-b2/g1-b2/g1-a2	mod. ballad, funny
It's good to be alive, Anna	c-b♭1	ballad
Look at 'er, Matt (Bar)	B♭-f1	mod. ballad
It's good to be alive reprise, Matt	A#-e1	ballad
Yer my friend, Marthy, Chris	d1-a2/d-f1	mod. ballad
Did you close your eyes?, Matt, Anna	B♭-g1/a-e♭2	ballad
Check apron ball, company		mod. uptempo
There ain't no flies on me, Alderman (Bar), Town Politician (Bar), Larry, chorus	all d-e1	uptempo/soft shoe/jelly roll
Ven I valse, Chris, Anna, chorus	B-e1/g-e♭2	flowing waltz
Sunshine girl reprise, chorus		mod. uptempo
If that was love, Anna	a♭-a♭1	ballad

Seaman's home, Marthy, chorus (many soli)   b♭-a2   mod. ballad

Bows: Sunshine girl, company   uptempo

*"Barbershop" trio.

The New Moon (1928)
Music by Sigmund Romberg
Lyrics by Oscar Hammerstein II, Frank Mandel, and Laurence Schwab

Song title, Character (Voice)	Range	Song Style
Dainty wisp of thistledown, chorus		march uptempo
Marianne, Robert (Bar)	b♭-e♭1	moving ballad
Marianne, we want to love you, Marianne (S), men's chorus	g1-a2 (opt. c2)	uptempo
The girl on the prow, Marianne, Besac (Bar)	a-g2 (opt. b♭2)/d-d1	mod. uptempo
Gorgeous Alexander, Julie (M), Alexander (Bar), women's chorus	c#1-d2/c#-d1	mod. uptempo
I'm seeking the hand of a maiden, Duval (Bar), Marianne	d-e1/d1-e2	ballad
Red wine in your glasses, chorus		uptempo waltz
Softly as a morning sunrise, Philippe (T), chorus	f-c2	ballad
Stouthearted men, Robert, Philippe, men's chorus	d-f#1 (opt. g1)/d-d1	march
Fair Maria, Marianne, women's chorus	f1-f2	uptempo tango
One kiss, Marianne, women's chorus	e♭1-b♭2	ballad
The trial, ensemble		mod. uptempo
Gentle airs, courtly manners, chorus		mod. ballad
Wanting you, Marianne, Robert	b♭-b♭2/B♭-f1 (opt. g1)	waltz ballad
Funny little sailormen, Clotilde (M), Besac	c1-e2/d-f1	fast character
Lover, come back to me, Marianne	d1-g2	ballad
Stouthearted men reprise, men's chorus		march
Love is quite a simple thing, Julie, Alexander, Besac, Clotilde	SMTB	mod. ballad
Just one year ago we were mated, chorus		moving ballad
Softly . . . morning sunrise reprise, Philippe, men	f-c2	ballad
Never for you, Marianne	f#1-a♭2	ballad
Lover, come back to me reprise, Robert, Marianne incidental	d-d1	ballad
One kiss reprise, Robert, Marianne	d-e♭1/d1-b♭2	ballad
Finale: Stouthearted men, company		march uptempo

Nick and Norah (1991)

Music by Charles Strouse   Lyrics by Richard Maltby, Jr.

Song title, Character (Voice)	Range	Song Style
Is there anything better than dancing?, trio	MMB	mod. uptempo
Everybody wants to do a musical, Tracy (M)	e-e2	mod. uptempo
Max's story, trio	MBB	scene
Swell, quartet	SMTB	mod. uptempo
As long as you're happy, Nick (Bar), Norah (M)	A-f1/g-g2	mod. ballad
People get hurt, Lily (M)	ab-db2	mod. ballad
Men, quartet	MMTB	ballad
May the best man win, company		mod. uptempo
Look who's alone now, Nick	Ab-d1	ballad
Class, Victor (T)	B-f#1	mod. ballad
Let's go home, Nora	g-b1	ballad
A busy night at Lorraine's, trio, company	MTB	mod. uptempo
Boom chicka boom, Maria (M), male chorus	a-bb1	uptempo
Let's go home reprise, Nick, Nora	Bb-c1/ab-c2	mod. ballad

Nine (1982)

Music and Lyrics by Maury Yeston

Song title, Character (Voice)	Range	Song Style
Not since Chaplin, chorus		uptempo
Guido's song, Guido (Bar), women's chorus	A-g1	uptempo
The Germans at the spa, Mama (M), chorus	g-e2	fast character
My husband makes movies, Luisa (M)	eb-c2	moving ballad
A call from the Vatican, Carla (S)	a-c3	mod. uptempo
Only with you, Guido	G#-d1	moving ballad
The script, Guido	d-f1	uptempo
Follies bergeres, La Fleur (M), Critic (Bar), chorus	g#-b1/B-b	mod. uptempo
Nine, Mama, Aunts	c1-a2	moving ballad
Be Italian, Saraghina (M), men's chorus	g#-db2	ballad
The bells of St. Sebastian, Guido, chorus	e-g1	moving ballad
Unusual way, Claudia (M), Guido	c#1-e2/G#-c#1	ballad
Contini submits/Grand canal, Guido, chorus*	d-g1	uptempo, patter
Every girl in Venice, Spa Lady (M), women's chorus	g1-e2	moderate
Amor, Guido, women's chorus	f-g1	ballad
Only with you, Guido, Nun's ensemble	c-e1	moving ballad
Simple, Carla	a-e2	ballad
Be on your own, Luisa	g#-a1	ballad
I can't make this movie, Guido	g-g1†	mod., driving
Getting tall, Boy (boy S)	ab-eb2	ballad

Finale: Nine reprise/Long ago, company   uptempo

*Chorus sings only on "Grand Canal."
†Song also provided in E minor (one step higher) and B-flat (a half-step lower).

No, No, Nanette (1925)

Music by Vincent Youmans   Lyrics by Irving Caesar and Otto Harbach

Song title, Character (Voice)	Range	Song Style
Too many rings around Rosie, Lucille (M), men's chorus	b-d2	ragtime ballad
I've confessed to the breeze, Nanette (S), Tom (T)	b-f2/d-f1	ballad
The call of the sea, Billy (T)	c#-f#2	uptempo
I want to be happy, Nanette, Jimmy (T), men	c1-e2/d-f#1	mod. uptempo
No, no, Nanette, Nanette, men	c1-eb2	uptempo
You can dance with any girl, Tom, Nanette, chorus	c-eb1/bb-d2	uptempo
Peach on the beach, Nanette, company	b-e2	uptempo
Tea for two, Tom	eb-f1	soft shoe ballad
You can dance with any girl at all, Lucille, Billy	a-eb2/c-f1	mod. uptempo
What a peach of a girl, company		mostly uptempo
Telephone girlie, Billy, SSA trio	c-f1	uptempo
Where-has-my-hubby-gone blues, Lucille, men	g-db2	blues ballad
Waiting for you, Nanette, Tom	ab-eb2/Bb-f1	moving ballad
Take a little one-step, Sue (M), company	g-ab1	uptempo
I want to be happy reprise, company		uptempo
Tea for two reprise, company		soft shoe ballad

No Strings (1962)

Music and Lyrics by Richard Rodgers

Song title, Character (Voice)	Range	Song Style
The sweetest sounds, Barbara (M), David (Bar)	a-d2/f-eb1	ballad
How sad, David	d-e1	uptempo
The sweetest sounds reprise, David	d-d1	ballad
Loads of love, Barbara	a-bb1	swing ballad
The man who has everything, Gregg (Bar)	d-d1	uptempo
Be my host, company		uptempo
La-la-la, Jeanette (M), Luc (Bar)*	b-c#2/e-d1	soft shoe ballad
You don't tell me, Barbara	ab-c2	uptempo

Love makes the world go round, Comfort (M), Mollie (M)	both a-d♭2	waltz ballad
Nobody told me, David, Barbara	d-e♭1/a-a#1	ballad
Look no further, Barbara, David	a-b♭1/B♭-b♭	uptempo
Maine, David, Barbara	d-e♭1/b-c2	moving ballad
An orthodox fool, Barbara	a-c2	uptempo
Eager beaver, Comfort, Mike (Bar)	c1-e2/c-e1	uptempo
No strings, David, Barbara	c#-d1/b♭-c2	moving ballad
Maine reprise, David, Barbara	B♭-ab1/b♭-a♭2	ballad (slower this time)
The sweetest sounds reprise, David, Barbara	e-d1/c1-g1	ballad
No strings reprise, company		mod. uptempo

*In French.

Nunsense (1985)
Music and Lyrics by Dan Goggin

Song title, **Character (Voice)**	**Range**	**Song Style**
Nunsense is habit forming, company		mod. uptempo
A difficult transition, company		uptempo
Benedicite, Sr. Mary Leo (S)	c#1-g2	mod. uptempo
The biggest ain't the best, Sr. Mary Hubert (M), Sr. Mary Leo	g-f#2/a-a1	moving ballad
Playing second fiddle, Sr. Robert Anne (M)	b-b1	uptempo
So you want to be a nun, Sr. Mary Amnesia (S)	c1-b2	uptempo
One last hope, company		uptempo
Turn up the spotlight, Sr. Mary Cardelia (M)	b-f1	uptempo
Lilacs bring back memories, Cardelia, Hubert, Leo, Amnesia	SSMM	ballad
Tackle that temptation with a time step, company		uptempo
Growing up Catholic, Robert Anne, Leo, Hubert, Amnesia	SSMM	moving ballad
We've got to clean out the freezer, company		uptempo
Just a coupl'a sisters, Cardelia, Hubert	both a-c2	jaunty ballad
Playing second fiddle reprise, Robert Anne	d1-b1	moving ballad
I just want to be a star, Robert Anne	g-c2	moving ballad
The drive in, Robert Anne, Amnesia, Leo	e♭-c2/g-c2/b♭-e2	50s ballad
I could've gone to Nashville, Amnesia	g-e2	country ballad
Holier than thou, Hubert, company	b♭-f2	uptempo gospel
Nunsense is habit forming reprise, company		uptempo

Of Thee I Sing (1932)

Music by George Gershwin   Lyrics by Ira Gershwin

Song title, Character (Voice)	Range	Song Style
Wintergreen for president, chorus		uptempo
Who is the lucky girl to be?/Because, because, chorus		uptempo
How beautiful, Diana (S), chorus	d1-f2	character
Love is sweeping the country, Miss Benson (S)	c1-f2	uptempo
Of thee I sing, Mary (S), Wintergreen (Bar)	d1-e2/d-e1	uptempo
Hello, good morning, chorus		mod. uptempo
Who cares?, Mary, Wintergreen, Reporters	d1-eb2/d-eb1	ballad
The illegitimate daughter, French Ambassador (Bar), company	d-e1	mod. uptempo
The senator from Minnesota, men's chorus		mod. ballad
The senate, Diana, Fr. Ambassador, men's chorus	d1-f#2/d-d1	uptempo
Prosperity is just around the corner, company		uptempo
Trumpeter blow your golden horn, chorus		uptempo
Of thee I sing reprise, company		uptempo

Oh, Kay! (1926)

Music by George Gershwin   Lyrics by Ira Gershwin

Song title, Character (Voice)	Range	Song Style
The woman's touch, women's chorus		uptempo
Don't ask, Potter (T); Dolly (S), Phillipa (S), women's chorus incidental	d-g1	mod. uptempo
Dear little girl, Jimmy (T)	eb-eb1	mod. ballad
Maybe, Jimmy, Kay (S)	c-f1/c1-f2	ballad
Clap yo' hands, Potter, company	c-d1	mod. uptempo
Do-do-do, Jimmy, Kay	d-f1/d1-f2	mod. ballad
Isn't it grand, chorus		uptempo
Never too late to Mendelssohn, company		uptempo
Someone to watch over me, Kay	eb1-f2	ballad
Fidgety feet, Potter, Phillipa incidental	eb-f1	mod. uptempo
Heaven on earth, Jimmy, women's chorus	eb-g1	mod. uptempo
Someone to watch over me reprise, unison chorus		ballad
Maybe reprise, unison chorus		ballad
Oh, Kay!, Kay, men's chorus	eb1-f2	uptempo
Finale: Do-do-do/Clap yo' hands, company		mod. ballad/ uptempo

Oklahoma! (1943)

Music by Richard Rodgers   Lyrics by Oscar Hammerstein II

Song title, Character (Voice)	Range	Song Style
Oh, what a beautiful morning, Curley (Bar)	d#-d#1	ballad
The surrey with the fringe on top, Curley	d#-e1	mod. ballad
Kansas City, Will (T)	e♭-f1	mod. uptempo
I cain't say no, Ado Annie (S)	c1-e2	fast character
Many a new day, Laurey (S)	d1-e2	mod. ballad
People will say we're in love, Curley, Laurey	d-f#1/d1-f#2	ballad
Pore Jud is daid, Curley, Jud (Bar)	both d-c#1	narrative ballad
Lonely room, Jud	d-c#1	ballad
Out of my dreams, Laurey, women's chorus	e1-f2	moving ballad
The farmer and the cowman, Old Man Carnes (T), Aunt Eller (M), chorus	f-f1/g-f2	fast character
All 'er nothin', Annie, Will	e♭1-e♭2/e-f1	character ballad
People will say . . . reprise, Curley, Laurey	d-f#1/d1-f#2	ballad
Oklahoma, company		uptempo
Finale: Beautiful morning/People will say, company		ballads

Oliver! (1963)

Music and Lyrics by Lionel Bart

Song title, Character (Voice)	Range	Song Style
Food, glorious food, boys' chorus		uptempo
Oliver, Mr. Bumble (T), Widow Corney (M), chorus		mod. uptempo
I shall scream, Widow Corney, Mr. Bumble	d♭-d♭1/d♭-f2	fast character
Boy for sale, Mr. Bumble	d-a1	ballad
That's your funeral, Mr. Sowerberry (Bar), Mrs. Sowerberry (M), Mr. Bumble	c-e1/c1-c2/c-f1	uptempo
Where is love?, Oliver (boy S)	c1-d2	ballad
Consider yourself, The Artful Dodger (boy T), Oliver, unison boys' chorus	b-c#2/a-b1	mod. uptempo
Pick a pocket or two, Fagin (Bar), boys	c-d♭1	fast character
It's a fine life, ensemble	MMTTB	mod. uptempo
Be back soon, Fagin, boys	c-d1	uptempo
Oom-pah-pah, Nancy (M), chorus	a-b1	fast character
My name, Bill Sykes (Bar)	d-d1	menacing ballad
As long as he needs me, Nancy	f-b♭1	ballad
Who will buy?, company		uptempo
Reviewing the situation, Fagin	c-f1	moving ballad
Oliver reprise, Mr. Bumble, Widow Corney	d-f1/d1-f2	mod. uptempo
As long as he needs me reprise, Nancy	b♭-c2	ballad

Finale: Food/Consider yourself/I'd do	uptempo/mod.
anything, company	ballad

On a Clear Day You Can See Forever (1965)

Music by Burton Lane   Lyrics by Alan Jay Lerner

Song title, Character (Voice)	Range	Song Style
On a clear day, chorus		mod. uptempo
Hurry! It's lovely up here!, Daisy (M)	a♭-d♭2	character
Solicitor's song, quartet	TTBB	fast character
He wasn't you, Daisy	g-c2	ballad
On a clear day reprise, Mark (Bar)	A#-e1	moving ballad
On the S.S. Bernard Cohn, Daisy, chorus	d#-d2	uptempo
She wasn't you, Edward (T), Daisy incidental	c-a♭1	ballad
Melinda, Mark	A#-d#1	ballad
When I come around again, company		uptempo
What did I have that I don't have?, Daisy	a♭-c2	ballad
Wait till we're sixty-five,Warren (T), Daisy, students	c-f1/c1-e2	uptempo
Come back to me, Mark	d-e1	uptempo
Finale: On a clear day, company		mod. uptempo

On the Town (1944)

Music by Leonard Bernstein   Lyrics by Betty Comden and Adolph Green

Song title, Character (Voice)	Range	Song Style
I feel like I'm not out of bed yet, men's chorus		moving ballad
New York, New York, Gabey (T), Chip (T), Ozzie (T)	all c-g1	uptempo
Come up to my place, Chip, Hildy (M)	B♭-g1/d1-d2	uptempo patter
Carried away, Claire (M), Ozzie	f-c2/F-a1	moving ballad
Lonely town, Gabey, chorus	d-a1	ballad
Carnegie Hall pavane, Ivy (M), Dilly (M), chorus	both c1-e♭2	mod. ballad
I can cook, too, Hildy	a-c#2	hot uptempo
Lucky to be me, Gabey	B♭-a1	mod. ballad
So long, baby, unison women's chorus		uptempo
I wish I was dead, Diana Dream (M)	c1-d2	blues ballad
Ya got me, Hildy, Ozzie, Claire, Chip	MMTT	mod. uptempo
I understand, Pitkin (Bar)	A-d1	narrative ballad
Some other time, Claire, Hildy, Ozzie, Chip	MMTT	uptempo
Finale: New York, New York, company		uptempo

On the Twentieth Century (1978)

Music by Cy Coleman   Lyrics by Betty Comden and Adolph Green

Song title, Character (Voice)	Range	Song Style
Stranded, chorus		uptempo
Saddle on the horse, company		uptempo
I rise again, Oscar (T), Oliver (T), Owen (T)	B-e1/others g#-e1	slow waltz
Indian maiden's lament, Imelda (S), girl (S)	e1-f2/c1-a2	character ballad
Veronique, Lily (S); Oscar, chorus incidental	e-g♭1	character ballad
I have written a play, Conductor (Bar)	c-f1	uptempo
Together, Oscar, chorus	c#-e1	uptempo
Never, Lily	b♭-f2	uptempo
Our private world, Oscar, Lily	A-e1/a-e2	moving ballad
Repent, Letitia (S)	e1-f#2	mod. uptempo
Mine, Oscar, Bruce (T)	A-e1/A#-f#1	mod. ballad
I've got it all, Lily, Oscar	b-e2/B-e1	mod. uptempo
I have written a play reprise, Congressman (T)	d-f1	uptempo, funny
Five zeros, Oscar, Owen, Letitia	B♭-a♭1/ab-db2/A♭-e♭1	mod. uptempo
I have written a play, Doctor (Bar)	c-e♭1	uptempo
Sign, Lily, sign, Lily, ensemble	b-f2	uptempo
She's a nut, company		uptempo
Max Jacobs, Max (Bar)	B♭-e♭1	moderate
Babette, Lily, chorus	f#-g2	ballad
Last will and testament, Oscar	B♭-f1	slow, recit.-like
Lily-Oscar, Lily, Oscar	g#1-g#2/c#-e1	ballad
Life is like a train, company		mod. uptempo

On Your Toes (1936)

Music by Richard Rodgers   Lyrics by Lorenz Hart

Song title, Character (Voice)	Range	Song Style
Two-a-day for Keith, Pa (Bar), Ma (M), Junior (Bar)	men: c-c1/her: c1-c2	uptempo
Questions and answers, Junior, chorus	c-d1	fast character
It's got to be love, Frankie (M), Junior, chorus	d1-d2/d-d1	moving ballad
Too good for the average man, Sergei (Bar), Peggy (M)	both g-a1	ballad, funny
There's a small hotel, Frankie, Junior	b-d2/B-d1	ballad
The heart is quicker than the eye, Peggy, Junior	a-a1/d-c♭1	uptempo
Glad to be unhappy, Frankie	c1-d2	ballad
Quiet night, Hank (Bar), chorus	c-e1	ballad

On your toes, Frankie, chorus	a-c2	uptempo
Quiet night reprise, Sergei, chorus	A-c#1	ballad

Once on This Island (1990)

Music by Stephen Flaherty   Lyrics by Lynn Ahrens

Song title, Character (Voice)	Range	Song Style
We dance, company		uptempo
One small girl, Mama (M), Tonton (Bar), Storytellers	b♭-b1/A-c1	narrative ballad
Waiting for life, Ti Moune (S)	c#1-e2	uptempo
And the gods heard her prayer, company		mod. ballad
Rain, Agwe (T)	f-d#1	mod. samba
Pray, company		uptempo
Forever yours, Ti Moune, Daniel (T), Papa Ge (T), chorus	a#-c#2/e#-f#1/c#-g1	ballad, then faster
The sad tale of the Beauxhommes, company	mostly spoken	mod. uptempo
Ti Moune, Mama, Tonton, Ti Moune	g♭-b♭1/g-e♭1/a-c2	mod. ballad
Mama will provide, Asaka (M), chorus	b-e2	bright calypso
Some say, company		mod. ballad
The human heart, Erzulie (M)	b-c#2	mod. ballad
Pray reprise, company		uptempo
Some girls, Daniel	B-e1	ballad
Promises/Forever yours reprise, Papa Ge, Erzulie	c#-g1/c1-d2	ballad
A part of us, Mama, Ti Moune, Tonton	b-b1/b-b1/B-b	ballad
Why we tell the story, company		mod. uptempo

Once Upon a Mattress (1959)

Music by Mary Rodgers   Lyrics by Marshall Barer

Song title, Character (Voice)	Range	Song Style
Many moons ago, Minstrel (T)	d-g1	narrative ballad
Opening for a princess, company		uptempo
In a little while, Harry (T), Larken (S)	d♭-f1/d♭1-f2	ballad
Shy, Winnifred (M), chorus	b-c#2	mod. character
The minstrel, the jester, and I, Minstrel, Jester (T), King (Bar)	all e-f#1	uptempo, funny
Sensitivity, Queen (M), Wizard (Bar) incidental, women's chorus	a-b1	character; in 5/4
The swamps of home, Winnifred, women's chorus	b♭-f2	ballad
Normandy, Minstrel, Jester, Larken	d-g1/d-b♭1/d1-g2	uptempo

Song of love, Dauntless (Bar); Winnifred, chorus incidental	B-e♭1	uptempo
Quiet, quiet, the Queen insists on quiet, chorus	spoken, with clapping	uptempo
Happily ever after, Winnifred	a♭-c♭2	fast character
Man to man talk, Dauntless, King	e-e1/mute	ballad
Very soft shoes, Jester	d-f1	ballad
Yesterday I loved you, Harry, Larken	c-g1/d-e♭2	ballad
How did she stay awake, company		mod. uptempo

110 in the Shade (1963)
Music by Harvey Schmidt   Lyrics by Tom Jones

Song title, Character (Voice)	**Range**	**Song Style**
Gonna be another hot day, company		mod. ballad
Lizzie's comin' home, Jim (Bar), Noah (Bar), chorus	both B-e1	uptempo
Love, don't turn away, Lizzie (S)	d1-f2	ballad
Poker polka, Jim, Noah, HC (Bar), File (T)	TTBB	fast character
The hungry men, chorus		uptempo
Rain song, Starbuck (T), chorus	e♭-a♭1	uptempo
You're not foolin' me, Starbuck, Lizzie	d-e♭1/e♭1-e♭2	ballad
Raunchy, Lizzie, HC incidental	g-g♭2	blues uptempo
A man and a woman, File, Lizzie	c-d1/d1-g2	ballad
Old maid, Lizzie	b-g2	uptempo
Everything beautiful happens at night, chorus		ballad
Melisande, Starbuck	G-g1	uptempo
Simple little things, Lizzie, Starbuck incidental	b-e2	ballad
Little red hat, Jim, Snookie (M)	c-f1/c1-e2	character ballad
Is it really me?, Lizzie, Starbuck	a-e2/B♭-e1	ballad
Wonderful music, Starbuck, File, Lizzie	men: d♭-f1/her: f1-e♭2	ballad
Finale: Rain song reprise, company		uptempo

Pacific Overtures (1976)
Music and Lyrics by Stephen Sondheim

Song title, Character (Voice)	**Range**	**Song Style**
The advantage of floating in the middle of the sea, Reciter (Bar), company	B-e♭1	mod. ballad
There is no other way, Observers (T, Bar)	e-g1/e-b	ballad

Four black dragons, Fisherman (T), Thief (Bar); chorus and Reciter incidental	c#-f#1/B-d1	narrative ballad
Chrysanthemum tea, ensemble		mod. uptempo
Poems, Kayama (T), Manjiro (S)	e♭-g1/d1-f2	ballad
Welcome to the Kanagawa, Madam (S), women's chorus	c1-e2	fast character
Someone in a tree, Old Man (T), Reciter, Boy (T), Warrior (T)	TTTB	uptempo
Please hello, ensemble	TTBBBB	fast character
A bowler hat, Kayama (M)	g-e♭1	narrative ballad
Pretty lady, Three British Soldiers (TBB)	I, III: G-f1/II: F-f1	ballad
Next, company		uptempo

Paint Your Wagon (1951)

Music by Frederick Loewe   Lyrics by Alan Jay Lerner

Song title, Character (Voice)	**Range**	**Song Style**
I'm on my way, men's chorus, many soli		uptempo
Rumson Town, Jake (Bar)	B-b	mod. ballad
What's goin' on here, Jennifer (M)	g#-c2	uptempo
I talk to the trees, Julio (T), Jennifer	c-f#1/g-c2	ballad
They call the wind Maria, Steve (Bar), Miners	c-f1	ballad
I still see Elisa, Ben (Bar)	G-c2	ballad
How can I wait, Jennifer	f-c2	ballad
I'm on my way reprise, ensemble		uptempo
Trio, Elizabeth (S), Sarah (M), Jacob (Bar)	e♭1-e♭2/b♭-e♭2/c-e1	prayerful ballad
Rumson Town reprise, Jake	B-b	ballad
Whoop-ti-ay, company		uptempo
Carino mio, Julio	B♭-f1	ballad
There's a coach comin' in, men's chorus		uptempo
Hand me down that can o' beans, Jake, chorus	c-c1	fast character
Another autumn, Julio	e♭-f1	ballad
Movin', ensemble		mod. uptempo
All for him, Jennifer	b-b1	waltz ballad
Wand'rin' star, Ben	d-e♭1	mod. uptempo
I talk to the trees reprise, Jennifer	g-c#2	ballad
The strike, company		uptempo
Wand'rin' star reprise, Miners		mod. uptempo
Finale: I'm on my way reprise, men's chorus		uptempo

The Pajama Game (1954)
Music and Lyrics by Richard Adler and Jerry Ross

Song title, **Character (Voice)**	**Range**	**Song Style**
Racing with the clock, chorus		uptempo
A new town is a blue town, Sid (T)	d♭-g1	uptempo
I'm not at all in love, Babe (M), women's chorus	a-b1	uptempo, funny
I'll never be jealous again, Mabel (S), Hines (T)	b-d2/B-f1	uptempo
Hey there, Sid, also a voice on tape	e♭-a♭1	ballad
Her is, chorus		uptempo
Once-a-year day, chorus		uptempo
Her is reprise, chorus		uptempo
Small talk, Sid, Babe	d♭-g♭1/a♭-d♭2	uptempo
There once was a man, Sid, Babe	B-b♭1/b♭-e♭2	uptempo
Slow down, women's chorus		moderate
Hey there reprise, Sid	f-g♭1	ballad
Steam heat, Gladys (M), men's chorus	c1-c2	jazzy uptempo
Hey there reprise, Babe	a-b♭1	ballad
Think of the time I save, Hines, women's chorus	c-c1	mod. uptempo, funny
Hernando's hideaway, Gladys, chorus	b-c2	Latin ballad
Seven and a half cents, Prey (Bar), Babe, chorus	d-e1/d1-f#2	uptempo
There once was a man reprise, Babe, Sid	b-b♭3/d♭-b♭1	uptempo

Pal Joey (1940)
Music by Richard Rodgers   Lyrics by Lorenz Hart

Song title, **Character (Voice)**	**Range**	**Song Style**
A great big town, Joey (Bar)	e♭-f1	uptempo
You musn't kick it around, Joey, Gladys (M)	e♭-e♭1/b♭-c2	uptempo
I could write a book, Joey, Linda (M)	e♭-e♭1/d-d1	mod. uptempo
A great big town reprise, women's chorus		uptempo
That terrific rainbow, Gladys, women's chorus	b♭-b♭1	blues ballad
What is a man?, Joey, Vera (M)	d-e♭1/d1-e♭2	ballad
Happy hunting horn, Joey	a♭-f1	uptempo
Bewitched, Vera	d1-d2	ballad
Pal Joey (What do I care for a dame?), Joey, chorus	d-c1	uptempo
The flower garden of my heart, Louis (T), Gladys	e♭-g1/d1-f#2	ballad
Zip, Melba (M)	f#-g1	ballad
Plant you now, dig you later, Gladys, chorus	d1-d2	fast character

Den of iniquity, Vera, Joey	e♭1-e♭2/e♭-e♭1	uptempo
Do it the hard way, Joey, chorus	c-c1	uptempo
Take him, Linda, Vera	both c1-d2	mod. uptempo
Bewitched reprise, Vera	e1-d2	ballad
I could write a book reprise, Joey	e♭-d♭1	uptempo

Parade (1998)

Music and Lyrics by Jason Robert Brown

Song title, Character (Voice)	Range	Song Style
The old red hills of home, Young Soldier (T)	d-a1	mod. uptempo
The old red hills of home 2, Old Soldier (T), chorus	c-g1	mod. uptempo
The dream of Atlanta, company		uptempo
How can I call this home?, Leo (Bar), company	A-f1	ballad
The picture show, Frankie (Bar), May (M)	e♭-f1/e♭1-c2	mod. uptempo
Leo at work/What am I waiting for?, Leo, Lucille (M), ensemble	c-f1/a-c2	fast march
Interrogation sequence, Newt Lee (Bar), Mrs. Phagan (M)	B♭-d♭1/b♭-b♭1	slow
Big news, Britt Craig (T)	f-a♭1	mod. blues
*Funeral sequence**		
There is a fountain, chorus		slow hymn
It don't make sense, Frankie	d-a♭1	slow
Watson's lullaby, Tom (Bar)	A-a	ballad
Somthin' ain't right, Dorsey (Bar)	c#-f#1	mod. ballad
Read big news, Craig, ensemble	b♭-e♭2	honky tonk
You don't know this man, Lucille	b♭-e♭2	ballad
The Trial:		
People of Atlanta, company		mod. uptempo
Twenty miles from Marietta, Dorsey	c1-e♭2	uptempo
Frankie's testimony, company		mod. uptempo
The factory girls/Come up to my office, girls' trio, Leo	SMM/G♭-f1	slow, then fast
Newt Lee's testimony, ensemble		uptempo
My child will forgive me, Mrs. Phagan	f#-a1	ballad
That's what he said, Conley (T), ensemble	d-g1	uptempo
It's hard to speak my heart, Leo	B-e1	ballad
Closing statement and verdict, ensemble		slow, then cakewalk
Opening, Act II, Craig	f-g1	mod. uptempo
Rumblin' and a rollin', quartet	MTTB	mod. uptempo
Do it alone, Lucille	a-d2	intense ballad
Pretty music, Stratton (Bar)	c-g1	mod. foxtrot
Judge Roan's letter, Roan (Bar)	E♭-d1	slow, then driving

This is not over yet, Leo, Lucille	d-f#1/a-d2	moving ballad
Factory girls reprise, trio	SMM	uptempo
Newt Lee reprise, Leo, Lucille; Newt incidental	d♭-f1/b♭-c2	uptempo
Blues: feel the rain, Conley, male chorus	d-b♭1	slow blues
Where will you stand when the flood comes?, trio, chorus	MMB	slow scene
All the wasted time, Leo, Lucille	B♭-f1/g-e♭2	mod. ballad
Sh'ma and finale, company		moving ballad

*These two songs sung separately, then combined.

Passion (1994)
Music and Lyrics by Stephen Sondheim

Song title, **Character (Voice)**	**Range**	**Song Style**
Happiness, Clara (S), Giorgio (Bar)	b♭-e2/A-d1	ballad
Happiness II, Clara, Giorgio	a-e2/A-d#1	ballad
First letter, Clara, Giorgio	f-e2/A-b*	moving ballad
Second letter, Clara, Giorgio		
Third letter, Clara, Giorgio, Soldiers (men's chorus)	2 solo Sol.: d-d1	
Fourth letter, Clara, Giorgio, Fosca (M)	Fosca: f-d2	
I do not read or think, Fosca, Giorgio incidental	f-d2	narrative ballad
How can I describe her, Giorgio, Fosca, Clara, Soldiers	c-d1/spoken/a♭-d♭2	mod. uptempo
Love that fills every waking moment, Clara, Giorgio	b-e2/a-e1	moving ballad
To speak to me of love, Fosca	a#-c#2	moving ballad
Fifth letter, Fosca, Giorgio, Clara, chorus	a-b/B-d1/b-d2	mod. ballad
I wish I could forget you, Fosca, Giorgio incidental	f-c2	slow ballad
Scene eight, Soldiers quintet	TBBBB	moderate
Flashback I, Colonel, Fosca, Mother, Father, Ludovic	SMTTB	slow ballad
Flashback II, Mistress (M)	g#-f2	mod. ballad
Flashback III, Ludovic (T)	c#-g1	mod. ballad
Flashback IV, Fosca, Colonel, Father, Mother, Ludovic, Mistress, others		ballad
Sunrise letter, Clara, Giorgio	a♭-e2/B♭-g1	mod. uptempo
Is this what you call love, Giorgio	A-f1	uptempo
Forty days, Clara	b♭-e2	mod. waltz
Loving you, Fosca	f#-c2	ballad
Giorgio, I didn't tell you, Clara	b♭-f2	mod. ballad
Christmas music, Torasso (T)	e♭-f1	uptempo, in 1
Scene 13, Clara, Giorgio	a-e2/A#-f1	mod. ballad

No one has ever loved me, Giorgio	B-d1	moving ballad
Finale: Your love will live in me, company		ballad

*Giorgio's and Clara's ranges are given once and apply to these four "Letters."

Peter Pan (1979)
Music by Mark Charlap and Jule Styne
Lyrics by Carolyn Leigh, Betty Comden, and Adolph Green

Song title, **Character (Voice)**	**Range**	**Song Style**
Tender shepherd, Mrs. Darling (M), Children	SSSM	mod. ballad
Crow, Peter Pan (M)	b♭-b♭1	uptempo
Neverland, Peter Pan	f-b♭1	ballad
I'm flying, Peter Pan, Children	a♭-b♭1	uptempo
Pirate's march, men's chorus		uptempo march
Hook's tango, Hook (T)	d-d1 (mostly spoken)	mod. tango ballad
Wendy, Peter, boys	a♭-g2	mod. uptempo
Tarantella, Hook, Pirates	e-e1 (mostly spoken)	mod. march
Grow up, Peter, boys	a-c2	mod. uptempo
Mysterious lady, Peter, Hook	f-a2/c-d♭1	ballad
Distant melody, Wendy (girl S)	a♭-b♭1	ballad
Captain Hook's waltz, Hook, Pirates	c-f1	quick waltz
Crow reprise, Peter, children	b♭-c2	mod. uptempo
Grow up reprise, company		mod. uptempo

Phantom (1991)
Music and Lyrics by Maury Yeston

Song title, **Character (Voice)**	**Range**	**Song Style**
Melody de Paris, Christine (S), chorus	c#1-a2	waltz ballad
Dressing for the night, company		uptempo
Where in the world, Phantom (T)	G-f1	slow ballad
This place is mine, Carlotta (S)	b♭-b♭2	uptempo
Home, Christine, Phantom	c1-a2/c-e1	moving ballad
Phantom fugue I, Phantom, Christine	e♭-g1/e♭1-g2	moving, vocalise
Phantom fugue II, company		mod. uptempo
You are music, Phantom, Christine	e♭-g1/e♭1-b♭2	ballad
The bistro/Melody de Paris reprise, Carlotta, Christine, chorus	c#1-e2/c#1-b2	uptempo
Who could ever have dreamed up you, Count (Bar), Christine	B♭-e♭1/b♭-e♭2	ballad

This place is mine reprise, Carlotta	d1-d2	mod. uptempo
Titania, Oberon (T), chorus	d-g1	moderate
Without your music, Phantom	c-f#1	mod. ballad
Where in the world reprise, Phantom	B♭-e♭1	mod. uptempo
The story of Eric, Carriere (Bar) (mostly spoken), Balladora (S), Young Eric (boy), chorus	G-a1/e1-g2/e1-c2	narrative ballad, anthem-like
My true love, Christine	c1-g2	ballad
My mother bore me, Phantom	c#-f#1	slow ballad
You are my own, Carriere, Young Eric	G-e1/g-e2	ballad

The Phantom of the Opera (1988)

Music by Andrew Lloyd Webber   Lyrics by Charles Hart and Richard Stilgoe

Song title, Character (Voice)	Range	Song Style
Opening scene, company		scene
Think of me, Carlotta (S), Raul (Bar)	d-g#2/e-g1	ballad
Angel of music, Meg (M), Christine (S)	b-d2/b-f2	moving ballad
Little Lotte/The mirror, Raul, Christine, Phantom (T) incidental	c#-d1/d1-f#2	moving ballad
The phantom of the opera, Christine, Phantom, chorus	g-e3/B-g1	mod. uptempo
The music of the night, Phantom	G#-g#1	ballad
I remember/Stranger than you dreamt it, Christine, Phantom	d1-e2/d-f#1	uptempo
Notes/Prima donna, company		uptempo
Il muto, company		uptempo
Why have you brought me here?, Raul, Christine	B♭-e♭1/a-e♭2	mod. uptempo
Raul, I've been there, Christine	b-a♭2	mod. ballad
All I ask of you, Raul, Christine	A♭-g1/a♭-a♭2	ballad
Masquerade, company		uptempo
Why so silent?, Phantom	e♭-g♭1	slow
Notes no. 2, quartet	STTB	uptempo
Twisted every way, Christine, Raul, company	b♭-e♭2/B♭-d1	slow
Wishing you were somehow here again, Christine	a-g2	ballad
Wandering child, trio	STB	moving ballad
Don Juan scene, Carlotta, company	a-a2	uptempo
Past the point of no return, Phantom, Christine	c-a1/c-g2	mod. uptempo
Down once more/Track down this murderer, company		scene

Pins and Needles (1937)
Music and Lyrics by Harold Rome

Song title, Character (Voice)	Range*	Song Style
Sing me a song with social significance	c1-f2	anthem ballad
Room for one (S)	b-c2	character ballad
Cream of mush song (Bar)	c1-e2	waltz ballad
One big union for two (Bar) (M)	B♭-c2/c1-e2	moving ballad
Mene, mene, tekel	c1-d2	character
What good is love	c1-d2	ballad
I'm just nuts about you	c1-d2	fast character
Four little angels of peace	e♭1-e♭2	ballad
Chain store daisy	c1-d2	narrative ballad
Back to work, unison chorus		uptempo
It's better with a union man	d1-e2	fast character
I've got the nerve to be in love	b♭-c2	ballad
Not cricket to picket	b♭-d2	uptempo
Sunday in the park	c1-e2	ballad
When I grow up (The G-man song) (Bar)	c1-d2	uptempo
Nobody makes a pass at me (S)	c1-f2	funny ballad
(Sitting on you) Status quo, solo, chorus	a-c2	swing ballad
Doing the reactionary	c1-e♭2	uptempo
We sing America, chorus, many soli		anthem ballad

*All ranges are given as notated in the score. Most numbers lack character names in the scores; when one is listed, that character is indicated here.

Pipe Dream (1955)
Music by Richard Rodgers   Lyrics by Oscar Hammerstein II

Song title, Character (Voice)	Range	Song Style
All kinds of people, Doc (T), Hazel (S)	e♭-e♭1/e♭1-e♭2	uptempo
The tide pool, Hazel, Doc, Mac (T)	c#1-f#2/e-f#1/d-f#1	character
Everybody's got a home but me, Suzy (M)	g-b1	ballad
On a lopsided bus, Mac, male chorus	f-f1	uptempo
Bum's opera, Joe (Bar), chorus	e♭-e♭1	uptempo
On a lopsided bus reprise, chorus		moving ballad
Sweet Thursday, Fauna (M)	c1-f2	uptempo
Suzy is a good thing, Fauna, Suzy	both d♭-d2	ballad
All at once you love her, Esteban (T), Doc, Suzy	e-f#1/A♭-c1/a♭-b♭1	ballad
The happiest house on the block, Fauna, girls	e1-f#2	moving ballad
The party that we're gonna have tomorrow night, company		uptempo
We are a gang of witches, women's chorus		character

Will you marry me?, Suzy, Fauna	both b♭-c2	ballad
Thinkin', Hazel	c#1-e2	mod. ballad
Serenade, Esteban	e-f#1	ballad
All at once . . . reprise, Fauna	a♭-b♭1	ballad
How long?, company		uptempo
The next time it happens, Suzy	a-e2	uptempo
Finale: Lopsided bus reprise, company		uptempo

Pippin (1972)
Music and Lyrics by Stephen Schwartz

Song title, Character (Voice)	Range	Song Style
Magic to do, Leading Player (T), company	e-f#1	uptempo
Corner of the sky, Pippin (T)	e-g1 (c2 in falsetto)	moving ballad
War is a science, Charles (Bar), Pippin, chorus	B♭-e1/g-g1	mod. character
Glory, company		mod. uptempo
Simple joys, Leading Player	e f#1	uptempo
No time at all, Berthe (M), male ensemble	f#-a1	uptempo
With you, Pippin	c-a2	ballad
Spread a little sunshine, Fastrada (M)	a-d2	mod. ballad
Morning glow, Pippin, chorus	d♭-g♭1	anthem ballad
Right track, Leading Player, Pippin	both e♭-a♭1	jazzy uptempo
Kind of woman, Catherine (M), girls incidental	g♭-d♭2	ballad
Extraordinary, Pippin	c-f1	uptempo
Prayer for a duck, Pippin	d-f#1	slow, funny
Love song, Pippin, Catherine	d♭-e♭1/c1-g2	ballad
I guess I'll miss the man, Catherine	f#-g1	ballad
Finale: Think about your life, company, Pippin	a-g1	fast, driving, then slower

The Pirates of Penzance (1981)
Music by Arthur Sullivan   Lyrics by W.S. Gilbert

Song title, Character (Voice)	Range	Song Style
Pour, o pour the pirate sherry, Samuel (B), chorus	B♭-d	uptempo
When Frederic was a little lad, Ruth (M)	g-b♭1	jaunty ballad
Oh, better far to live and die, Pirate King (Bar), Pirates (men's chorus)	B-d1	character
Oh, false one, you have deceived me!, Frederic (T), Ruth	B-g1/a-e2	ballad

Song	Range	Style
Climbing over rocky mountains, Edith (S), Kate (S), women's chorus	b♭-f2/e♭-f2	uptempo
Oh, is there not one maiden breast, Frederic, Mabel (S), women	f-g♭1 (opt. b♭1)/ e♭1-b♭2	ballad
Poor wandering one!, Mabel, women's chorus	e♭1-b♭2	moving ballad
How beautifully blue the sky, Mabel, Frederic, women's chorus	f#1-b2/d-g1	fast chorus; solos slower
Stay, we must not lose our senses, chorus		uptempo
Hold, monsters!, ensemble		character
I am the very model of a modern major-general, Major General (Bar), Pirates	B♭-c1	character; patter
Oh, men of dark and dismal fate, company		uptempo
Oh, dry the glistening tear, Mabel, women	f1-g♭2	ballad
When the foeman bares his steel, company		mod. uptempo
When you had left our pirate fold, Ruth, Frederic, Pirate King	a-f#2/f#-f#1/F#-d#1	uptempo
Away! Away! My heart's on fire, Ruth, Pirate King, Frederic	b-f#2/B-d1/a-a1	uptempo
Stay, Frederic, stay!, Mabel, Frederic	d1-b♭2/d-g1	uptempo
When a felon's not engaged in his employment, Sergeant (Bar), men	c-c1	character
With cat-like tread, upon our prey we steal, company, many soli		slow march
Sighing softly to the river, company		uptempo

Note: Ranges taken from score of the operetta.

Plain and Fancy (1955)

Music by Albert Hague   Lyrics by Arnold Horwitt

Song title, Character (Voice)	Range	Song Style
You can't miss it, Dan (T), Ruth (M), chorus	B-c1/a♭-c2	uptempo
It wonders me, Katie (S), chorus	b♭-b♭2	ballad
Plenty of Pennsylvania, Emma (M), chorus	f-b♭1	uptempo
Young and foolish, Peter (Bar)	c#-e1	ballad
Why not Katie?, Ezra (Bar), male ensemble	B♭-d1	ballad, then faster
Young and foolish reprise, Peter, Katie	d-f1/d♭1-a♭2	ballad
It's a helluva way to run a love affair, Ruth	g-c2	uptempo
This is all very new to me, Hilda (S), girls	b-e2	mod. ballad
Plain we live, Papa Yoder (Bar), Amish men	B-e1 (opt. g1)	anthem ballad
Plain we live reprise, company		mod. ballad
How do you raise a barn, company		uptempo
Follow your heart, Peter, Katie, Hilda	B-f#1/b-f#2/b-g2	ballad
City mouse, country mouse, Emma, girls	f-b1	fast character
I'll show him, Hilda	b♭-f2	uptempo, angry

Take your time and take your pick, Ruth, Dan, Hilda	g-c2/G-d1/c1-f2	mod. ballad
Finale: It wonders me, company		mod. ballad

Porgy and Bess (1935)

Music by George Gershwin — Lyrics by Dubose Heyward and Ira Gershwin

Song title, Character (Voice)	**Range**	**Song Style**
Jasbo Brown blues, scat chorus		mod. uptempo
Summertime, Clara (S)	f#1-f#2	ballad
A woman is a sometime thing, Jake (Bar)	d-d1	mod. uptempo
Here come de honey man, chorus		uptempo
They pass by singin', Porgy (Bar)	B-d1	ballad
Dice scene: Oh little stars, company		uptempo
Gone, gone, gone/Overflow, company		spiritual
My man's gone now, Serena (S)	e1-b2	ballad
Leavin' for the promise' land, Bess (S), chorus	f1-f2	gospel spiritual
It take a long pull to get there, Jake, chorus	e-e1	gospel ballad
I got plenty o' nuttin', Porgy, chorus	B-d1	uptempo
Bess, you is my woman, Porgy, Bess	B-c1/c#1-a#2	ballad
Oh, I can't sit down, chorus		uptempo
I ain't got no shame, chorus		uptempo
It ain't necessarily so, Sporting Life (T), chorus	d-gb1	uptempo
What you want wid Bess?, Bess, Crown (T)	f#1-a2/f-f1 (opt. gb)	dramatic ballad
I loves you, Porgy, Bess, Porgy	d1-a2/db-db1	dramatic ballad
Oh, hev'nly father/Oh, de Lawd shake de heavens/Oh, dere's somebody knockin' at de do', chorus, many soli		mod. to quick
A red-headed woman, Crown, chorus	db-gb1	character
There's a boat dat's leavin' soon for New York, Sporting Life	d-bb1	uptempo
Good mornin', sistuh!, chorus		uptempo
Oh, Bess, oh where's my Bess, Porgy, Serena, Maria (M)	c#-e#1/g#1-g#2/b-c2	ballad
Oh Lawd, I'm on my way, Porgy, chorus	e-e1	uptempo gospel

Note: The music is continuous; the reader may discover additional soli or ensembles to excerpt.

The Producers (2000)
Music and Lyrics by Mel Brooks

Song title, **Character (Voice)**	**Range**	**Song Style**
It's opening night, company		uptempo
The king of Broadway, Max (Bar), chorus	c-e1	mod. uptempo
We can do it, Max, Leo (Bar)	B♭-e♭1/B♭-e#1	mod. uptempo
I wanna be a producer, Leo, chorus	A-f1	uptempo
We can do it reprise, Max, Leo	B♭-e♭1/d-f1	uptempo
In old Bavaria, Franz (B)	F-d2	character ballad
Der guten tag hop-clop, Franz; Max and Leo incidental	d-f1	mod. waltz
Keep it gay, company		uptempo
When you've got it, flaunt it, Ulla (M)	a-e♭2	character ballad
Along came Bialy, Max, company	B♭-e♭1	uptempo
That face!, Leo, Ulla	B-f1/b♭-c2	flowing ballad
Have you ever heard the German band?, Franz	A-g1	march uptempo
It's opening night reprise, 2 Usherettes	both b♭-c2	uptempo
It's bad luck to say good luck on opening night, company		uptempo
Springtime for Hitler, company		uptempo
Where did we go right?, Max, Leo	A-d1/B-f#1	moderate
Leo goes to Rio, Leo, Ulla incidental	c-e1	mod. samba
Betrayed!, Max	A-f#1	uptempo
'Til him, Leo, Max, women's chorus	c-f1/B-e1	mod. ballad
Prisoners of love, company		uptempo
Goodbye!, company		uptempo

Promises, Promises (1968)
Music by Burt Bacharach   Lyrics by Hal David

Song title, **Character (Voice)**	**Range**	**Song Style**
Half as big as life, Chuck (Bar)	B♭-e♭	mod. uptempo
Grapes of Roth, unison scat chorus		uptempo
Upstairs, Chuck	c-f1	mod. uptempo
You'll think of someone, Fran (M), Chuck	b-a1/b-e1	ballad
It's our little secret, Chuck, Sheldrake (Bar)	B♭-f1/c-e1	uptempo
She likes basketball, Chuck	B-d1	waltz ballad
Knowing when to leave, Fran	a-c2	driving uptempo
Where can you take a girl, Dobitch (Bar), chorus	d-d1	uptempo
Wanting things, Sheldrake	c-d1	ballad
Christmas party/Turkey lurkey time, chorus		uptempo
A fact can be a beautiful thing, Marge (M), Chuck, chorus	a-d2/a-d1	mod. ballad

Whoever you are, I love you, Fran	g-b1	ballad
Christmas day, chorus		mod. uptempo
A young pretty girl like you, Doctor (T), Chuck	b♭-g1/b♭-d1	mod. ballad
I'll never fall in love again, Fran, Chuck	b-b1/c#-d1	moving ballad
Promises, promises, Chuck	A-e1	uptempo
Bows: Christmas party, company		uptempo

Ragtime (1998)

Music by Stephen Flaherty   Lyrics by Lynn Ahrens

Song title, Character (Voice)	Range	Song Style
Ragtime, company		mod. uptempo
Goodbye, my love, Mother (M)	g-d♭2	ballad
Journey on, Father (Bar), Tateh (Bar), Mother	MBB	mod. ballad
The crime of the century, Evelyn (M), ensemble	b♭-d2	sassy ragtime
What kind of woman, Mother	b♭-e♭2	stirring ballad
A shtetl iz Amereke, company		slow
Success, Tateh, company	c-f#1	mod. uptempo
His name was Coalhouse Walker, chorus		mod. uptempo
The gettin' ready rag, Coalhouse (T), chorus	c-d1 (mostly spoken)	mod. ragtime
Henry Ford, Ford (T), chorus, Coalhouse incidental	d-f#1	uptempo
Nothing like the city, ensemble		ballad
Your daddy's son, Sarah (M)	g-f2	ballad
The courtship, company		mod. ballad
New music, company		mod. ballad
The wheels of a dream, Coalhouse, Sarah	A♭-f♭1/e♭1-e♭2	ballad
The night that Goldman spoke at Union Square, Younger Brother (T), Emma (M), chorus	B-f#1/b-d♭2	mod. uptempo
Gliding, Tateh	A-f#1	moving ballad
Justice, Coalhouse, Sarah	d-f1/a♭-c2	mod. uptempo
President, Sarah	a-d2	moving ballad
Till we reach that day, company		stirring ballad
Harry Houdini, master escapist, Houdini (T)	d♭-g♭1	mod. uptempo
Coalhouse's soliloquy, Coalhouse, company	G-f1	uptempo
What a game!, Father, Little Boy, male chorus	c-e♭1	uptempo
Atlantic City, Evelyn, Father, Houdini, chorus	MTT	mod. uptempo
Buffalo nickel photo play, inc., Tateh	B-f#1	uptempo
Our children, Mother, Tateh	a-d2/a-e1	moving ballad

Sarah Brown eyes, Coalhouse, Sarah	A-e1/a-e2	ballad
He wanted to stay, Emma, Young Boy, Coalhouse, male chorus	MTT	mod. uptempo
Back to before, Mother, offstage women's chorus	g-c#2	moving ballad
Look what you've done, company		mod. uptempo
Make them hear you, Coalhouse	eb-g#1	mod., then fast
Ragtime reprise, company		uptempo

Raisin (1973)

Music by Judd Woldin   Lyrics by Robert Brittan

Song title, Character (Voice)	Range	Song Style
Man say, Walter (Bar)	B-a1	uptempo
Angry man, Ruth (M)	c1-e2	mod. ballad
Runnin' to meet the man, Walter, chorus	d-a1	mod. uptempo
A whole lotta sunlight, Mama (M)	ab-cb2	ballad
Booze, company		uptempo
Alaiyo, Asagai (Bar), Beneatha (M)	Bb-eb1/bb-d2	ballad
African dance, chorus		uptempo
Sweet time, Ruth, Walter	g#-e2/c#-f#1	ballad
You done right, Walter	B-e1	mod. uptempo
He come down, company		mod. uptempo
It's a deal, Walter	B-f1	uptempo
Sweet time reprise, Ruth, Walter	g-eb1/G-g1	ballad
Sidewalk tree, Travis (Bar)	B-d#1	uptempo
Not anymore, trio, chorus	MMB	gospel uptempo
Alaiyo reprise, Asagai	Bb-g1	mod. ballad
It's a deal reprise, Walter	spoken	uptempo
Measure the valleys, Mama	g-c2	ballad

The Red Mill (1906)

Music by Victor Herbert   Lyrics by Henry Blossom

Song title, Character (Voice)	Range	Song Style
Opening chorus, chorus		uptempo
Mignonette, Tina (M), women's chorus	d1-f2	uptempo march
You can never tell about a woman, Burgomaster (Bar), Willem (Bar)*	both c-d1	mod. ballad, funny
Whistle it, Tina, Kid (Bar), Con (Bar)*	c1-c2/men c-c1	funny ballad
A widow has ways, Bertha (M)	b-e2	waltz ballad
The isle of our dreams, Capt. Doris (Bar), Gretchen (M)	d-e1/d1-f#2	ballad
Go while the goin' is good, company		mod. ballad

Ensemble, company		uptempo
The day is gone, Gretchen, company	c1-f2	ballad
Why this silence?, chorus		uptempo
The legend of the mill, Bertha, chorus	c1-e2	narrative ballad
Good-a-bye, John, Kid, Con (done w/ accent)	both e-d1	uptempo
I want you to marry me, Tina, chorus incidental	c#1-e2	waltz ballad
Every day is ladies' day with me, Governor (Bar), men's chorus	c-eb1	uptempo march
Because you're you, Berthe, Governor	d1-d2/d-d1	ballad
The streets of New York, Kid, Con	unison, f-f1	waltz ballad
Entrance of wedding guests, chorus		stately ballad
In old New York, company in unison		mod. uptempo

Added Song:

If you love but me, Tina, chorus	b-d2	mod. uptempo

*Either number could also work as a solo—they present two sides of the same story—and would also work well sung as a duet.

Redhead (1959)

Music by Albert Hague   Lyrics by Dorothy Fields

Song title, **Character (Voice)**	**Range**	**Song Style**
The Simpson sisters, chorus		mod. uptempo
The right finger of my left hand, Essie (M)	g-a1	character
Just for once, ensemble		mod. uptempo
I feel very marvelous, Essie	ab-bb1	uptempo
Uncle Sam rag, chorus		quick ragtime
'Erbie Fitch's dilemma, Essie	g-bb1	uptempo
She's not woman enough for me, George (T), Tom (Bar)	c-f1/c-e1	ballad, funny
Behave yourself, Sarah (M), Maude (M)	both a-e2	uptempo
Look who's in love, Tom, Essie	A-c1/a-bb1	ballad
My girl is just woman enough for me, Tom, chorus incidental	c-e1	ballad
Two faces in the dark, chorus		ballad
I'm back in circulation, Tom	B-d1	uptempo
We loves ya, Jimey, chorus		uptempo
Look who's in love reprise, Tom	c-e1	ballad
I'll try, Tom, Essie	A-d1/a-a1	moving ballad
Finale: Look who's in love, company		ballad

Rent (1996)
Music and Lyrics by Jonathan Larson

Song title, Character (Voice)	Range	Song Style
Tune up A, Mark (T), Roger (Bar)	e-g1/a-e1	scene
Voice mail no. 1, Mom (M)	c-d1	recitative
Tune up B, company		scene
Rent, company		mod. uptempo
You OK, honey, Angel (T), Collins (Bar)	b♭-g♭1/G-f1	moderate
One song glory, Roger	d♭-a♭1	ballad
Light my candle, Roger, Mimi (M)	e♭-g1/e♭-c2	ballad
Voice mail no. 2, Mr. Jefferson (B)	c-c1	recitative
Today for you, quartet	TTBB	mod. uptempo
You'll see, ensemble		moderate
Tango Maureen, Mark, Joanne (M)	c-fd#1/f#-d2	uptempo
Support group, company		moderate
Out tonight, Mimi	a-e2	mod. uptempo
Another day, Roger, Mimi, chorus	e♭-g♭1/b-c#2	mod. ballad
Will I?, company		ballad
On the street, company		scene
Santa Fe, trio	TTB	mod. uptempo
I'll cover you, Angel, Collins	d-a1/c-g1	ballad
We're OK, Joanne	c-d2	moderate
Christmas bells, company		mod. ballad
Over the moon, Maureen (M), chorus	c1-e♭2	mod. uptempo
La vie boheme, company*		uptempo
I should tell you, Mimi, Roger*	g-b1/B♭-g1	ballad
Seasons of love A, company		ballad
Happy New Year A, company		mod. ballad
Voice mail no. 3, Mrs. Cohen (M)	c1-e2	recitative
Voice mail no. 4, Alexi (S)	b♭1-b♭2	recitative
Happy New Year B, company		scene
Take me or leave me, Maureen, Joanne	c1-f2/c1-e2	uptempo
Seasons of love B, chorus		ballad
Without you, Mimi, Roger	f#-b2/F#-f#1	ballad
Voice mail no. 5, Alexi	b1-b2	recitative
Contact, company		uptempo
I'll cover you reprise, Collins, chorus	F#-a1	ballad
Halloween, Mark	e♭-e♭1	ballad
Goodbye love, company		ballad
What you own, Mark, Roger	d-f1/d-a1	uptempo
Voice mail no. 6, quartet	MMMB	recitative
Finale A, company		moderate
Your eyes, Roger	B-g1	ballad
Finale B, company		mod. uptempo

*These two songs are sung together.

Note: Mimi and Joanne are notated in the score an octave higher than sung.

The Rink (1984)

Music by John Kander   Lyrics by Fred Ebb

Song title, **Character (Voice)**	**Range**	**Song Style**
Colored lights, Angel (M)	a-c2	ballad
Chief cook and bottle washer, Anna (M)	e♭-b♭1	uptempo
Don't ah ma me, Anna, Angel	f-b♭1/a♭-c2	uptempo
Blue crystal, Dino (T)	A-f#1	mod. ballad
Under the roller coaster ("Familiar things"), Angel	a#-a1	mod. ballad
Not enough magic, ensemble		mod. uptempo
We can make it, Anna	e♭-b♭1	ballad
After all these years, The Wreckers (male sextet)	TTTBBB	fast, easy two
Angel's rink and social center, Angel, Wreckers	g♭-c2	mod. uptempo
What happened to the old days?, Anna, Mrs. Silverman (S), Mrs. Jackson (S)	b♭-c2/b♭-g2/b♭-g2	mod. ballad
Colored lights reprise, Angel	a-c2	ballad
The apple doesn't fall, Anna, Angel	e-c2/e-c2	uptempo, funny
Marry me, Lenny (T)	c#-e1	ballad
We can make it reprise, Anna	d-a1	ballad
Mrs. A, Anna, Angel; Suitors (T, T), Lenny incidental	a♭-c2/b♭-c2/Suitors both B-f#1	uptempo
The rink, Wreckers	all f#-a1 or d#-f1	mod. uptempo
Wallflower, Anna, Angel	f-c2/g-a1	mod. ballad
All the children in a row, Angel, Danny (Bar) incidental	f#-c2/e♭-c1	ballad

The Roar of the Greasepaint—
The Smell of the Crowd (1965)

Music and Lyrics by Leslie Bricusse and Anthony Newley

Song title, **Character (Voice)**	**Range**	**Song Style**
Beautiful land, company, many soli		mod. uptempo
A wonderful day like today, Sir (Bar), Cocky (T), Urchins (chorus)	B♭-g1/B♭-e♭1	uptempo
It isn't enough, Cocky, Urchins	A-f1	mod. ballad
Things to remember, Sir, Kid (boy S), Urchins	A-e♭1/a#-c#2	uptempo waltz
Put it in the book, Kid, Urchins	d#1-b1	mod. uptempo
This dream, Cocky	A-f#1	ballad
Where would you be without me, Sir, Cocky	B-f1/c-f1	uptempo
Look at that face, Sir, Kid, Urchins	B-e♭1/f#-d2/c-f1	uptempo

My first love song, Cocky, Girl (M)	c-g1/bb-f2	mod. ballad
The joker, Cocky	d-g1 (opt. a1)	uptempo
Who can I turn to?, Cocky, Urchins incidental	Gb-g1	moving ballad
A very funny funeral/That's what it is to be young, Urchins		mod. uptempo
What a man, Cocky, Urchins	e-eb1	uptempo
Feeling good, Negro (T), Urchins incidental	d-ab1	ballad
Nothing can stop me now, Cocky, Urchins	Bb-g#1	uptempo
Things to remember reprise, Sir	c-d1	moving ballad
My way, Cocky, Sir	c-f1/c-d1	mod. uptempo
Who can I turn to reprise, Sir	G-e1	ballad
Beautiful land reprise, Urchins		mod. uptempo
Sweet beginning, Cocky, Sir, company	c-f#1/d-g#1	mod. uptempo

The Robber Bridegroom (1976)

Music by Alfred Uhry   Lyrics by Robert Waldman

Song title, **Character (Voice)**	**Range**	**Song Style**
Once upon the Natchez Trace, Jamie (T), company	d-g#1	uptempo
Two heads, Big Harp (Bar), Little Harp (T), ensemble	both e-e1	mod. ballad
Steal with style, Jamie, chorus	B-g1	uptempo
Hell among the yearlings, Salome (M)	spoken	square-dance
Rosamund's dream, Rosamund (M), Jamie incidental	bb-eb1	ballad
Prickle pear and lilybud, Salome, chorus incidental	b-d2	fast character
Soldier's joy, Salome, chorus	spoken	march tempo
Ain't nothin' up, Rosamund, chorus	c1-e2	ballad
Cluck old hen, chorus	spoken	uptempo
Deeper in the wood, chorus, many soli		ballad
Flop-eared mule, chorus	spoken	mod. uptempo
Marriage is riches, company		moving ballad
Little piece of sugarcane, chorus	humming	slow ballad
Love stolen, Jamie, chorus incidental	c-g1	moving ballad
Poor tied up darlin', Little Harp, Goat (T)	d-g1/g-c2	uptempo
Goodbye, Salome, company		uptempo
Sleepy man, Rosamund, chorus	d1-f2	ballad
Where, oh where, Jamie, company	d-g#1	uptempo
Richmond cotillion, Preacher	spoken	uptempo
Finale/Bows: Goodbye, Salome, company		uptempo

Roberta (1933)

Music by Jerome Kern   Lyrics by Otto Harbach

Song title, Character (Voice)	Range	Song Style
Let's begin, unison male quartet	e♭-e♭1	uptempo
Madrigal, John (Bar), men's chorus	B#-e1	uptempo
You're devastating, Huck (T)	B♭-f1	ballad
You're devastating reprise, Stephanie (M)	g-d2	ballad
Yesterdays, Minnie (S)	c-g2	ballad
Something bad had to happen, Schwarenka (M)	a-f2	moving ballad
You're devastating reprise, Stephanie	g-d2	ballad
The touch of your hand, Stephanie, Ladislaw (T)	b-c2/e-a1	mod. ballad
I'll be hard to handle, Schwarenka	b♭-d2	ballad, funny
Hot spot, Schwarenka	b-c2	mod. character
Smoke gets in your eyes, Stephanie	a♭-f2	ballad
Let's begin reprise, Huck, Stephanie	e♭-d1/e♭1-d2	uptempo
Something bad had to happen reprise, John	G-e♭1	moving ballad
Don't ask me not to sing, company		uptempo
The touch of your hand reprise, Stephanie, Ladislaw	b-c2/e-a1	ballad
Finale, company		uptempo

Robin Hood (1891)

Music by Reginald de Koven   Lyrics by Harry B. Smith

Song title, Character (Voice)	Range	Song Style
Holla, holla, company		uptempo
Auctioneer's song, Outlaws, chorus	MBBB	uptempo
Milkmaid's song, Annabel (S), Allan a Dale (M), women's chorus	g1-a2/d1-f2	mod. ballad
Come the bowmen in Lincoln Green, Robin (T), Outlaws, chorus	f-g1	uptempo
Though it was within this hour, Robin, Marian (S)	g-g1/g1-b2	ballad
I am the Sheriff of Nottingham, Sheriff (Bar), Sir Guy (T), chorus	c-d1/f#-g1	uptempo
When a peer makes love, Sheriff, Sir Guy, Marian	d-e1/d-a1/e1-b♭2	uptempo
Come the bowmen . . . reprise, company		uptempo
Finale act I, company		uptempo
Oh, cheerily sounds the hunter's horn, Outlaws, men's chorus		uptempo
Song of brown October ale, Little John (Bar), men's chorus	e♭-e♭1	uptempo

Oh promise me, Marian	d1-e2 (opt. g2)	ballad
Tinker's song, Sir Guy, Sheriff, Tinkers (chorus)	unison d-g1	fast character
Oh see the little lambkins play, Robin, Outlaws	TTBBBB	uptempo
Forest song, Marian	f#1-b2 (opt. d3)	ballad
A troubadour sang to his love, Robin, Marian, others incidental	e-a1/b♭-b♭1	ballad
Let us put him in the stocks, Outlaws		waltz uptempo
Armorer's song, Will Scarlet (B)	G-d1 (opt. D)	mod. uptempo
When a maiden weds, Annabel	d1-g2	light ballad
The legend of the chimes, Allan, chorus	c-f1	narrative ballad
There will come a time, Robin, Marian	e♭-b♭1/e1-b♭2	ballad
When life seems made of pains and pangs, ensemble	SSTBB	uptempo
Country dance, company		uptempo

Romance/Romance (1988)

Music by Keith Herrmann   Lyrics by Barry Harman

Song title, Character (Voice)	**Range**	**Song Style**
The little comedy, Alfred (T), Josefine (M)	d♭-f1/d♭1-e♭2	waltz ballad
Goodbye, Emil, Josefine	b♭-f2	mod. bal., funny
It's not too late, Alfred, Josefine	B♭-f1/a♭-e♭2	mod. ballad
Great news, Alfred, Josefine	f#-f#1/c#1-d#2	uptempo
Oh what a performance, Alfred, Josefine	c-f#1/g-d#2	mod. uptempo
Happy, happy, happy, Alfred	B♭-f#1	ballad
Women of Vienna, Alfred	c#-f#1	moving ballad
Yes, it's love, Josefine	a♭-c2	uptempo waltz
A rustic country inn, Alfred, Josefine	c-f1/a-e2	mod. uptempo
The night it had to end, Josefine	a♭-d♭2	ballad
The little comedy reprise, Alfred, Josefine	d♭-f1/c-c2	waltz ballad
Summer share, company	SMTB	uptempo
Think of the odds, Barb (S), Lenny (T)	b-e♭2/b-g1	uptempo
Let's not talk about it, Sam (T), Barb	b-e1/b-c2	ballad
So glad I married her, company	SMTB	mod. uptempo
Small craft warnings, Barb, Lenny	b-b♭1/B-c1	ballad
How did I end up here?, Monica (M)	g-c2	uptempo
Words he doesn't say, Sam	A♭-g♭1	ballad
My love for you, Lenny, Barb	B♭-g1/d-e♭2	ballad, funny
Moonlight passing through a window, Sam	d-f1	ballad
Now, Monica	a-d#2	uptempo
Romantic notions, Sam, company	A-e♭1	ballad
Romance! Romance!, company		uptempo

Note: The roles of Alfred/Sam and Josefine/Monica are played by the same two people.

Rose Marie (1924)

Music by Rudolph Friml and Herbert Stothart
Lyrics by Otto Harbach and Oscar Hammerstein II

Song title, Character (Voice)	Range	Song Style
Prelude and opening, Emile (T), chorus (some in French)	f#-g1	slow
Hard-boiled Herman, Herman (Bar), women's chorus	B♭-e♭1 (much spoken)	fast character
Rose Marie, Jim (T), Malone (T)	both e♭-g1	ballad
The mounties, Malone, men's chorus	e-f#1 (opt. a1)	uptempo march
Lak jeem, Rose Marie (S), men's chorus	c1-a2	uptempo
Rose Marie reprise, company		ballad
Indian love call, Rose Marie, Jim	c1-a2 (opt. b♭2)/c-f1	ballad
Pretty things, Rose Marie, chorus	d1-b♭2	moving ballad
Why shouldn't we?, Herman, Jane (M)	B-f1/b-f2	ballad
Totem tom-tom, Wanda (M), chorus	f1-f2	character ballad
Pretty things!, Ethel (M), women's chorus	c1-g2	uptempo
Only a kiss, Herman, Jane, Malone	d-f#1/e1-f#2/d-f#1	mostly uptempo
Sextet, Rose Marie, Jim, Hawley, Emile, Ethel, Wanda	SMMTTB	ballad
Minuet of the minute, Rose Marie, Herman, chorus	b-g#2/B-f#1	uptempo
Door of my dreams/Bridal finale, Rose Marie, chorus	e1-b♭2	ballad
Indian love song reprise, Jim, Rose Marie, company	c-d1/c1-f2	ballad

The Rothchilds (1970)

Music by Jerry Bock   Lyrics by Sheldon Harnick

Song title, Character (Voice)	Range	Song Style
Pleasure and privilege, Prince William (Bar), chorus	c-f1	mod. uptempo
One room, Gutele (M), Mayer (Bar)	b♭-c2/c-e1	mod. uptempo
The fair, Mayer, chorus incidental	c-e1	mod. ballad
Sons, Meyer, 4 sons, Gutele incidental	c-e1/sons all c-d1	uptempo
Everything, Gutele, sons	MBBBB	ballad
Rothschild and sons, Mayer, sons	c-e1	march uptempo
The French auction, Fouché (B), male chorus	B-f1	uptempo
Finale, Act I, Gutele, Mayer, sons	d-c1/f-d1/spoken	mod. uptempo
The English auction, Herries (Bar), Nathan (Bar), male chorus	d-e1/A-e1	hymn
I'm in love! I'm in love!, Nathan	d-d1	uptempo

I'm in love! reprise, Hannah (M), Nathan incidental	b-b1	uptempo
In my own lifetime, Mayer	A-d1	ballad
The congress auction, Metternich (Bar), chorus	G-e♭1	mod. uptempo
Bonds, company		mod. uptempo

Ruthless (1992)

Music by Marvin Laird   Lyrics by Joel Paley

Song title, Character (Voice)	Range	Song Style
Tina's mother, Judy (M)	g-g2	mod. uptempo
Born to entertain, Tina (S)	g-f♭2	mod. uptempo
Talent, Sylvia (M)	a-d2	uptempo
To play this part, Tina	f#-e2	mod. uptempo
Teaching third grade, Miss Thorn (M)	e♭-b1	moderate
Where Tina gets it from, Judy, Sylvia	b-e2/c#1-e2	ballad
The Pippi song, Tina	c1-c2	mod. uptempo
Kisses and hugs, Tina, Judy	b♭-d♭2/c1-c2	mod. ballad
Talent reprise, Sylvia	b♭-d2	uptempo
I hate musicals, Lita (M)	g-d2	uptempo
Angel mom (false start), Tina, Sylvia	b♭-b♭1/b-b♭1	moderate waltz
Angel mom, Judy, Tina	b-d2/d1-d2	moderate waltz
Montage, Judy, Tina	g-c♭2/g-c21	scene
Penthouse apartment, Sylvia	f#-c#2	jazzy uptempo
It can never be that way again, Ginger (M)	b-c#2	moderate
I want the girl, Sylvia	g-f2	uptempo
Parents and children, Judy, Tina	f-e2/g-c#2	uptempo
Ruthless, trio	SMM	uptempo
Talent reprise no. 2, Tina	a♭-d♭2	uptempo
Ruthless reprise, company		uptempo
I'll be an unkie's muncle, Ruth (M)*	f#-d2	uptempo

*Pre-recorded for show.

Sarah, Plain and Tall (2002)

Music by Laurence O'Keefe   Lyrics by Nell Benjamin

Song title, Character (Voice)	Range	Song Style
Lady of the house, Anna (M), Caleb (T)	g-d♭2/e-g1	mod. uptempo
The letter sequence, company		uptempo
Sarah, plain and tall, company		mod. uptempo
Would you miss me?, quartet	SMTB	mod. uptempo
Sixty cents, trio	TTB	uptempo

Make it through tonight (The dinner song), company		uptempo
Quartet, quartet	SMMT	mod. uptempo
Is it me you want to kiss?, Sarah (M)	b♭-c2	mod. ballad
Sing you to sleep, Anna, Jacob (Bar); Caleb incidental	b-e2/c-e♭1	ballad

Saturday Night Fever (1999)
Music and Lyrics by the Bee Gees

Song title, Character (Voice)	Range	Song Style
Stayin' alive, company		uptempo
Boogie shoes, men		mod. uptempo
Disco inferno, Monty (T), chorus	f#-b1	uptempo
Night fever, Tony (T), Annette (M), chorus	B-f1/f-e2	mod. uptempo
Disco duck, chorus		mod. uptempo
If I can't have you, women's chorus		ballad
More than a woman, Tony, Stephanie (M), chorus	f-e1/c1-c2	moving ballad
If I can't have you reprise, Annette, chorus	c1-d2	ballad
It's my neighbourhood, chorus		mod. uptempo
You should be dancin', Tony, chorus	c-g1	mod. uptempo
Jive talkin', Annette, chorus	a-c#1	mod. uptempo
More than a woman reprise, Stephanie	c#1-a1	ballad
Tragedy, Bobby (T), chorus	e-g#1	mod. uptempo
What kind of fool, Stephanie	b♭-d♭2	ballad
Nights on Broadway, Annette, Stephanie	d1-e♭2/e1-b1	ballad
Open sesame, chorus		mod. uptempo
More than a woman reprise 2, chorus		mod. uptempo
Immortality, Tony, chorus	d-g1	ballad
How deep is your love?, Tony, Stephanie, chorus	B♭-g1/e♭1-d2	moving ballad

The Scarlet Pimpernel (1997)
Music by Frank Wildhorn   Lyrics by Nan Knighton

Song title, Character (Voice)	Range	Song Style
Storybook, Marguerite (M), chorus	a♭-c2	uptempo
Madame Guillotine, Chauvelin (Bar), chorus; St. Cyr incidental	B-a♭1	uptempo
You are my home, Percy (T), Marguerite, chorus	B-g1/b-f#2	mod. ballad
Prayer, Percy	B♭-a♭1	ballad
Into the fire, Percy, male chorus	B-a♭1	uptempo

Falcon in the dive, Chauvelin	G#-g1	mod. uptempo
Scarlet Pimpernel transition, trio, women's chorus	SMT	uptempo
When I look at you, Marguerite	b-e2	ballad
When I look at you reprise, Percy, Marguerite	db-f1/db1-f2	ballad
Where's the girl?, Chauvelin	B-e1 (opt. g1)	mod. ballad
You are my home (garden reprise), Marguerite, Armand (Bar)	g#-c#2/g#-f#1	ballad
The creation of man, Percy, male ensemble	B-f#1	uptempo
The riddle part 1, trio	MTB	mod. uptempo
Who is the Scarlet Pimpernel?, Percy, Marguerite, chorus	c-f1/c1-d2	uptempo
They seek him here, company		uptempo
She was there, Percy	d#-g#1	ballad
Storybook reprise, Marguerite, women's chorus	b-e2	uptempo
Where's the girl reprise, Chauvelin	B-g1	ballad
Into the fire reprise, male ensemble		uptempo
I'll forget you, Marguerite, chorus	g#-db2	ballad
When I look at you, Percy, Marguerite, chorus	c-f1/eb-f2	mod. ballad
Into the fire (finale reprise), company		uptempo

The Secret Garden (1991)

Music by Lucy Simon   Lyrics by Marsha Norman

Song title, **Character (Voice)**	**Range**	**Song Style**
Opening: India, chorus		mod. uptempo
There's a girl/The house upon the hill, chorus		mod. ballad
I heard someone crying, Mary (girl S), Lily (S), Archie (T), chorus	c1-d2/d1-b2/d-eb1	moving ballad
If I had a fine white horse, Martha (M)	g-d2	narrative ballad
A girl in the valley, Lily, Archie	d1-d2/d-e1	ballad
It's a maze, Mary, Martha, Dickon (T), Ben (Bar)	cb1-c2/eb1-c2/cb-fb1/e-d1	uptempo
Winter's on the wing, Dickon	f#-f#1	uptempo
Show me the key, Mary, Dickon	c1-c#1/d-f1	mod. ballad
A bit of earth, Archie	db-gb1	dramatic ballad
Storm I, chorus		uptempo
Lily's eyes, Dr. Craven (Bar), Archie	c-f1/c-g1	ballad
Storm II, chorus		uptempo
Round-shouldered man, Colin (boy S), Mary	a-d1/bb-bb1	moving ballad
Final storm, company		uptempo
The girl I mean to be, Mary	bb-c2	ballad

Quartet, Craven, Archie, Rose (M), Lily	c-e♭1/c-a1/c1-d2/c1-a2	mod. ballad
Race you to the top of the morning, Archie	e♭-a♭1	narrative ballad
Wick, Dickon, Mary	f-f#1/b-d2	mod. uptempo
Come to my garden, Lily, Colin	c1-g2/c1-e2	ballad
Come spirit come charm, company		mod. uptempo
Disappear, Craven	c-f1	dramatic ballad
Hold on, Martha	f-b♭1	ballad
Where in the world, Archie	f-f1	uptempo
How could I ever know?, Lily, Archie	b♭-a1/d-f#1	ballad

See What I Wanna See (2005)
Music and Lyrics by Michael John LaChiusa

Song title, Character (Voice)	Range	Song Style
Kesa and Morito, Kesa (M)	g-e2	mod. uptempo
R. Shomon, Janitor (Bar)	B♭-d♭1	swing uptempo
The thief/She looked at me, Thief (T)	A-e1 (yodeled a1)	uptempo
See what I wanna see, Wife (M), Thief incidental	e#-d♭2	uptempo
Big money, Thief, Husband incidental	B♭-f#1	mod. uptempo
The park, Thief	A-f1	moderate
Best not to get involved, Janitor	B♭-e♭1	uptempo
Louie, Wife	g-e2	uptempo
The medium and the husband, Medium (M), Husband (B)	b♭-c2/B♭-e1	moderate
You'll go away with me, quartet	MMTB	uptempo
No more, Wife, quartet	g♭-f♭2/MMTB	ballad
Death, Husband, Medium	B♭-f1/f-b1	mod. uptempo
Light in the east, Janitor	B♭-e♭1	mod. uptempo
Finale, Act I, company		mod. uptempo
Kesa and Morito reprise, Morito (Bar)	G-e1	mod. uptempo
Confession/Last year, Priest (Bar), chorus	A-e1	uptempo
The greatest practical joke, Aunt Monica (M)	b♭-e♭1	uptempo
First message, Priest, trio	d-e1	moderate
Central Park, C.P.A. (T)	A-c2	uptempo
Second message, Priest, Actress (M)	d♭-f1/d1-d2	mod. ballad
Coffee, Actress	g-d2	mod. ballad
Glory day, Priest, chorus	g-g♭1	uptempo
Curiosity/Prayer, Reporter (T), trio	B-f#1/MTT	mod. ballad
Third message/Feed the lions, Priest	d-g♭1	uptempo
There will be a miracle, Aunt	a-c2	mod. ballad
Prayer reprise, trio	MTB	uptempo
Rising up/Finale, company		mod. uptempo

Seesaw (1973)

Music by Cy Coleman   Lyrics by Dorothy Fields

Song title, **Character (Voice)**	**Range**	**Song Style**
Seesaw, company		uptempo
My city, chorus		mod. uptempo
Nobody does it like me, Gittel (M)	g-ab1	mod. uptempo
In tune, Jerry (Bar), Gittel, chorus	Ab-c1/ab-c2	mod. uptempo
In tune reprise, soprano solo, chorus	eb2-c3	uptempo
Spanglish, company		uptempo
Welcome to the Holiday Inn, Gittel	db1-a1	mod. uptempo
You're a loveable lunatic, Jerry	c-c1	mod. ballad
He's good for me, Gittel	f#-bb1	ballad
Ride out the storm, chorus, many soli		uptempo
We've got it, Jerry	B-eb1	uptempo
Poor everybody else, Gittel*	g-bb1	mod. ballad
Salt, Jerry	f-eb1	uptempo
Salt II, Jerry, chorus*	f-f1	uptempo
It's not where you start it's where *you finish*, David (T), chorus	A-gb1	uptempo
Finale		
You're a loveable lunatic reprise, Gittel	ab-bb1	ends uptempo
I'm way ahead, Gittel	g#1-a3(+)	mod. ballad
Thank you, Jerry, Gittel	ab-bb1	mod. ballad
It's not where you start . . . reprise, company		uptempo

*These two numbers are combined after "Salt" is first sung.
+Range given here as in the score, but sung an octave lower.

Seussical (2000)

Music by Stephen Flaherty   Lyrics by Lynn Ahrens

Song title, **Character (Voice)**	**Range**	**Song Style**
Oh, the thinks you can think!, company		uptempo
Horton hears a Who!, Horton (B), company	A-e1	mod. uptempo
Biggest blamed fool, ensemble		driving uptempo
Here on Who, company		uptempo
Oh, the thinks reprise, Cat in the Hat (Bar)	c-e1	moderate
It's possible, JoJo (Bar), chorus	d-b1	mod. ballad
How to raise a child, Mr. Mayor (Bar), Mrs. Mayor (M)	d-e1/a-a1	uptempo
The military, Schmitz (Bar), company	B-f1	uptempo
Alone in the universe, Horton, JoJo	B-e1/ab-eb2	mod. ballad
The one feather tail of Ms. Gertrude McFuzz, Gertrude (M)	g-c2	character folk ballad
Amazing Mayzie, Mayzie (M), Gertrude, girls' trio	g#-d2/e-c2	Latin uptempo

Amazing Gertrude, Gertrude, others	b1-c#2	Latin uptempo
Monkey around, quartet	TTBB	mod. uptempo
Chasing the Whos, company		uptempo
How lucky you are, Cat in the Hat	d-f1	soft shoe ballad
Notice me, Horton, Gertrude, Horton	f#-f2/d-f1	flowing ballad
How lucky you are reprise, Mayzie, Cat in the Hat incidental	b♭-e2	blues ballad
Finales, company		uptempo
Our story resumes, company		scene
Egg, nest, and tree, company		uptempo
The Circus McGurkus, Cat in the Hat, chorus	d-d#1 (mostly spoken)	moderate
How lucky you are reprise, Horton, chorus	d-e1	uptempo
Mayzie in Palm Beach, Mayzie, Cat in the Hat	a-c2/spoken	mod. Latin uptempo
Amazing Horton, Mayzie	c#-c2	Latin uptempo
Alone in the universe reprise, Horton	c-c2	ballad
Solla sollew, Horton, company	c-e1	lullabye
Alone in the universe reprise, JoJo	d♭-b1	ballad
Havin' a hunch, Cat in the Hat, chorus	c#-d1	mod. uptempo
All for you, Gertrude, company	f-c2*	uptempo
The people versus Horton the Elephant, company		scene
Yopp!, company	mostly spoken	moderate
Alone in the universe reprise, Horton, Gertrude	e-e1/a-b1	mod. ballad
Oh, the thinks reprise, company		mod. uptempo
Green eggs and ham, company		military swing

*Also in the score a step higher.

Seven Brides for Seven Brothers (1982)
Music by Johnny Mercer, Al Kasha, and Joel Hirschhorn
Lyrics by Gene de Paul, Al Kasha, and Joel Hirschhorn

Song title, Character (Voice)	Range	Song Style
Bless your beautiful hide, Adam (Bar)	c-f1	mod. uptempo
Get a wife, 7 brothers		uptempo
Wonderful day, Milly (M), girls' trio	a♭-d♭2	mod. uptempo
I'm jumpin' in, Milly	a-b♭1	uptempo
One man, Milly	g-b♭1	ballad
I married seven brothers, Milly	g-a1	character
Goin' courtin', Milly, brothers	b♭-b♭1	mod. uptempo
Love never goes away, trio	MTB	mod. ballad
Sobbin' women, Adam, brothers	c-f#1	uptempo
Suitor's lament, company		mod. uptempo
A woman ought to know her place, Adam	e-f#1	mod. ballad

We gotta make it through the winter, brothers   uptempo
Lonesome polecat, brothers   country ballad
A woman ought to know . . . reprise, Adam,   both g♭-f1   ballad
   Gideon (T)
I'm glad that you were born, Milly, chorus   d♭-a♭1   ballad
   incidental
Wonderful day reprise, company   uptempo

1776 (1969)
Music and Lyrics by Sherman Edwards

Song title, **Character (Voice)**	**Range**	**Song Style**
For God's sake, John, sit down, Adams (T), Congress (men's chorus)	b♭-e♭1	slow waltz
Piddle, twiddle, Adams	d♭-e♭1	mod. uptempo
The Lees of old Virginia, Lee (T), Franklin (Bar), Adams	c-f#1/c-d1/a-d1	mod. uptempo
But, Mr. Adams, Adams, Franklin, Jefferson (T), Sherman (Bar), Livingston (Bar)	TTBBB	mod. ballad
Yours, yours, yours, Adams, Abigail (S)	d♭-f2/d♭-e♭1	ballad
He plays the violin, Martha (S), Franklin, Adams	b♭-d2/c-a/c-d1	waltz ballad
Cool, cool, considerate men, Dickinson (Bar), men's chorus	B♭-e1	slow ballad
Momma look sharp, Courier (T), two men	all B♭-d♭1	ballad
The egg, company		mod. uptempo
Molasses to rum, Rutledge (T)	e♭-a♭1	waltz ballad
Compliments, Abigail	e♭1-e♭2	mod. ballad
Is anybody there?, Adams, Franklin, Jefferson, Thompson (Bar)	c-e1/d-d1/c1-d1/e♭-e1	mod. uptempo

70, Girls, 70 (1971)
Music by John Kander   Lyrics by Fred Ebb

Song title, **Character (Voice)**	**Range**	**Song Style**
Old folks, company		mod. uptempo
Home, Ida (M), company		mod. ballad
Broadway, my street, Melba (M), Fritzi (M) chorus	g♭-b1/f#-f2	uptempo
The caper, Man (B)	c-e1	uptempo
Coffee in a cardboard cup, Fritzi, Melba	both f-d♭2	uptempo
You and I, ensemble		moderate
Do we, Walter (T), Eunice (S)	f#-g♭1/f#-g♭2	uptempo
Hit it, Lorraine, company		mod. uptempo

See the light, Gert (M), male chorus	f-c2	uptempo
Entracte, Act. II, company		uptempo
Boom ditty boom, company		mod. uptempo
Believe, Melba, company	a-b2	ballad
Go visit your grandmother, Eddie (T), Sadie (M)	d#-f#1/f#-e2	uptempo
70, girls, 70, company		mod. uptempo
The elephant song, Ida, company	f-b♭1	uptempo
Yes, Ida, company	a-g2	mod. uptempo

She Loves Me (1963)

Music by Jerry Bock   Lyrics by Sheldon Harnick

Song title, Character (Voice)	Range	Song Style
Good morning, good day, company		uptempo, light
Sounds while selling, company		mod. uptempo
Days gone by, Maraczek (Bar)	B♭-c1	mod. ballad
No more candy, Amalia (S)	d♭1-f♭2	ballad
Three letters, Amalia, Georg (T)	d1-e2/d-e1	mod. ballad
Tonight at eight, Georg	d-e1	uptempo
I don't know his name, Amalia, Ms. Ritter (M)	c#1-d#2/f#-d♭2	ballad
Perspective, Sipos (Bar)	A-d1	moving ballad
Goodbye, Georg, company		moderate
Will he like me, Amalia	d1-f#2	ballad
Ilona, Kodaly (T); Sipos, Arpad incidental	d-e1	beguine ballad
I resolve, Ritter	a-b♭1	uptempo march
A romantic atmosphere, Waiter (T), customers	c#-b2/spoken	slow character
Tango tragique, Georg	B-g1	tango ballad
Mr. Novak, will you please, Amalia	e1-f2	angry ballad
Dear friend, Amalia	d♭1-f2	ballad
Try me, Arpad (T)	B-e1	uptempo
Days gone by reprise, Maraczek	B-b♭1	ballad
Where's my shoe, Amalia, Georg	e1-g2/f-f1	uptempo waltz
Vanilla ice cream, Amalia	d1-b2	mod. uptempo
She loves me, Georg	e♭-f1	uptempo
A trip to the library, Ritter	g-c#2	uptempo bolero
Grand knowing you, Kodaly	d-a1	mod. uptempo
Twelve days to Christmas, chorus		uptempo
Vanilla reprise, Amalia, Georg	d1-e2/d-e1	mod. uptempo

Shenandoah (1975)

Music by Gary Geld   Lyrics by Peter Udell

Song title, **Character (Voice)**	**Range**	**Song Style**
Raise the flag, men's choruses		angry ballad
I've heard it all before, Charlie (Bar)	c-e1	mod. ballad
Pass the cross to me, chorus		ballad
Why am I me?, Boy (S), Gabriel (Bar)	a-d2/B♭-d1	bright ballad
Next to lovin' I like fightin' best, company		uptempo
Over the hill, Jenny (M)	c1-d2	waltz ballad
The pickers are comin', Charlie	A♭-e♭1	ballad
Next to lovin' . . . reprise, company		uptempo
Meditation I, Charlie	B♭-f1	narrative ballad
We make a beautiful pair, Anne (M), Jenny	g-c2/g-d2	ballad
Violets and silverbells, Sam (Bar), Jenny, chorus	G-b♭/g-b♭1	waltz ballad
It's a boy, Charlie	B♭-d1	uptempo
Freedom, Anne, Gabriel	g#-c#2/G#-e1	uptempo
Silverbells reprise, James (Bar), Anne	d-d1/b-d2	ballad
Papa's gonna make it alright, Charlie	A-c1	waltz ballad
The only home I know, Corporal (T), chorus	d-f1	ballad
Papa . . . reprise, Jenny	f#-a1	mod. waltz
Meditation II, Charlie	c-e1	reflective ballad
Pass the cross . . . reprise, company		mod. ballad

Show Boat (1927)

Music by Jerome Kern   Lyrics by Oscar Hammerstein II and P.G. Wodehouse

Song title, **Character (Voice)**	**Range**	**Song Style**
Opening: Cotton Blossom, company		mod. uptempo
Where's the mate for me?, Ravenal (T)	d-f#1	ballad
Make believe, Ravenal, Magnolia (S)	B-e1/c1-f2	ballad
Ol' man river, Joe (B), men's chorus	G-e1	ballad
Can't help lovin' dat man, Julie (S), Queenie (M); chorus, Joe incidental	b♭-f2/g-b♭1	ballad
Life upon the wicked stage, Ellie (M), women's chorus	b♭-f2	uptempo
Queenie's bally-hoo, Queenie	g-c2	character
You are love, Ravenal, Magnolia	d-f1/d1-f2	ballad
At the world's fair, chorus		uptempo
Why do I love you?, Magnolia, Ravenal, chorus	c#1-g2/c#-f#1	ballad
Dahomey, chorus		uptempo
Bill, Julie	c1-d2	mod., funny
Can't help . . . reprise, Magnolia	c♭-f2	ballad
After the ball, Magnolia*	d1-f2	ballad

Ol' man river reprise, Joe	G-e1	ballad
You are love reprise, Ravenal	c-ab1	ballad
Finale: Ol' man river, company		ballad

*Turn-of-the-century song by Charles K. Harris, interpolated here.

Side Show (1997)

Music by Henry Krieger   Lyrics by Bill Russell

Song title, **Character (Voice)**	**Range**	**Song Style**
Come look at the freaks, company		uptempo
On the midway, trio	TTB	scene
Behind the bleachers, trio	SMT	scene
(I want to be) Like everyone else, Violet (M),	g#-c#2/g#-e2	ballad
Daisy (M), Jake and Terry incidental		
You deserve a better life, Buddy (T), Terry	both e-f#1	mod. ballad
(T)		
Your girls could play vaudeville, Boss (T),	c-g1	mod. uptempo
company		
So lovely to meet you ladies, company		scene
The devil you know, Jake (T), company		uptempo
More than we bargained for, Terry, Buddy	c#-fba/A-ab1	mod. ballad
Sideshow's about to explode, company		scene
Feelings you have got to hide, Daisy, Violet	a-b1/g-d2	ballad
When I'm by your side, Daisy, Violet	both c#1-d#2	moving ballad
They came to hear us sing, company		mod. uptempo
Say goodbye to the freak show, company		mod. uptempo
The press conference (Overnight sensation),		scene
company		
Leave me alone, Daisy, Violet; Terry	e-c#2/e-d2	mod. uptempo
incidental		
We share everything no. 1, chorus		uptempo
We share everything no. 2, Daisy, Violet	a-f#2/a-c#2	uptempo
I knew they were meant to sing, company		mod. uptempo
The interview, company		mod./scene
Buddy kissed me, Violet, Daisy	db-eb2/cb-eb2	ballad
Who will love me as I am?, Violet, Daisy	eb-f2/ab-e2	driving ballad
Rare songbirds on display, company		uptempo
Good show, you two, trio	MMT	scene
New Year's Day, company		mod. uptempo
Private conversations, Terry, Daisy	G-g1/b-f2	uptempo
One plus one equals three, Buddy, trio	e#-a1/MMT	mod. uptempo
I need to talk to you, company		scene
Oh Daisy, how can I make this easier?, trio	MMT	scene
You should be loved, Jake, Violet	c-e1/a-f#2	moving ballad
Cannibal King reprise, Jake	c-g1	uptempo

Tunnel of love, quartet, company	MTTT	mod. uptempo
Celebrate love, Man (Bar), company	d#-g1	uptempo
Violet, I always knew, company		scene
Marry me, Terry, Daisy, others	b-f#2	ballad
I will never leave you, Daisy, Violet	g-e♭2/a-e♭2	mod. ballad
Daisy, can you hear what I'm thinking?, Daisy, Violet, company	b♭-d2/c1-d2	mod. ballad

Silk Stockings (1955)
Music and Lyrics by Cole Porter

Song title, Character (Voice)	Range	Song Style
Too bad, company		mod. uptempo
Paris loves lovers, Canfield (Bar), Ninotchka (M)	A♭-d♭1/g♭-f1	mod. ballad
Stereophonic sound, Janice (M), men's chorus incidental	a-b♭1	uptempo
It's a chemical reaction, Ninotchka, Canfield	f#-f2/A-d1	mod. uptempo
Satin and silk, Janice	g-b1	mod. ballad
Without love, Nina (M)	e♭-f1	mod. ballad
Hail Bibinski, company		uptempo
As on the seasons we sail, Canfield, Nina	A-d1/g-g1	moving ballad
Josephine, Janice, chorus	a♭-b♭1	fast character
Siberia, ensemble		uptempo
Silk stockings, Canfield	B♭-d♭1 (opt. f1)	mod. ballad
Stereophonic . . . reprise, Janice, men	a-b♭1	uptempo
Red blues, chorus		blues ballad
Too bad reprise, company		uptempo

A Slice of Saturday Night (1989)
Music and Lyrics by the Heather Brothers

Song title, Character (Voice)	Range	Song Style
A slice of Saturday night, company		uptempo
Club a go-go, Eric (T)	e-e1	uptempo
Waiting, women's ensemble		mod. uptempo
Saturday night chat, company		uptempo
Seventeen, Rick (T), Sharon (S)	c#-c#1/c#1-c#2	mod. ballad
Don't touch me, Eric, Gary (T), Rick, Bridget (M)	men b♭-f1/f1-f2	mod. uptempo
Twiggy, Sue (M)	g-c2	country ballad, character
Cliff, company		mod. uptempo
Love on our side, Terry (Bar), Shirley (M)	d-e1/d1-d2	ballad

What do I do now?, Sharon, Rick	c#1-f#2/c#-f#1	moving ballad
What do you do?, company		mod. uptempo
If you wanna have fun, Eric, company	a-f#1	uptempo
Long walk back, Rick	A-g1	ballad
Romance/Wham bam, company		mod. uptempo
Boy of my dreams, Bridget	a-d2	ballad
It wouldn't be Saturday night without a fight, company		mod. uptempo
Eric's hokey cokey shuffle, Eric, chorus	g-e1	uptempo
I fancy you, Rick, Sharon, chorus	eb-d1/d1-e2	mod. uptempo
Sentimental eyes, Sharon, Rick	f#-d2/a-e1	uptempo
Heart breaker, girls' chorus		mod. uptempo
Eric's gonna keep going, Eric, boys' chorus	a-g1	uptempo
Oh so bad, Eddie (Bar), Gary	d#-f1/c-f1	mod. uptempo
Please don't tell me, company		country ballad
You're oh so . . . , girls' chorus		"cool" uptempo
Lies, Eric, male ensemble	d-f1	uptempo
Baby, I love you, Gary, company	f-e1	uptempo
P.E., Gary, boys incidental	d-g1	mod. character
Who'd be seventeen?, Eric, girls	A-d1	mod. uptempo
Last Saturday night, Rick, Sharon	c-e1/c1-c2	mod. ballad
Finale, company		uptempo

Smile (1986)

Music by Marvin Hamlisch   Lyrics by Howard Ashman

Song title, Character (Voice)	**Range**	**Song Style**
Typical high school senior, company		uptempo
The very best week of your lives, Brenda (M)	g-bb1	mod. uptempo
Dear Mom no. 1, Robin (S)	c#-db2	ballad
Disneyland, Doria (M)	g-d2	country ballad
Shine, Brenda (M), Tommy, girls' chorus	ab-e2/spoken	uptempo
Dear Mom no. 2, Robin	c#-db2	ballad
Bob's song, Bob (Bar)	a-f#1	country ballad
Nerves, company		mod. uptempo
Young and American, girls' chorus, some incidental soli		uptempo
Until tomorrow night, company		driving uptempo
Dear Mom no. 3, company		uptempo
Smile, Ted (Bar), girls' chorus	c-eb1	mod. uptempo
We wish you were here, girls' chorus		uptempo
In our hands, girls' chorus		ballad
There goes the girl, Ted	d-f1	mod. uptempo
Finale/Tomorrow, company		mod. uptempo

Song and Dance (1985)

Music by Andrew Lloyd Webber   Lyrics by Don Black and Richard Maltby, Jr.

Song title, **Character (Voice)**	**Range**	**Song Style**
Take that look off your face, Woman (M), girls' chorus	g-d2	mod. uptempo
Let me finish	g#-e♭2	uptempo
It's not the end of the world (if I love him)	a-e♭2	mod. uptempo
First letter home	a-d2	ballad
Sheldon Brown	g#-e2	mod. uptempo
Capped teeth and caesar salad	a-b1	mod. uptempo
You made me think you were in love	a-c2	uptempo
It's not the end of the world (if he's younger)	a-e♭1	mod. uptempo
Second letter home	a-a1	ballad
Unexpected song	f#-g2	flowing ballad
The last man in my life	g-e♭2	moving ballad
Come back with that same look in your eyes	a-c2	mod. uptempo
Let's talk about you	g#-e2	uptempo
Tell me on a Sunday	g-e2	moving ballad
It's not the end of the world (if he's married)	f-e2	mod. uptempo
Married man	g#-c#2	uptempo
I'm very you	a-c2	uptempo
Third letter home	g-a1	ballad
Nothing like you've ever known	g#-c#2	flowing ballad
Let me finish reprise	g#-e♭2	uptempo
Take that look off your face reprise, + girls	b-d2	uptempo

Song of Norway (1944)

Music by Edvard Grieg

Musical Adaptation and Lyrics by Robert Wright and George Forrest

Song title, **Character (Voice)**	**Range**	**Song Style**
The legend, Rikaard (T)	e-a♭1	mod. ballad
Hill of dreams, Nina (S), Edvard (Bar), Rikaard	d♭1-b♭2/B♭-f1/e♭-a♭1	mod. uptempo
Freddy and his fiddle, Einar (T), Sigrid (S)	c#-g1/d1-g2	mod. uptempo
Now, Louisa (S), chorus	c1-a♭2	uptempo, then waltz ballad
Strange music, Nina, Edvard	d1-b♭2/B-g1	moving ballad
Midsummer's eve, Rikaard, Louisa	d-g1/d♭1-a2	ballad
March of the Trollgers, company		uptempo
Hymn of betrothal, Mother Grieg (M), Rikaard incidental, chorus	e1-d2	anthem ballad
Now! Now!, company		mostly uptempo
Bon vivant, company		uptempo
Three loves, Louisa, Edvard	c1-a2/B-e♭1	moving ballad

One love alone, chorus		uptempo
Waltz eternal, chorus		uptempo
I love you, Nina	f#1-g2	ballad
At Christmas time, Father Grieg (Bar), Mother Grieg, Nina, ensemble	G-b/b♭-d2/e1-e2	uptempo

Songs for a New World (1996)
Music and Lyrics by Jason Robert Brown

Song title, **Character (Voice)**	**Range**	**Song Style**
The new world, company		mod. uptempo
On the deck of a Spanish sailing ship, 1492, Man 1 (T), company	B♭-b♭1	uptempo
Just one step, Woman 2 (M)	f#-c#2	mod. uptempo
I'm not afraid, Woman 1 (S)	a-e2	mod. uptempo
The river won't flow, company		uptempo
Stars and the moon, Woman 2	a-d2	uptempo
She cries, Man 2 (Bar)	c-g#1	mod. uptempo
The steam train, Man 1, company	f-c2	uptempo
The world was dancing, Man 2, company	c-f2	mod. ballad
Surabaya Santa, Woman 2	g-e♭2	moderate character
Christmas lullaby, Woman 1	a-e2	ballad
King of the world, Man 1	e-c2	funky uptempo
I'd give it all for you, Woman 1, Man 2	f#-f2/f#-g1	mod. ballad
The flagmaker, 1775, Woman 2	a-e2	mod. uptempo
Flying home, Man 1, company	d-f2	moving ballad
The new world reprise, company		mod. uptempo
Hear my song, company		moving ballad

The Sound of Music (1959)
Music by Richard Rodgers   Lyrics by Oscar Hammerstein II

Song title, **Character (Voice)**	**Range**	**Song Style**
Dixit Dominus/Alleluia (chant), women's chorus		slow
The sound of music, Maria (S)	b-b1	ballad
Maria, women's ensemble		mod. uptempo
My favorite things, Maria, Mother Abbess incidental	b-e♭2	mod. waltz
Do-re-mi, Maria, Children	c1-g2	uptempo
Sixteen going on seventeen, Liesl (S), Rolf (T)	b-c2/d-e♭1	waltz ballad
The lonely goatherd, Maria, Children	c1-b♭2	fast character
How can love survive?, Max (T), Elsa (M)	d-f1/d1-f2	ballad

The sound of music reprise, Captain (Bar), Children	B-b1	ballad
So long, farewell, Children		mod. uptempo
Nuns' processional/Morning hymn, women's chorus		slow
Climb ev'ry mountain, Mother Abbess (M)	c1-a♭2	anthem ballad
The sound of music reprise, Children		ballad
My favorite things reprise, Children		mod. waltz
No way to stop it, Max, Elsa, Captain	c-e1/c1-b2/c-e1	uptempo
An ordinary couple, Captain, Maria	G-d1/b-d2	ballad
Processional, Nuns		ballad
Canticle: Confitemini Domino, Nuns		ballad
Sixteen going on seventeen reprise, Maria, Liesl	b-c#2/b1-b2	ballad
The concert: Do-re-mi, Trapp family		uptempo
So long, farewell reprise, Family		mod. uptempo
Finale: Climb every mountain, Mother Abbess, Nuns	c1-g2	ballad

South Pacific (1949)

Music by Richard Rodgers   Lyrics by Oscar Hammerstein II

Song title, Character (Voice)	**Range**	**Song Style**
Dites-moi, ensemble w/ incidental soli		slow
A cockeyed optimist, Nellie (M)	a-c2	uptempo
Twin soliloquies, Nellie, Emile (Bar)	c1-b1/B-b	ballad
Some enchanted evening, Emile	c-e1	ballad
Bloody Mary, men's chorus		uptempo
There is nothing like a dame, men's chorus		uptempo
Bali ha'i, Mary (M)	g-g1	ballad
Cable hears Bali ha'i, Cable (T)	d-d1	ballad
I'm gonna wash that man right out-a my hair, Nellie, women's chorus	b-b1	fast character
Some enchanted evening reprise, Emile, Nellie	c-e1/c1-f1	ballad
I'm in love with a wonderful guy, Nellie, women	b-c2	uptempo
Bali ha'i reprise, French girls		ballad
Younger than springtime, Cable, women incidental	e-g1	ballad
I'm in love with a wonderful guy reprise, Nellie	c1-c2	uptempo
This is how it feels, Nellie, Emile	b♭-d2/B♭-c1	mod. ballad
I'm gonna wash that man . . . reprise, Emile	B-b	fast character
Happy talk, Mary	a-b1	character
Honey bun, Nellie, chorus	b♭-f2	fast character

This nearly was mine, Emile	B-d	waltz ballad
Honey bun reprise, chorus		uptempo

Spamalot (2005)
Music and Lyrics by Eric Idle and John du Prez

Song title, Character (Voice)	Range	Song Style
Fisch schlapping dance, company		uptempo
I am not dead yet, company		march uptempo
The lady of the lake, Lady (M)	a-c2	ballad
The Laker girls, Arthur (Bar), chorus	d-e1	march uptempo
The song that goes like this, Dennis (T), Lady	c-f#1/c1-f#2	character ballad
We are not dead yet reprise, chorus		uptempo
Burn her, Belvedere (T), Witch (M), chorus	f-f1/b♭-a♭1	mod. uptempo
All for one, Knights		mod. uptempo
Find your grail, Lady, chorus, Arthur incidental	c#1-e2	pop ballad
Knights of the Roundtable, company		uptempo
The cow song, Marlene (M), chorus	f-b♭1	waltz ballad
Run away!, chorus		uptempo
Always look to the bright side of life, Patsy (S), Arthur, Knights	b-f2/d-d1	mod. ballad
Brave Sir Robin, Minstrel (Bar)	a-d1	ballad
You won't succeed on Broadway, Robin (Bar), chorus incidental	d-e1	uptempo
Whatever happened to my part?, Lady, chorus incidental	f#-e2	pop ballad
He's going to tell/Here you are, Herbert (Bar), chorus	G-b♭	mod. uptempo
His name is Lancelot, company		mod. uptempo
I'm all alone, Arthur, Patsy, Knights	G-c1/g-a1	ballad
Why does he never notice me?, Lady	f-d♭2	pop ballad
Finale, company		scene

Spring Awakening (2006)
Music by Duncan Sheik   Lyrics by Steven Slater

Song title, Character (Voice)	Range	Song Style
Mama who bore me, Wendla (M)	g-a1	ballad
Mama who bore me reprise, company		uptempo
All that's known, Melchior (T)	c-e1	ballad
The bitch of living, Moritz (Bar), company	c-d1	mod. uptempo
My junk, company women		uptempo
Touch me, company		uptempo

The word of your body, Wendla, Melchior	b-c2/B-d#1	ballad
The dark I know well, Martha (M), company	a-a1	uptempo
And then there were none, Moritz, company	d#-g#1	uptempo
Mirror blue night, Melchior, company men	B-a1	ballad
I believe, company		mod. uptempo
The guilty ones, company		ballad
Don't do sadness, Moritz*	B-f1 (falsetto a1)	mod. uptempo
Blue wind, Ilse (S)*	g-a1	mod. ballad
Left behind, Melchior, company	c-f# (falsetto b1)	ballad
Totally fucked, Melchior	B♭-f1	mod. uptempo
Word of your body reprise, company		ballad
Whispering, Wendla	b-g1	ballad
Those you've known, trio	MTB	ballad
The song of purple summer, company		ballad

*These two songs then combined.

Starlight Express (1987)
Music by Andrew Lloyd Webber
Lyrics by Richard Stilgoe, Don Black, and David Yazbeck

Song title, Character (Voice)	Range	Song Style
Rolling stock, company		uptempo
Nobody can do it like a steam train, Rusty (T), company	b-b1	uptempo
Taunting Rusty, company		uptempo
This is going to be the day, quartet	SMMT	moderate
A lotta locomotion, quartet	SMMM	mod. uptempo
Freight is power, chorus		mod. uptempo
AC/DC, Elektra (M), chorus	g-ab2*	uptempo
Pumping iron, Greaseball (Bar), company	c-e1	uptempo
Hitching and switching, company		mod. uptempo
Pearl, you've been honoured, trio	MMT	uptempo
Make up my heart, Pearl (M)	a-e2 (also down a step)	ballad
That was cheating, Dinah (M), Greaseball	f-g2/c-d1	uptempo
There's me, Caboose (T), Dinah	d-f1/d1-d2	flowing ballad
Poppa's blues, Poppa (T)	g-g1	uptempo blues
After the blues, Poppa, Rusty, others incidental	G-bb1/c-g1	mod. slow
Boy, boy, boy, company		uptempo
Starlight express, Rusty	c-bb1	ballad
The rap, company	spoken	mod. uptempo
U.n.c.o.u.p.l.e.d., Dinah	a-bb1	country ballad
Girl's rolling stock, trio	SMM	uptempo
Dinah, you've been honoured, company		scene

Wide smile, high style, Caboose	e-g2 (opt. g3 in falsetto)	uptempo
That was cheating reprise, company		uptempo
Right place right now, quartet	TTBB	uptempo
Only you, Poppa, Rusty	c#-f#1/c#-a1	ballad
Hello Rusty, Rusty, Dustin (T)	c-c1/c-f1	slow
Dinah's disco, Dinah, Elektra	b-b1/b1-f#2	uptempo
Locomotion, company		uptempo
One rock and roll too many, company		mod. blues
Only you reprise, Pearl, Rusty	f-d2/f-a1	ballad
Well done, Rusty, company		uptempo
Light at the end of the tunnel, Poppa, company	d-f1	uptempo

*Some passages marked 8va optional.
Note: Annotated from the revised 1992 German version.

Starmites (1989)
Music and Lyrics by Barry Keating

Song title, **Character (Voice)**	**Range**	**Song Style**
Superhero girl, Eleanor (M)	f#-d2	samba uptempo
Starmites, Space Punk (T), trio	d-g1/TTB	mod. uptempo
Afraid of the dark, Space Punk, Mites (chorus); Eleanor incidental	A♭-a♭1	mod. uptempo
Lullaby (Little hero), Eleanor, Mites	g-d2	ballad
Trink's narration, Trinkulus (T), Mites	B-e1	scene
Attack of the Banshees, Shotzi (M), Banshees	g-f2/SMM	mod. uptempo
Hard to be a diva, Diva (M), Banshees	g-f2	uptempo
Love duet, Space Punk, Eleanor	d-b♭1/g#-e♭2	ballad
The connuptial dance of spousal arousal, Balbraka (M), Banshees	d-d2	mod. uptempo
Finaletto, company		uptempo
Bizarbara's wedding, Bizarbara (M), Banshees	g-d♭2	uptempo
Milady, Space Punk, Mites	c-c2	uptempo
Beauty within, Diva, Bizarbara	e-c2/g-e2	pop ballad
The cruelty stomp, Trink, company	A-a1	uptempo
Reach right down, company		mod. gospel ballad
The immolation, Eleanor, Shak Graa (T), Space Punk, Mites	a-d2/c#-a1/a-a1	moderate
Starmites/Diva reprise, Diva, company	f1-d♭2	uptempo
Finale, company		mod. uptempo

Starting Here, Starting Now (1977)

Music by David Shire   Lyrics by Richard Maltby, Jr.

Song title, Character (Voice)	Range	Song Style
I am in love, Woman 1 (S), Woman 2 (M), Man (Bar)	d1-f2/d1-eb2/f-e	mod. ballad
Starting here, starting now, Woman 1, 2, Man	b-d2/b-c2/d-e1	mod. uptempo
I'm a little bit off, Woman 2	ab-eb2	quick ragtime
I may want to remember today, Woman 1, 2	both c1-eb2	uptempo
Beautiful, Woman 1, 2, Man	bb-gb1/bb-f2/Bb-e1	ballad
We can talk to each other, Man	c-eb1	uptempo
Just across the river, Woman 1, 2, Man	c1-f#2/bb-d2/Bb-d1	mod. rock uptempo
Crossword puzzle, Woman 2	c-e2	mod. uptempo
Autumn, Woman 1	bb-eb2	ballad
I don't remember Christmas, Man	c-e1	uptempo samba
I don't believe it, Woman 1, 2, Man	c#1-eb/c#1-d2/c#-eb1	uptempo
I hear bells, Man; Women (on syllables)	Bb-d1/f1-f2/c1-f2	ballad
I'm going to make you beautiful, Woman 1	bb-g1	uptempo
Pleased with myself, Woman 1, 2, Man	ab-c3/f-f2/ab-f1	mod. uptempo
Hey there, fans, Man	A-d1	uptempo
The girl of the minute, Woman 1, Man	db1-eb2/db-eb1	ballad
Travel, Woman 1, 2, Man	a-c#2/bb-c#2/Ab-c#1	mod. uptempo
Watching the big parade go by, Woman 1	bb-d2	mod. uptempo
Flair, Man	A-d1	uptempo
What about today?, Woman 2	bb-bb1	hard ballad
One step, Woman 1, 2, Man	b-f2/b-d2/c-f1	mod. uptempo
Song of me, Woman 1	d1-f#2	mod. uptempo
Today is the first day, Women	both db1-eb2	mod. ballad
A new life coming, Woman 1, 2, Man	c1-e2/c1-e2/c-f1	uptempo
Flair reprise, Woman 1, 2, Man	d1-g2/d1-eb2/d-e1	uptempo

Optional Song:

Barbara, Man	Gb-bb	ballad

Stop the World—I Want to Get Off (1962)

Music and Lyrics by Leslie Bricusse and Anthony Newley

Song title, Character (Voice)	Range	Song Style
The abc song, chorus		character
I wanna be rich, Little Chap (T), girls	d-g1	uptempo

	b-d1/c-d1/b-b1	mod. ballad
Typically English, Evie (M), Little Chap, solo M, girls	d-f1	uptempo
Lumbered, Little Chap, incidental girl solo	c-f1	uptempo
Gonna build a mountain, Little Chap, girls	G-a	mod. character
Glorious Russian, Anya (Bar), chorus	e♭-e♭1/g-f1	mod. ballad
Meilinki meilchik, Little Chap, Anya	e♭-e♭1/a-c2/a-d2/a-d2	mod. uptempo
Family fugue, Little Chap, Evie, Susan (M), Jane (M)	f#-c2	character ballad
Typische deutsche, Ilse (M)	A♭-g♭1/a♭-d♭2	uptempo
Family fugue reprise, Little Chap, Evie		mod. uptempo
Nag, nag, nag, company	a-a1	uptempo
All American, Ginnie (M)	c-f1/d1-c2	ballad
Once in a lifetime, Little Chap, solo M	spoken	fast character
Mumbo jumbo, Little Chap, chorus	B♭-f1	ballad
Once in a lifetime reprise, Little Chap, chorus	a♭-b♭1/c-e♭1	ballad
Someone nice like you, Evie, Little Chap	a♭-f1	ballad
What kind of fool am I?, Little Chap		

Street Scene (1947)

Music by Kurt Weill   Lyrics by Langston Hughes and Elmer Rice

Song title, **Character (Voice)**	**Range**	**Song Style**
Ain't it awful, the heat?, ensemble		mod. uptempo
I got a marble and a star, Henry (Bar)	B♭-f1	blues ballad
Get a load of that, Mrs. Jones (M), Mrs. Fiorentino (S), Mrs. Olson (M)	c1-e♭2/g1-g2/a♭-c2	uptempo
When a woman has a baby, Buchanen (T)	d-g♭1	moving ballad
Somehow I never could believe, Mrs. Maurrant (S)	d♭1-g2	ballad
Ice cream sextet	SMTTBB	uptempo, funny
Let things be like they always was, Maurrant (Bar)	A-d1	mod. ballad
Wrapped in a ribbon and tied in a bow, ensemble		mod. uptempo
Lonely house, Sam (T)	f-b♭1	ballad
Wouldn't you like to be on Broadway, Easter (Bar)	d-f1	mod. uptempo
What good would the moon be?, Rose (S)	d1-g2	moving ballad
Moon faced, starry eyed, Dick (T), Mae (M)	f-f1/d1-d2	uptempo
Remember that I care, Sam, Rose	f-a1/d1-a2	ballad
Catch me if you can, Children's chorus		uptempo
There'll be trouble, Mrs. Maurrant, Rose, Maurrant	e♭1-a2/d1-g2/A#-f1	angry uptempo
A boy like you, Mrs. Maurrant	g1-g2	mod. ballad

We'll go away together, Rose, Sam	e♭1-g2/e♭-g1 (opt. b♭1)	uptempo
The woman who lived up there, chorus		slow, narrative
Lullaby, two nursemaids (S, M), chorus	c1-g2/a♭-e2	ballad
I loved her too, chorus		ballad
Don't forget the lilac bush, Sam, Rose	e♭-a♭1/d1-g2	ballad

Strike Up the Band (1930)

Music by George Gershwin   Lyrics by Ira Gershwin

Song title, **Character (Voice)**	**Range**	**Song Style**
Fletcher's American cheese choral society, Timothy (T), Sloane (Bar), Fletcher (T), chorus	d♭-e♭1/c- d♭1/d♭-e♭1	uptempo
17 and 21, Timothy, Anne (S)	e♭-e1/e♭1-f2	mod. ballad
Typical self-made American, Fletcher, Jim (Bar), men's chorus	B-e1/e-e1	mod. uptempo
Meadow serenade, Jim, Joan (S)	d-f1/d1-b2	mod. ballad
Unofficial spokesman, Fletcher, Holmes (T), chorus	c-e1/c-e♭1	uptempo
Patriotic rally, chorus		march uptempo
The man I love, Joan, Jim	d1-a2/f-f1	ballad
Yankee doodle rhythm, Spelvin (Bar), chorus	e-e1	uptempo
17 and 21 reprise, Mrs. Draper (S), Fletcher	e♭1-f2/e♭-f1	mod. ballad
He knows mild, company		uptempo
Strike up the band, Timothy, chorus	f-g1	uptempo
Oh this is such a lovely war, chorus		waltz uptempo
Come-look-at-the-war choral society, women's chorus		mod. uptempo
Hoping that someday you'd care, Jim, Joan	d-f1/d1-f2	ballad
Military dancing drill, Timothy, Anne, chorus	c-f1/c1-f2	march uptempo
How about a man?, Mrs. Draper, Holmes, Fletcher	e♭1-g2/c-g1/e♭1- a♭2	mod. uptempo
Homeward bound/The girl I love reprise, Soldier (T)	g-b♭1	uptempo/ballad
The war that ended war, chorus		march uptempo
Strike up the band reprise, company		uptempo

Note: Many songs here were added in a later revision.

The Student Prince (1924)

Music by Sigmund Romberg   Lyrics by Dorothy Donnelly

Song title, **Character (Voice)**	**Range**	**Song Style**
Prologue, quartet	TTBB	mod. uptempo

Golden days, Prince (T), Engel (Bar)	c#-g#1/f-e♭1	ballad
Garlands bright, women's chorus		mod. uptempo
To the inn we're marching, men's chorus		uptempo
Drinking song, men's chorus		uptempo
Where is the maid?, Kathie (S), chorus	e1-c3	uptempo
Drinking song reprise, men's chorus		uptempo
Heidelberg, beloved vision, chorus		anthem ballad
Gaudeamus, men's chorus		anthem ballad
Golden days reprise, Engel	c-e♭1	ballad
Come sir, will you join?, ensemble, men's chorus		uptempo
Overhead the moon is beaming, company		mod. ballad
Farmer Jacob lay a-snoring, men's chorus		mod. character
Student life, company		uptempo
Just we two, Princess (S), Tarnitz (T), men's chorus	d1-g2/d-g1	mod. uptempo
What memories, sweet Rose, company		mod. ballad
Let us sing a song, men's chorus		uptempo
To the inn we're marching reprise, company		uptempo march

Sugar (1972)

Music by Jule Styne   Lyrics by Bob Merrill

Song title, Character (Voice)	**Range**	**Song Style**
When you meet a girl in Chicago, Sugar (M), women's chorus	a-c2	uptempo
Turn back the clock, women's chorus		easy ballad
Penniless bums, Joe (Bar), Jerry (Bar), men's chorus	both c-e1	mod. uptempo
Tear the town apart, Spats, men's chorus	spoken	jazzy uptempo
The beauty that drives men mad, Joe, Jerry, chorus	both d-f1	blues ballad
We could be close, Sugar, Jerry	b#-d2/B#-d1	ballad
Sun on my face, ensemble, women's chorus		uptempo
November song, Osgood (Bar), men's chorus	c-d1	easy ballad
Doin' it for Sugar, Joe, Jerry	B-e1/c-e♭1	swing ballad
Hey, why not?, Sugar, men's chorus	b♭-b♭1	mod. uptempo
Beautiful through and through, Osgood; Jerry incidental	c#-e♭1	uptempo waltz
What do you give to a man who's had everything, Joe; Sugar incidental	d-e1	uptempo
Magic nights, Jerry	e-f1	uptempo
It's always love, Joe	c-d1	ballad
When you meet a man in Chicago reprise, company		uptempo

Sugar Babies (1979)

Music by Jimmy McHugh, Arthur Malvin, Jay Livingston, and Ray Evans
Lyrics by Arthur Malvin, Dorothy Fields, George Oppenheimer,
Eugene West, Irwin Dash, Jay Livingston, Ray Evans,
Ted Koehler, Jack Frost, and Irving Mills

Song title, **Character (Voice)**	**Range**	**Song Style**
Good old burlesque show, Mickey (T), chorus	B-f1	mod. swing
Let me be your sugar baby, women's chorus		uptempo
I feel a song comin' on, Ann (M), chorus	b♭-f1	uptempo
Sally, Production Tenor	c#-g1	uptempo
Immigration Rose, solo T, male quartet	d-f#1	ballad
Don't blame me, Ann	a-a2	mod. uptempo
Sugar baby bounce, Linda (M), Chris (M), Ann	all a♭-e2	ballad
Down at the Gaiety burlesque, women's chorus		uptempo
Mr. Banjo Man, Ann, Mickey, chorus	b♭-b2/B♭-a	uptempo
I'm keepin' myself available for you/ Exactly like you, Ann, women	a-c2	mod. uptempo/ mod. swing
Warm and willing, Rosita Royce (M)	a♭-c2	ballad
Cuban love song, Production Tenor	A-g1	beguine ballad
McHugh medley, Mickey, Ann	B♭-e♭1/f-c#2	mostly uptempo
Uncle Sammy finale, Mickey, Ann, chorus	d-e1/a-e♭2	uptempo

Sunday in the Park with George (1984)

Music and Lyrics by Stephen Sondheim

Song title, **Character (Voice)**	**Range**	**Song Style**
Sunday in the park with George, Dot (M)	e-d♭2	ballad, often funny
No life, Jules (Bar), Yvonne (M)	G-d1/a-d2	ballad
Color and light, Dot, George (T)	b-e2/d-g1	mod. uptempo
Gossip sequence, ensemble		uptempo
The day off, company		mod. uptempo
Everybody loves Louis, Dot	a-c2	uptempo
Finishing the hat, George	B♭-a♭1	mod. uptempo
We do not belong together, Dot, George	g-d2/A-e1	ballad
Beautiful, Old Lady (M), George	f#-b1/c#-f#1	ballad
Sunday, company		moving ballad
It's hot up here, company		mod. uptempo
Putting it together, George, company	d♭-g♭1	uptempo
Children and art, Marie (M), George incidental	g♭-d♭2	moving ballad
Lesson no. 8, George	G♭-f1	ballad

Move on, George, Dot	d#-g1/g#-c#2	moving ballad
Sunday reprise, company		mod. uptempo

Note: The characters of Dot and Marie are played by the same actress.

Sunny (1925)

Music by Jerome Kern   Lyrics by Otto Harbach and Oscar Hammerstein II

Song title, **Character (Voice)**	**Range**	**Song Style**
Here we are together again, chorus		uptempo
Here you come a-running, Tom (T)	e♭-f1	ballad
Who?, Sunny (S), Tom	b-e2/B-e1	uptempo
So's your old man, Wendell (T), chorus	d-g1	uptempo
Let's say goodnight, Weenie (M), Jim (T)	b♭-e♭2/B♭-e♭1	mod. ballad
D'ye love me, Sunny	b-g2	waltz ballad
It won't mean a thing, Sunny, Tom, Jim, men's chorus	b-a2/B-f1/A-f1	ballad
The wedding knell, Sunny, men's chorus	b-g#2	uptempo
Two little bluebirds, Weenie, Wendell	d1-e♭2/d-e♭1	ballad
Ev'ry guest is in the room, company		uptempo
We're gymnastic, Sue (S), women's chorus	c#1-f2	uptempo
Divorce, Sunny, Jim	b-e2/B-e1	uptempo
Sunshine, Marcia (M), chorus	d1-a2	waltz ballad
The chase, company		mod. uptempo
I might grow fond of you, Weenie, Wendell	c1-e2/c-e1	ballad
The fox has left his lair, unison quartet*	c-f1 (c1-f2)	character
The hunt ball, chorus		mod. uptempo
Who reprise, Jim	d-e1	uptempo
D'ye love me reprise, company		waltz ballad

*Could be performed as a solo.

Sunset Boulevard (1994)

Music by Andrew Lloyd Webber   Lyrics by Don Black and Christopher Hampton

Song title, **Character (Voice)**	**Range**	**Song Style**
I guess it was five a.m., Joe (T)	d-g♭1	recitative-like
Let's have lunch, company		swing uptempo
Betty's pitch, Beth (M), Joe	b-c2/B-f1	recitative
Surrender, Norma (M)	f-b♭1	ballad
Once upon a time, Norma	a-a1	uptempo
With one look, Norma	g#-c#2	ballad
Salome, Norma, Joe	a-d2/A-d♭1	uptempo
The greatest star of all, Max (Bar)	B-g♭1	ballad
Schwab's drugstore (Every movie's a circus), company		swing uptempo

Girl meets boy, trio	MTT	moderate
I started work, Joe, Max incidental	c-g1	uptempo
New ways to dream, Norma	b♭-d♭2	ballad
The lady's paying, trio, company	MTT	mod. uptempo
New Year tango, Joe, Max	A-b/c-d1	uptempo
The perfect year, Norma, Joe	a-d♭2/A-d1	mod. ballad
I had to get out, Joe	c-e♭1 (opt. g1)	driving uptempo
This time next year, company		mod. uptempo
Sunset Boulevard, Joe	c-g1	uptempo
There's been a call, Norma	a-d2	recitative
It took her three days, Joe	A-e1	uptempo
As if we never said goodbye, Norma	g#-c#2	ballad
Paramount conversations, company		scene
Girl meets boy reprise, Joe, Betty	c-f1/a-f2	mod. uptempo
A little suffering, company		uptempo
I should have stayed there, Joe	A-e1	uptempo
Too much in love to care, Betty, Joe	a-g2/d-g1	mod. ballad
New ways to dream reprise, Max	B-e1	ballad
Phone call, Norma	f-a1	recitative
What's going on, Joe?, Betty, Joe	b-d2/c-f#1	uptempo
Final scene, Max, Norma	c-e♭1/f-c2	scene

Sweeney Todd (1979)
Music and Lyrics by Stephen Sondheim

Song title, Character (Voice)	Range	Song Style
No place like London, Todd (B), chorus	G-c#1	mod. uptempo
The worst pies in London, Mrs. Lovett (M)	b-e♭2	character
Poor thing, Mrs. Lovett	f#-b1	ballad
My friends, Todd, Mrs. Lovett	B♭-e1/b-e♭2	mod. ballad
Green finch and linnet bird, Johanna (S)	c1-g2	uptempo
Johanna, Anthony (T)	c-e♭1	ballad
Pirelli's miracle elixir, Tobias (T), chorus	d-a♭1	mod. character
The contest, Pirelli (T), chorus	d-c2	mod. uptempo
Johanna, Judge Turpin (Bar)	B♭-f1	angry ballad
Wait, Mrs. Lovett	b♭-e♭2	ballad
Kiss me I, Johanna, Anthony	c#1-g#2/c#-f#1	flowing ballad
Ladies in their sensitivities, Beadle (T)	d-f#1	character ballad
Kiss me II, Johanna, Anthony, Beadle, Judge	STTB	ballad
Pretty women, Judge, Todd	G-d1/d-e1	mod. ballad
Epiphany, Todd, Mrs. Lovett incidental	c-f1	angry uptempo
A little priest, Mrs. Lovett, Todd	g#-b1/G-g♭1	grizzly, mod.
God, that's good, chorus		mod. uptempo
Johanna, Todd, Anthony, Beggar Woman, Johanna	A♭-c/A♭-e♭1/ women: a♭1-e♭2	ballad

By the sea, Mrs. Lovett, Todd	g#-e2/ G#-e1	jaunty ballad
The letter, ensemble		mod. ballad
Not while I'm around, Tobias	e♭-a♭1	ballad
Parlor songs, Beadle, others incidental	d-g1	mod. ballad
City on fire!, chorus		uptempo
Searching, ensemble		mod. ballad
The ballad of Sweeney Todd, company		mod. uptempo

Sweet Charity (1965)

Music by Cy Coleman   Lyrics by Dorothy Fields

Song title, Character (Voice)	**Range**	**Song Style**
You should see yourself, Charity (M)	b♭-b♭1	uptempo
Big spender, women's chorus		quick, striptease
Charity's soliloquy, Charity	a♭-a1	mod. uptempo
If my friends could see me now, Charity	g#-b♭1	uptempo, jazzy
Too many tomorrows, Vidal (T)	B♭-g1	40s ballad
There's gotta be something better, Charity, Nickie, Helene	all a-c#2	driving uptempo
I'm the bravest individual, Charity, Oscar (Bar)	f#-b♭1/c-g1	mod. uptempo
Rhythm of life, Daddy Brubeck (Bar), two assistants, chorus	all d-d1	jazzy chorus
Baby, dream your dream, Nickie, Helene	both f#-c#2	mod. ballad
Sweet Charity, Oscar, chorus incidental	d♭-e1	uptempo
Where am I going?, Charity	g-g1	ballad
I'm a brass band, Charity, men's chorus	a-a1	uptempo march
I love to cry at weddings, Herman (T), company	e-b1 (in falsetto)	uptempo
See me now reprise, company		uptempo

Sweet Smell of Success (2002)

Music by Marvin Hamlisch   Lyrics by Craig Carnella

Song title, Character (Voice)	**Range**	**Song Style**
The column, company		uptempo
Voodoo club (I can get you in, J.J.), ensemble		scene
Welcome to the night (I cannot hear the city), J.J. (Bar), chorus	c♭-f1	mod. uptempo
At the fountain, Sidney (T)	c#-a1	mod. uptempo
Don't know where you leave off, Dallas (T), Susan (M)	A-g♭1/b♭-f2	ballad mod. uptempo
What if, Susan, chorus	g-f2	mod. ballad

For Susan, J.J.	c-e♭1	mod. ballad
One track mind, Dallas, chorus incidental	e-a1	uptempo
At the Club Elysian, Dallas, chorus	A-b♭1	mod. uptempo
Break it up, company		uptempo
Rita's tune, Rita (M)	g-d2	mod. uptempo
Dirt, chorus		uptempo
I could get you in, J.J. reprise, Sidney, Dallas incidental	d-g#1	mod. uptempo
I cannot hear the city reprise, Susan	b-f♭1	moving ballad
Don't look now, J.J. chorus		moderate
At the fountain reprise, Sidney, chorus	A-a1	ballad
Finale, company		scene

Sweethearts (1913)

Music by Victor Herbert   Lyrics by Robert B. Smith

Song title, **Character (Voice)**	**Range**	**Song Style**
Iron! Iron! Iron!, women's chorus		uptempo
On parade, chorus		uptempo march
There is magic in a smile, Liane (S), chorus	c1-b♭2	ballad
Sweethearts, Sylvia (S), chorus	b♭-b♭2	ballad
Every lover must meet his fate, Prince (T), chorus	c-f1	ballad
Mother Goose, Sylvia, women's chorus	c1-f#2	character ballad
Jeanette and her little wooden shoes, Liane, ensemble	c1-f2	uptempo
The angelus, Sylvia, Prince	f1-a2/c-f1	anthem ballad
The game of love, Karl (T), chorus	e-a2	ballad
May the god of fortune attend you, company		mod. uptempo
Waiting for the bride, double men's chorus		uptempo
Pretty as a picture, Van Tromp (Bar), chorus	B♭-d1	character ballad
What she wanted—and what she got, Paula (M), women's chorus	d1-e2	uptempo, funny
In the convent they never taught me that, Sylvia, chorus incidental	d1-a2	uptempo
Talk about this—talk about that, Liane, Karl	c1-g2/d-g1	moving ballad
I don't know how I do it, but I do, Slingsby (T)	c-e♭1 (mostly spoken)	mod. ballad
The cricket on the hearth, Sylvia, Prince	c#1-f#2/c#-e1	ballad
Pilgrims of love, Slingsby, Van Tromp, Caniche (S)	d-a1/G-c1/d1-f1	march ballad
The ivy and the oak, Sylvia	d1-g2	ballad
Reprises, company		uptempo
Sweethearts, Indian summer, Pretty as a picture		

Taboo (2002)

Music by Boy George and Kevan Frost   Lyrics by Boy George

Song title, Character (Voice)	Range	Song Style
Ode to attention seekers, Philip (T), ensemble	B♭-f1	mod. uptempo
Safe in the city, Billy (T), chorus	g-f1	uptempo
Freak, Philip, chorus	d-f1	uptempo
Stranger in this world, George (T)	c-g1	ballad
Genocide peroxide, Marilyn (S), chorus	b♭-g2	uptempo
I'll have you all, Leigh (Bar), Billy incidental	e♭-f1	mod. uptempo
Love is a question mark, Kim (M), Billy	g#-b1/g#-g#1	uptempo
Shelter, Petal (Bar), trio	A-c1/SMM	mod. uptempo
Pretty lies, Kim, George, chorus	b♭-b♭1/b♭-g1	ballad
Guttersnipe, Marilyn, George, chorus	d#1-g#2/d#-e1	uptempo
Talk amongst yourselves, Josie (M)	g#-b1	ballad
Do you really want to hurt me?, George	e-g1	mod. uptempo
Touched by the hand of cool, company		uptempo
Church of the poisoned mind, Leigh	c-c1	uptempo
Stranger in this world reprise, Billy, chorus	c-a♭1	moving ballad
Everything taboo, company		uptempo
Independent women, Josie; Kim, Philip incidental	b-a1	uptempo
I see through you, Billy	e-g1	moving ballad
Petrified, Philip	g-c2	ballad
Ich bin kunst, Leigh	B-e1	ballad
Out of fashion, quartet	MTTB	mod. uptempo
I adore, Big Sue (M)	c-c2	mod. uptempo
Pie in the sky, George, Billy	g-b1/e-g1	mod. uptempo
Bow down mister, company		uptempo
Karma chameleon, company		uptempo

Take Me Along (1959)

Music and Lyrics by Bob Merrill

Song title, Character (Voice)	Range	Song Style
Opening chorus, Nat (Bar), chorus	spoken	mod. uptempo
Oh, please, Essie (M), Nat, chorus	b♭-e♭2/B♭-e♭1	mod. ballad
I would die, Muriel (M), Richard (T)	b♭-b♭1/c-f1	mod. uptempo
Sid, ol' kid, Sid (Bar), men's chorus	B-f1	fast character
Staying young, Nat	A-d1	mod. uptempo
I get embarrassed, Lily (S), Sid	b♭-f2/F-f	mod. ballad
We're home, Lily	c♭-d♭1	ballad
Take me along, Nat, Sid	both c-c1	uptempo

For sweet charity, Nat, chorus	d♭-f1/f-f1	uptempo
Pleasant beach house, Wint (T)	B-f1	mod. ballad
That's how it starts, Richard	d-a♭1	uptempo
Oh, please reprise, Nat, Essie	B♭-c1/b♭-c2	mod. ballad
Slight detail, Lily	b-d2	mod., funny
Staying young reprise, Nat	A-c1	mod. ballad
Little green snake, Sid	c-e♭1	mod. ballad
Nine o'clock, Richard	d-d1	mod. uptempo
But yours, Sid, Lily	B♭-f1/b♭-d2	mod. uptempo
Sid, ol' kid reprise, company		uptempo

Tap Dance Kid (1983)

Music by Henry Krieger   Lyrics by Robert Lorick

Song title, Character (Voice)	Range	Song Style
Dipsey's comin' over, Willie (Bar)	G-d1	mod. uptempo
High heels, "Someting better," Dipsey (T)	d-d1	mod. ballad
Four strikes against me, Emma (M)	a♭-d♭1	mod. uptempo
Class act, Dipsey, Ginnie (M), Daddy Bates (Bar)	B♭-g1/b♭-e♭2/a-d1	big band swing ballad
Four strikes reprise, Emma	c1-d♭2	mod. uptempo
They never hear what I say, Emma, Willie	b♭-d2/c-c1	uptempo
Dancing is everything, Willie	B♭-d1	quick shuffle
Fabulous feet, Dipsey	d-c2	medium shuffle
I could get used to him, Carole (M)	f-e2	ballad
Man in the moon, Dipsey	d♭-e♭1	ballad
Like him, Emma, Ginnie	b♭-d♭2/g-c2	moving ballad
My luck is changing, Dipsey	d♭-f1	uptempo
Someday, Emma, Willie*	a-d2/A-d1	uptempo
I remember how it was, Ginnie	e-b1	moving ballad
Lullaby, Ginnie	g-g1	ballad
Tap tap, Daddy Bates	d♭-f1	mod. uptempo
Audition, chorus		mod. 4, shuffle
William's song, William (T)	B♭-g♭1	ballad
Class act finale, company		uptempo

*Could be performed as a solo for her.

Tenderloin (1960)

Music by Jerry Bock   Lyrics by Sheldon Harnick

Song title, Character (Voice)	Range	Song Style
Prologue: Bless this land, chorus		slow hymn
Little old New York, Nita (M), Gertie (M), chorus	a-d1/a-c1	uptempo
Dr. Brock, Dr. Brock (Bar)	c-e1	uptempo
Artificial flowers, Tommy (Bar), girls' chorus incidental	G-c#1	ballad
What's in it for you?, Tommy, Brock	B-f1	mod. uptempo
Reform, trio, Gertie incidental	SSM	uptempo
Tommy, Tommy, Laura (M), Tommy incidental	c1-e2	mod. ballad
Picture of happiness, Margie (M), Tommy, chorus	a-c2/G-f1	mod. uptempo
Dear friend, Brock, chorus	B-e1	mod. ballad
Army of the just, Brock, male chorus	B-d1	mod. march
The money changes hands, company		uptempo
Good clean fun, Brock, chorus	db-f1	uptempo
My Miss May, company		uptempo
My gentle young Johnny, Nita	g#-a1	mod. waltz ballad
Picture of happiness reprise, girls' chorus		mod. uptempo
The trial, company		scene
Reform reprise, chorus		uptempo
Tommy, Tommy reprise, Laura	d1-d2	mod. ballad
Epilogue: Little old New York reprise, company		uptempo

They're Playing Our Song (1979)

Music by Marvin Hamlisch   Lyrics by Carole Bayer Sager

Song title, Character (Voice)	Range	Song Style
Falling, Vernon (Bar)	A-d1	ballad
Falling reprise, Sonia (M)	e-a1	ballad
Workin' it out, Vernon, Sonia, chorus	eb-gb1/f-bb1	mod. uptempo
If he really knew me, Sonia, Vernon	g-b1/b-d#1	ballad
They're playing my song, Vernon, Sonia	Bb-f1/gb-cb2	uptempo
If she really knew me reprise, Vernon, Sonia	c-d1/g-a1	ballad
Right, Sonia, Vernon, chorus	a-g1/c-g1	mod. uptempo
Just for tonight, Sonia	g#-a1	ballad
When you're in my arms, Vernon, Sonia, chorus	e-g1/e-e1	mod. uptempo
A lyricist? (To the studio), woman on tape (M)	f-bb1	ballad

I still believe in love, Sonia	e-a1	ballad
Fill in the words, Vernon, men's chorus	g-e1	mod. ballad
They're playing . . . reprise, company		uptempo

Thoroughly Modern Millie (2002)

Music by Jeanine Tesori   Lyrics by Dick Scanlan

Song title, Character (Voice)	Range	Song Style
Not for the life of me, Millie (M)	a-e2	dixie uptempo
Thoroughly modern Millie, company		uptempo
Not for the life tag, Millie, girls' chorus	a-c#2	uptempo
How the other half lives, Millie, Dorothy (S)	b-d2/b-e♭2	mod. uptempo
Not for the life reprise, Ching Ho (Bar), Bun Foo (Bar)	both B♭-d1	uptempo
The speed test, Trevor (T), Millie, chorus	A-f1/a-e2	uptempo
They don't know, Mrs. Meers (M)	d#-f1	mod. ballad
The nuttycracker suite, chorus incidental		various
What do I need with love, Jimmy (T)	d-g1	mod. uptempo
Only in New York, Muzzy (M)	g#-d2	sexy ballad
Jimmy, Millie	a#-d♭2	uptempo
Forget about the boy, Millie, chorus	a-c#2	mod. uptempo
Falling in love, Trevor, Dorothy	a-g1 (falsetto a1)/c-a1	ballad
I turned the corner, Jimmy, Millie incidental	d1-d2	flowing ballad
Falling in love reprise, quartet	SMTB	ballad
Muqin (My mammy), trio	MBB	character uptempo
Long as I'm here with you, Muzzy, male chorus	a-c#2	uptempo
Gimme gimme, Millie	a♭-d2	ballad, then faster
Thoroughly modern Millie reprise, company		uptempo

The Threepenny Opera (1959)

Music by Kurt Weill   Lyrics by Marc Blitzstein

Song title, Character (Voice)	Range	Song Style
The ballad of Mack the Knife, Narrator (T)	d-d1	ballad
Peachum's morning song, Peachum (Bar)	e-e♭1	uptempo
Army song, Peachum, Mrs. Peachum (M)	e♭-f♭1/e♭1-f♭2	mod. ballad
Wedding song, chorus		anthem ballad
Pirate Jenny, Polly (M)	b-d2	sprightly ballad
Canon song, Macheath (T), Brown (Bar)	d#1-g♭2/G#-d1	uptempo
Love song, Polly, Macheath	d#1-g♭2/d#-g♭1	ballad
Barbara's song, Polly	c1-f2	ballad

First Threepenny finale, Polly, Peachum, Mrs. Peachum	d#1-e2/c-e1 (opt. f1)/d#1-e2	uptempo
Polly's song, Polly	e1-c2	ballad
Tango ballad, Jenny (M), Macheath	b-f2/B-f1	uptempo tango
Ballad of an easy life, Macheath	e-f#1	ballad
Jealousy duet, Lucy (S), Polly	e1-f#2/e1-g♭2	uptempo
Second Threepenny finale, Macheath, Mrs. Peachum, chorus	d-e1/d1-e2	mod. uptempo
Useless song, Peachum	e-e1	mod. ballad
Solomon's song, Jenny	b-f2	ballad
Rest from the tomb, Macheath	e-e1	uptempo
Grave letter, Macheath	d-f1	slow ballad
Third Threepenny finale, company		mod. uptempo

Tick, Tick . . . Boom! (2001)
Music and Lyrics by Jonathan Larson

Song title, **Character (Voice)**	**Range**	**Song Style**
Thirty/ninety, Jonathan (T), company	e-a1	uptempo
Green green dress, Jonathan, Susan (M)	c#1-g1/c1-c2	mod. uptempo
Johnny can't decide, trio	MTB	moving ballad
Sunday, trio	MTB	mod. ballad
No more, Michael (Bar), Jonathan	c-f#1/e-g1	mod. uptempo
Therapy, Jonathan, Susan	A-g1/a-d2	gradually faster
Real life, Michael, company	B♭-e♭1	mod. uptempo
Sugar, Jonathan, company	f-g1	uptempo
See her smile, Jonathan, company	d-a1	mod. ballad
Come to your senses, Karessa (M)	a♭-c2	ballad
Why?, Jonathan	d-f1	ballad
Thirty/ninety reprise, Jonathan	a-f1	uptempo
Louder than words, trio	MTB	uptempo

Titanic (1997)
Music and Lyrics by Maury Yeston

Song title, **Character (Voice)**	**Range**	**Song Style**
In every age, Andrews (Bar)	A-g1	mod. ballad
How did they build Titanic?, Barrett (T)	g-f1	uptempo
There she is, company		uptempo
I must get on that ship, company		uptempo
The first-class section, Alice (M)	b♭-d2	uptempo
Godspeed Titanic, chorus		hymn
Barrett's song, Barrett	A-g1	uptempo

What a remarkable age, chorus		uptempo
To be a captain, Murdoch (Bar)	d-e1	ballad
Lady's maid, company		mod. uptempo
The proposal, Barrett, Bride incidental	g-f1	mod. ballad
The night was alive, Bride (S), Barrett	c-g2/g-f1	mod. uptempo
God lift me up, chorus		hymn
Doing the latest rag, company		uptempo
I have danced, Alice, Edgar (Bar)	a-d2/G-b	mod. waltz
No morn, company		ballad
Autumn, Harley (Bar)	b-f#1	ballad
No morn reprise, company		ballad
Wake up, wake up, chorus		uptempo
Dressed in your pajamas in the grand salon, company		mod. ballad
The staircase, company		uptempo
The blame, trio	TBB	uptempo
To the life boats, company		mod. uptempo
We'll meet tomorrow, company		mod. uptempo
To be a captain reprise, Etches (Bar)	B-c#1	ballad
Still, Ida (M), Isidor (Bar)	g-d2/F-f1	ballad
Mr. Andrew's vision, Andrews	e-g1	uptempo
In every age reprise, company		mod. ballad
Godspeed Titanic reprise, company		hymn ballad

Tommy (1993)
Music and Lyrics by Pete Townshend
Additional Music and Lyrics by John Entwhistle and Keith Moon

Song title, Character (Voice)	Range	Song Style
It's a boy, company		mod. uptempo
Twenty-one, Mrs. Walker (M), Lover (T), Mr. Walker (T)	g-c2/g-ab1/f-ab1	ballad
Amazing journey, Narrator (T)	a-g1	uptempo
Christmas, company		uptempo
Do you think it's alright, Mrs. Walker, Capt. Walker	eb1-eb2/g-eb1	mod. uptempo
Fiddle about, Uncle Ernie (T), offstage men's chorus	G-bb1	fast character
Cousin Kevin, Kevin (T)	c-ab1	uptempo
Sensation, Narrator, chorus	f-a1	uptempo
Eyesight to the blind, Hawker (T), Harmonica Player (T), chorus	a-g1/c#-b1	mod. uptempo
Acid queen, Gypsy (M)	g-g2	uptempo
Pinball wizard, Lad 1 (T), Lad 2 (T), Kevin	d-c2/f#-a1/a-b1	uptempo
Go to the mirror, boy, ensemble		mod. uptempo

Tommy, can you hear me?, male ensemble		uptempo
I believe my own eyes, Mrs. Walker, Mr. Walker	a-b1/f-a1	mod. uptempo
Smash the mirror, Mrs. Walker	b-d1	uptempo, hard
I'm free, Tommy (T)	f#-b1	uptempo
Sensation reprise, Tommy, chorus	g-a1	uptempo
I'm free/Pinball wizard reprise, Tommy; Kevin and Guards incidental	e-a1	uptempo
Tommy's holiday camp, Uncle Ernie	d-f#1	mod. character
Sally Simpson, company		uptempo
Welcome, Tommy, chorus	d♭-a♭1	mod. ballad
We're not gonna take it, Tommy, chorus	d-b♭1	uptempo
Finale: See me, feel me, company		mod. uptempo

25th Annual Putnam County Spelling Bee (2005)
Music and Lyrics by William Finn

Song title, Character (Voice)	Range	Song Style
The 25th annual . . . , company		mod. uptempo
The rules, Panch, Rona (M), company	d1-d2	uptempo
My friend, the dictionary, Olive (M)	b-d2	mod. uptempo
Pandemonium, Chip (T), company	f#-b1	uptempo
I'm not that smart, Leaf (T), company	A-a1	moderate
Magic foot, William (Bar), company	f-a1	swing uptempo
Pandemonium reprise, Mitch (T), company	g-a1	uptempo
My favorite moment no. 2, Rona	d1-d2	mod. uptempo
Prayer of the comfort counselor, Mitch, company	e-a1	character ballad
My unfortunate erection, Chip	d♭-a♭1	funny uptempo
Woe is me, Schwartz (M), company	g-c2	mod. uptempo
I'm not that smart reprise, Leaf	d-f#1	mod. ballad
I speak in six languages, Marcy (M), company	d-f#1	uptempo
Jesus, Marcy, company	a-b1	uptempo
The I love you song, trio	MMT	ballad
Woe is me reprise, Schwartz, Mitch incidental	e1-c2	ballad
My favorite moment no. 3, Rona	d♭1-d♭2	ballad
Second, company		slow
Epilogues, company		moderate
The 25th annual . . . reprise, company		mod. uptempo

Two by Two (1970)

Music by Richard Rodgers   Lyrics by Martin Charnin

Song title, **Character (Voice)**	**Range**	**Song Style**
Why me?, Noah (T)	d-f#1 (opt. d3), some spoken	uptempo
Put him away, chorus		mod. uptempo
Something, somewhere, Japheth (T), chorus	e♭-g1	uptempo
You have got to have a rudder on the ark, Noah, Sons	Noah: B-e1/Sons: f-f#1	uptempo
Something doesn't happen, Rachel (S), Esther (M)	c#1-e2/d-c#1	ballad
An old man, Esther	b♭-c2	uptempo
Ninety again, Noah	c-a♭1	uptempo
Two by two, chorus		mod. uptempo
I do not know a day I did not love you, Japheth	d♭-g♭1	ballad
When it dries, Noah, family	c-g1	uptempo
You, Noah	B-b	ballad
The golden ram, Goldie (S)	a♭-c3	moving ballad
Poppa knows best, Noah, Japheth, Sons	e-e1/f#-d1	uptempo
I do not know . . . reprise, Rachel, Japheth	c1-d2/c-f1	ballad
As far as I'm concerned, Shem (Bar), Leah (M)	c-g1/e1-e♭2	uptempo, funny
Hey, girlie, Noah	A#-d1	ballad
The covenant, Noah	d-g1	ballad

Two Gentlemen of Verona (1971)

Music by Galt MacDermot   Lyrics by John Guare

Song title, **Character (Voice)**	**Range**	**Song Style**
Summer, summer, chorus		mod. uptempo
I love my father/That's a very interesting question, Girl No. 4 (S)	f1-f2	mod. ballad
I'd like to be a rose, Valentine (T), Proteus (Bar), chorus	c-a1/A-e1	mod. ballad
Symphony, Proteus, chorus	B♭-e♭1	ballad
I am not interested in love, Julia (M)	a-c2	ballad
Love, is that you?, Thurio (T), women's chorus incidental	g-c2	recitative
Thou hast metamorphosed me, Julia	a-g2	ballad
What does a lover pack?, Julia, Proteus	c1-e♭2/c-f1	mod. ballad
Pearls, Launce (Bar)	A-c#1	waltz ballad
I love my father reprise, Proteus	e♭-e♭1	ballad

Two gentlemen of Verona, Julia, Lucetta (M), women's chorus	both b♭-e♭2	uptempo
Follow the rainbow, company		mod. uptempo
Where's north, company		uptempo
Bring all the boys back home, Duke (Bar), chorus	c-e1	uptempo march
Who is Silvia?, Silvia (M), Valentine	d1-d2/d-d1	ballad
Love's revenge, Valentine	c-a1	ballad
To whom it may concern me, Silvia, Valentine	g-e2/G-e1	narrative ballad
Night letter, Silvia, Valentine	c1-a2/c-a1	uptempo
Love's revenge reprise, Valentine, men's chorus	c-c2	ballad
Calla lily lady, Proteus	e-g1	fast calypso
I come from the land of betrayal, Lucetta	c1-c2	mod. ballad
Thurio's samba, Thurio, Duke, chorus	c-c2/c-f1	uptempo
Hot lover, Launce, Speed (Bar)	d-g1/d-e♭1	quick dixieland
What a nice idea, Julia, chorus incidental	a-b1	ballad
Who is Silvia reprise, Proteus, chorus	d-f1	mod. ballad
Love me, Silvia, chorus	a-d2	driving ballad
Eglamour, Eglamour (Bar), Silvia incidental	B-e1	moving ballad
Kidnapped, company		uptempo
Howl, Valentine	G#-e1	mod. uptempo
What's a nice girl like her?, Proteus	c#-f#1	mod. ballad
Don't have the baby, Lucetta, Speed, Launce, Julia	men: B-c1/her: b-c2*	mod. uptempo
Milkmaid, Milkmaid (M), Launce	b-d2/c-d1	uptempo
Love has driven me sane, Silvia, company	c1-c2	mod. uptempo

Alternate for "Howl":
Mansion, Valentine	c#-f#1	ballad

*Could be performed as a solo.

The Unsinkable Molly Brown (1960)
Music and Lyrics by Meredith Willson

Song title, Character (Voice)	Range	Song Style
I ain't down yet, Molly (M), Brothers	b♭-f2/spoken	uptempo
Belly up to the bar, boys, unison men's chorus		uptempo
Colorado, my home, Johnny (T)	B-f1	uptempo
Belly up to the bar, boys reprise, Molly, men's chorus	a-a1	uptempo
Cabin sequence, Johnny, Molly	d♭-f1/g-a♭1	ballad
Beautiful people of Denver, Molly	f-a1	ballad

Song title, Character (Voice)	Range	Song Style
Are you sure?, Molly, chorus	f#-c2	uptempo
We're going to learn to read and write, Molly, Johnny	ab-eb2/Ab-f1	uptempo
Happy birthday, Mrs. J.J. Brown, Princess (S), chorus	a-f2	uptempo
Bon jour, ensemble		mod. uptempo
If I knew, Johnny	c-f1	ballad
Keep a-hoppin', chorus		uptempo
Leadville Johnny Brown, Johnny	d-e1	ballad
Dolce far niente, Prince (Bar), Molly	G-eb1/ab-ab1	ballad

Urinetown (2001)

Music by Mark Hollmann   Lyrics by Mark Hollman and Greg Kotis

Song title, Character (Voice)	Range	Song Style
Urinetown, company		moving ballad
It's a privilege to pee, Pennywise (S), chorus	c1-c3	uptempo
It's a privilege reprise, Lockstock (T), chorus	c-g1	uptempo
Mr. Cladwell, Cladwell (Bar), company	Bb-gb1	ballad
Cop song, Lockstock, Barrel (Bar), chorus	both Bb-eb1	uptempo
Follow your heart, Hope (S), Bobby (T)	bb-f2/Bb-g1	waltz ballad
Look at the sky, Bobby, company	Bb-g1	mod. uptempo
Don't be the bunny, Cladwell, company	A-e1	mod. uptempo
Free! People are free!, company		uptempo
What is Urinetown?, company		uptempo
Snuff that girl, Harry (T), Becky (M), chorus	d-f1/d1-e2	jazzy uptempo
Run, freedom, run, Bobby, chorus	d-c2	gospel uptempo
Follow your heart reprise, Hope	bb-db2	ballad
Why did I listen to that man?, company		uptempo
Tell her I love her, Sally (M), Bobby	a-e2/B-e1	moving ballad
We're not sorry, company		mod. uptempo
I see a river, Hope, company		mod. ballad

The Vagabond King (1925)

Music by Rudolph Friml   Lyrics by Brian Hooker

Song title, Character (Voice)	Range	Song Style
Life is like a bubble in our glasses, company		uptempo
Love for sale, Huguette (S), chorus	eb1-g2	mod. uptempo
Drinking song, Tabary (T), chorus	d-a1	uptempo
Song of the Vagabonds, Villon (T), chorus	c-f1	mod. ballad
Some day, Katherine (S)	f#1-a2	ballad
Only a rose, Katherine, Villon	d1-g2/d-f1	ballad

Hunting, chorus		uptempo
Scotch archer's song, B solo, men's chorus	D-d1	march uptempo
To-morrow, Villon, Katherine	e♭-f1/e♭1-a♭2	mod. uptempo
Some day, company		ballad
Nocturn, S, Bar soli, chorus	c1-b♭2/c-e♭1	ballad
Serenade, Tabary, Oliver (T), Mary (M)	c-e1/c-e1/c1-e2	waltz ballad
Huguette waltz, Huguette	d1-f2	waltz ballad
Love me tonight, Katherine, Villon	c1-a2/c-e1	waltz ballad
Sons of toil and danger, company		march uptempo
Church music, Bar solo, chorus	e♭-e♭1	anthem ballad
Only a rose reprise, company		mod. ballad

Victor/Victoria (1995)

Music by Henry Mancini and Frank Wildhorn   Lyrics by Leslie Bricusse

Song title, **Character (Voice)**	**Range**	**Song Style**
Paris by night, Toddy (Bar)	B♭-e♭1	mod. uptempo
If I were a man, Victoria (M)	g-a1	mod. ballad
Trust me, Toddy, Victoria	A-d1/a-a♭1	uptempo
Le jazz hot, Jazz Singer (T), Victoria, chorus	c-f#1/f-f2	uptempo
Paris makes me horny, Norma (M)	b♭-e♭2	mod. uptempo
Crazy world, Victoria	e♭-c2	ballad
Louis says, Victor, men's chorus	e-b1	uptempo
King's dilemma, King (Bar)	A-f1(much spoken)	uptempo
You and me, Toddy, Victoria	B-b1/g-g#1	ballad
Paris by night reprise, La Parisienne (M)	a-c2	mod. ballad
Almost a love song, Victoria, King	g-c2/G-e♭1	ballad
Chicago, Illinois, Norma, women's ensemble	a-e2	uptempo
Living in the shadows, Victoria	e-a1	ballad
Living in the shadows reprise, Victoria	e-a1	ballad
Victor/Victoria, company		uptempo

The Wedding Singer (2006)

Music by Matthew Sklar   Lyrics by Chad Beguelin

Song title, **Character (Voice)**	**Range**	**Song Style**
It's your wedding day, Robbie (T), company	e-a1	uptempo
Someday, Julia (M), women's chorus	a-e♭2	moderate shuffle
Awesome, Robbie, Julia	e-g#1/b-d2	freely
Linda's note, Linda (M)	a-c#2	ballad
Pop!, trio	SMM	uptempo

Somebody kill me, Robbie	a-a1	mod. uptempo
Grandma's note, Rosie (M)	c1-c2	ballad
Casualty of love, Robbie, company	f#-a1	uptempo
Come out of the dumpster, Julia, Robbie incidental	a-e2	ballad
Today you are a man, trio	TTB	uptempo
George's prayer, George (T)	e-a1	ballad
Not that kind of thing, company		mod. ballad
Saturday night in the city, company		uptempo
All about the queen, Glen (T), company	f-g1	uptempo
Right in front of your eyes, Hally (M), Sammy (Bar)	b-c#2/d♭-f1	uptempo
Single, male ensemble		moderate blues
If I told you, Robbie, Julia	B-g1/g-e2	flowing ballad
Let me come home, Linda	b-d2	mod. rock ballad
Not that kind/If I told you reprise, Robbie, Julia	f#-d#1/b-b1	ballad
Move that thing, Rosie, George	c1-c2 (mostly spoken)/B♭-e♭1	mod. uptempo
Grow old with you, Robbie, Julia incidental	e-f#1	ballad
It's your wedding day finale, company		uptempo

West Side Story (1957)

Music by Leonard Bernstein   Lyrics by Stephen Sondheim

Song title, Character (Voice)	Range	Song Style
Jet song, Riff (Bar), Jets (male ensemble)	b♭-g1	mod. uptempo
Something's coming, Tony (T)	e-f#1	jazzy ballad
Maria, Tony	b-a♭1	ballad
Balcony scene, Maria (S), Tony	b♭-a♭2/B♭-a♭1	ballad
America, Anita (M), Rosalie (M), women	both a-d1	uptempo
Cool, Riff, Jets	c#-e♭1	mod. uptempo
One hand, one heart, Tony, Maria	g♭-g♭1/g♭-a♭2	ballad
Tonight, Maria, Tony, Anita, Riff, Bernardo	SMTBB	uptempo
I feel pretty, Maria, girls	c1-g2	mod. uptempo
Gee, Officer Krupke, Action (Bar), Jets	G-f1	fast character
Boy like that/I have a love, Maria, Anita	b♭-b♭2/f-d2	driving ballad

Where's Charley? (1948)
Music and Lyrics by Frank Loesser

Song title, Character (Voice)	Range	Song Style
The years before us, men's chorus		mod. ballad
Better get out of here, Amy, Kitty, Charley, Jack	SSTB	mod. ballad
The new Ashmolean marching society and students' conservatory band, company		uptempo
My darling, my darling, Jack (T), Kitty (S)	c-f1/eb1-g2	ballad
Make a miracle, Amy (S), Charley (Bar)	bb-eb2/Bb-eb1	uptempo
Serenade with asides, Spettigue (Bar)	B-c1	character ballad
Lovelier than ever, Sir Francis (T), Donna Lucia (S), chorus	d-g1/d1-g2	ballad
The woman in his room, Amy	d-fb2	waltz ballad
Pernambuco, chorus		uptempo
Where's Charley, Jack, company	d-g1	uptempo
Once in love with Amy, Charley	Bb-bb	moving ballad
The gossips, women's chorus		uptempo
The years before us reprise, men's chorus		mod. ballad
Lovelier than ever reprise, chorus		ballad
At the red rose cotillion, Jack, Kitty, chorus	d-g1/d1-g2	waltz ballad
Finale: My, darling, my darling, company		uptempo

Whistle Down the Wind (1996)
Music by Andrew Lloyd Webber   Lyrics by Jim Steinman

Song title, Character (Voice)	Range	Song Style
Keep to the vaults of heaven, company		ballad
I never get what I pray for, trio	SMT	uptempo
Home now, ensemble		mod. ballad
Grown ups kill me, Boone (T)	Bb-ab1	ballad
Whistle down the wind, Boone, Swallow (M)	d-d1/db1-db2	ballad
Cold, company		uptempo
Soliloquy, Man (T)	B-a1	ballad
If only, Man, Swallow	B-g1/a-d2	mod. uptempo
Tire tracks, Candy (M), Amos (T)	c1-d2/f-a1	mod. uptempo
Safe haven, company		mod. uptempo
Long overdue for a miracle, company		uptempo
When children rule the world, company		ballad
The gang, Man, chorus	d-g1	uptempo blues
No matter what, company		mod. ballad
Opening, Act 2, company		uptempo
Try not to be afraid, Man, Swallow	A-a1/c1-d2	mod. ballad
Let's make a promise, Amos	f-ab1	uptempo

A kiss is a terrible thing to waste, trio	MTT	mod. ballad
No matter what reprise, company		ballad
So many cries, Man	d-b♭1	ballad
Now the noose, company		uptempo
Wrestle with the devil, Preacher (T), company	e♭-a1	uptempo
No matter what the outrage, chorus		uptempo
The nature of the beast, Man, Swallow	c-b♭1/a-f2	ballad
The thunder is rolling, company		mod. uptempo

Wicked (2003)
Music and Lyrics by Stephen Schwartz

Song title, **Character (Voice)**	**Range**	**Song Style**
No one mourns the wicked, company		uptempo
Dear old Shiz, chorus		hymn ballad
The wizard and I, Morrible (M), Elphaba (A)	g♭-b♭1/g-e2	uptempo
What is this feeling?, Glinda (M), Elphaba	b♭-f♭2/b-d♭2	uptempo
Something bad, Dillamond (Bar), Elphaba incidental	c#-e♭1	mod. uptempo
Dancing through life, Fiyero (T), trio	d-a1/MMT	uptempo
Popular, Glinda	g-c2	uptempo
I'm not that girl, Elphaba	e-b1	mod. ballad
One short day, Glinda, Elphaba, chorus	a-c1/a-e1	mod. uptempo
A sentimental man, Wizard (T)	B-f#1	mod. uptempo
Defying gravity, Glinda, Elphaba, chorus	a-d♭2/g♭-f2	uptempo
No one mourns the wicked reprise, company		uptempo
Thank goodness, Glinda, Morrible, company	b♭-a2/f#-b1	mostly uptempo
The wicked witch of the East, trio	MMT	scene
Wonderful, Wizard, Elphaba incidental	A-e1	mod. ballad
I'm not that girl reprise, Glinda	g-d1	ballad
As long as you're mine, Elphaba, Fiyero	b♭-d♭1/g-b♭1	mod. ballad
No good deed, Elphaba	a-d#2	uptempo
March of the witch-hunters, Boq (T), chorus	e-g1	uptempo
For good, Glinda, Elphaba	a♭-d♭2/g#-d♭2	ballad
Good news!, company		uptempo

The Wild Party (2000)
Music and Lyrics by Michael John LaChiusa

Song title, **Character (Voice)**	**Range**	**Song Style**
Queenie was a blonde, company		uptempo
Marie is tricky, Burrs (T), chorus	d-g1	uptempo
Queenie is so, Queenie (M), Burrs incidental	g-b♭	moderate

Wild party, Burrs, Queenie	c#-f#1/e#-d2	uptempo
Dry, company		uptempo
Welcome to my party, Queenie, Nadine incidental	g-c2	boogie uptempo
Like Sally, Madeleine (M)	b♭-c2	moderate swing
Breezin' through another day, Jackie (S)	a-a2	moderate swing
Uptown, trio	TTB	uptempo
Eddie and Mae, Eddie (T), Mae (M)	B-a♭1/b♭-e♭2	uptempo
Gold and Goldberg, Gold (T), Goldberg (T)	e-c#2/B-a♭1	moderate
Moving uptown, Dolores (S)	f-a1	Latin ballad
The black bottom, Queenie, company	spoken	swing uptempo
Best friend, Queenie, Kate (M)	both a♭-b♭1	moderate
A little m-m-m, Oscar (T), Phil (T)	e-e1/e-g1	moderately slow
Tabu, Oscar	f-e♭1	moderate foxtrot
Takin' care of the ladies, Black (T)	B-g1	swing uptempo
Wouldn't it be nice, Burrs	c-a♭1	moderate
Lowdown-down, Queenie	a-b1	moderate
Gin, company		moderate
Wild, company		uptempo
Need, company		slow
Black is a moocher, Kate, chorus	e-d2	mod. slow
People like us, Queenie, Black	e-b1/c-f#1	ballad
After midnight dies, Sally (M)	a1-a2	ballad
Golden boy, Eddie; Oscar, Phil incidental	A-e1	blues ballad
The movin' uptown blues, Goldberg, Gold	both B♭-g♭1	mod. blues
The lights of Broadway reprise, Nadine (M)	b-e2	uptempo
More, Jackie	c1-g2	moderate
Love ain't nothin', Kate	f-e♭2	uptempo
Welcome to her party, Burrs	c-d1	uptempo
What I need, Queenie	a♭-a1	ballad
How many women in the world?, Burrs	B-a♭1	mod. ballad
When it ends, Dolores	d#1-g2	moderate
This is what it is, Queenie	a♭-e♭2	slow
Finale, company		moderate

The Wild Party (2000)
Music and Lyrics by Andrew Lippa

Song title, **Character (Voice)**	**Range**	**Song Style**
Queenie was a blonde, Queenie (M), male chorus	g-d2	mod. uptempo
Before too long, Burrs (T), chorus, Queenie incidental	B♭-g1	uptempo
The apartment, company		mod. ballad

Out of the blue, Queenie	g#-d#2	slow, then faster
What a party, company		uptempo
Raise the roof, Queenie, chorus	f#-d2	uptempo
Look at me now, Kate (M)	a-e2	swing uptempo
He was calm, company		scene
Poor child, quartet	MMTB	ballad
An old fashioned love story, Madeleine (M)	a-e2	character uptempo
By now the room was moving, company		uptempo
The juggernaut, quartet, chorus	MMTB	blues ballad
A wild, wild party, company		uptempo
Two of a kind, Eddie (Bar), Mae (M)	B-e1/a-d2	moderate swing
Of all the luck, Black (Bar), Queenie incidental	f-e♭1	uptempo
Maybe I like it this way, Queenie	a-d♭2	ballad
What is it about her?, Burrs, Queenie	c-a♭1/c1-c2	moving ballad
The life of the party, Kate	f#-d♭2	moderate swing
Who is this man?, Queenie	g-c2	mod. uptempo
The gal for me, Black, Queenie incidental	A-d1	mod. uptempo
I'll be here, Black	d#-d#1	driving ballad
Listen to me, quartet	MMTB	scene
Let me down, Burrs, chorus, Kate incidental	d-a1	gospel swing
The fight, company		uptempo
I know nothing about you, Black, Queenie	F#-d1/g#-d2	moderate
Come with me, Black, Queenie, chorus	f#-f#1/f#-e♭2	ballad
Make me happy, trio	MTB	uptempo
Poor child reprise, Black, Queenie	G-e1/a-b1	ballad
How did we come to this?, Queenie, company	g#-c#2	ballad

Wildcat (1960)

Music by Cy Coleman   Lyrics by Carolyn Leigh

Song title, **Character (Voice)**	**Range**	**Song Style**
Oil, chorus		uptempo
Hey, look me over!, Wildy (M), Janie (M)	a-c#2/f#-e2	uptempo march
You've come home, Joe (Bar)	B♭-e♭1	ballad
What takes my fancy, Sookie (Bar), Wildy	A♭-c1/a♭-c2	uptempo hoedown
You're a liar, Joe, Wildy	B-c1/c1-b1	uptempo, funny
One day we dance, Hank (T), Janie	d-f♭1/c1-c2	waltz ballad
Give a little whistle, Wildy, Joe, chorus	g-c2/B♭-e♭1	uptempo polka
Tall hope, Tattoo (T), Oney (Bar), men	a♭-e♭1/d♭-e♭1	blues ballad
Dancing on my tippy-tippy toes, Countess (M), Wildy	a-d2/a-c#2	waltz ballad
El sombrero, Wildy, Cisco (Bar), Oney	all b-e1	uptempo

Corduroy road, Joe, chorus   B♭-e♭1   uptempo
Hey, look me over reprise, company   uptempo

The Will Rogers Follies (1993)

Music by Cy Coleman   Lyrics by Betty Comden and Adolph Green

Song title, Character (Voice)	Range	Song Style
Let's go flying, chorus		uptempo
Will-a-mania, Ziegfeld's Favorite (M), chorus	g-a1	mod. uptempo
Give a man enough rope, Will (Bar), Cowboy quartet	B♭-f1	mod. ballad
It's a boy, Clem (Bar), girls' sextet	c-e1	mod. ballad
It's a boy reprise, Will	B-d1	mod. ballad
My unknown someone, Betty Blake (M)	a♭-c2	mod. ballad
The big time, Will, Betty, four children	B-d#1/b-d#2	uptempo
My big mistake, Betty; Will, incidental	f-d2	ballad
Marry me now/Without you, company		uptempo
Entr'acte, men's chorus; Will incidental		mod. uptempo
Look around, Will	c#-d1	mod. uptempo
The campaign, "Our favorite son," Will, chorus	c-e♭1	mod. uptempo
No man left for me, Betty	a-c#2	blues ballad
Presents for Mrs. Rogers, Will, Cowboy quartet	B-c#1	moving ballad
Never met a man I didn't like, Will, chorus	B-d#	moving ballad

Wish You Were Here (1952)

Music and Lyrics by Harold Rome

Song title, Character (Voice)	Range	Song Style
Camp Kare-free, chorus		uptempo
There's nothing nicer than people, Teddy (S), chorus	b♭-e♭2	uptempo
Ballad of a social director, Itchy (Bar), chorus	d-e1	fast character
Shopping around, Fay (M)	c1-b♭1	jazzy ballad
Waiter's song, men's chorus		fast, fight song
Mix and mingle, Chick (T), chorus, many soli	c-f1	uptempo
Could be, company		ballad
Light fantastic, chorus		uptempo
Where did the night go?, Chick, Teddy, chorus	c-e♭1/f1-b♭2	ballad

Certain individuals, company		uptempo
They won't know me, Chick	B-g1	ballad
Summer afternoon, Pinky (T), chorus	B#-f#1	moving ballad
Where did the night go reprise, chorus		ballad
Don Jose of Far Rockaway, Itchy, chorus	c#-e♭1	tango uptempo
Everybody love everybody, Fay, company	b♭-b1	uptempo
Wish you were here, Chick, background chorus	e♭-a♭1	ballad
Relax, Pinky, Teddy	c-e♭1/mostly spoken	ballad
Gone with the night, company		be-bop uptempo
Flattery, Itchy, Teddy, chorus	c-c1/c1-c2	moving ballad
Summer afternoon, company		moving ballad

The Wiz (1975)
Music and Lyrics by Charlie Smalls

Song title, **Character (Voice)**	**Range**	**Song Style**
The feeling we once had, Aunt Em (M)	g-c2	gospel ballad
He's the Wiz, Addaperle (S)	f-c3	jazzy mod.
Soon as I get home, Dorothy (S)	b♭-c#2	ballad
I was born on the day before yesterday, Scarecrow (T)	e-a1	uptempo
Ease on down the road, Dorothy, chorus	g-d♭1	uptempo
Slide some oil to me, Tinman (T)	g-b♭1	mod. uptempo
Mean ole lion, Lion (T)	G-b♭1	mod. uptempo
Be a lion, Dorothy, Lion	b♭-d♭2/a♭-a♭1	anthem ballad
So you wanted to meet the Wizard, Wiz (T)	e-g1	driving uptempo
What would I do if I could feel, Tinman	d-a1	blues ballad
Don't nobody bring me no bad news, Evillene (M), chorus	g-d♭2	uptempo
Everybody rejoice ("Brand new day"), Dorothy, chorus	e-b♭1	uptempo
Who do you think you are, company		mod. uptempo
Believe in yourself, Wiz	c-g1	ballad
Y'all got it, Wiz, chorus	g-a1	fast, hard jazz
A rested body, Glinda (M)	f-d2	moving ballad
When I think of home, Dorothy	g-e2	moving ballad

Woman of the Year (1981)

Music by John Kander   Lyrics by Fred Ebb

Song title, Character (Voice)	Range	Song Style
Opening, Tess (M), women's chorus	e-f1	mod. uptempo
Woman of the year, Tess, women's chorus	e-g1	mod. uptempo
See you in the funny papers, Sam (Bar)	A-db1	mod. uptempo
Right, Tess, Gerald (Bar)	ab-c2/G-a	uptempo
Shut up, Gerald, Sam, Tess, Gerald	all c-c1	uptempo, funny
So what else is new?, Sam, Katz (M)	Bb-db1/Ab-db1	mod. ballad
Second poker game, male ensemble		uptempo
One of the boys, Tess, men	e-g1	mod. uptempo
Table talk, Tess, Sam	f-g1/F-g	ballad
The two of us, Sam, Tess, company	both f-bb1	mod. ballad
It isn't working, chorus		uptempo
I told you so, Gerald, Helga (M)	B-e1/b-c#2	uptempo
Woman of the year reprise, Tess	gb-e2	driving ballad
I wrote the book, Tess, men's chorus	b-d2	ballad
Happy in the morning, Alex (M)	a-f1	mod. ballad
Sometimes a day goes by, Sam	A-c2	ballad
The grass is always greener, Jan (M), Tess	bb-db2/ab-eb2	mod. ballad, funny
Open the window, Tess, chorus	e-f2	uptempo
Finale: Table talk reprise, company		uptempo

Wonderful Town (1953)

Music by Leonard Bernstein   Lyrics by Betty Comden and Adolph Green

Song title, Character (Voice)	Range	Song Style
Washington Square, Guide (M), chorus	c1-eb2	mod. uptempo
Ohio, Eileen (S), Ruth (M)	bb-ab2/d-ab1	mod. ballad
100 easy ways to lose a man, Ruth	g-a1	jazzy, funny
What a waste, Baker (Bar), men's chorus	A-e1	mod. uptempo
Little bit in love, Eileen	c1-c#2	mod. ballad
Pass the football, Wreck (Bar)	A-e1	mod. character
Nice people, Eileen, chorus	d1-d3	ballad, then fast
Quiet girl, Baker, men's chorus	G-c1	ballad
Conga, Ruth, Admirals (male ensemble)	f-ab1	uptempo
Eileen, Eileen, men's chorus, several soli	g1-g2	ballad
Swing, Ruth, chorus	e1-e2	uptempo
Ohio reprise, Eileen, Ruth	bb-bb1/db-ab1	mod. ballad
It's love, Eileen, Baker, chorus incidental	g-c2/G-e1	uptempo

Wrong note rag, chorus; Eileen, Ruth incidental	b-d#2/B-d1	uptempo rag
It's love reprise, Eileen, Baker, company		uptempo

Working (1978)

Music and Lyrics by Stephen Schwartz, Micki Grant, Craig Carnella, James Taylor, Graciela Daniele, Matt Landers, Susan Birkhead, and Mary Rodgers

Song title, **Character (Voice)**	**Range**	**Song Style**
All the livelong day, company		uptempo
Lovin' Al, Al (T), chorus	B♭-f1 (one b♭1)	mod. uptempo
Newsboy, Newsboy (boy S), men's chorus	c1-d2	mod. uptempo
Nobody tells me how, Rose (S)	e1-a2	ballad
Un mejor dia vendra, Emilio (Bar), chorus	c-c1	ballad
Just a housewife, Housewife (M), chorus	a-b1	mod. ballad
Millwork, Millworker (M)	a-a1	mod. uptempo
The mason, Mason (T)	B♭-g1	ballad
If I could've been, company, many soli		mod. uptempo
It's an art, Dolores (M), chorus	a-c#2	mod. ballad
Brother trucker, Trucker (T), chorus	g-b1	rock uptempo
Joe, Joe (Bar)	d-d1	narrative ballad
Cleanin' women, Woman (M), women's chorus	b♭-e2	uptempo
Fathers and sons, Man (Bar), men's chorus incidental	c#-e1	hard ballad
Something to point to, company		driving ballad

The World Goes 'Round (1991)

Music by John Kander   Lyrics by Fred Ebb

Song title, **Character (Voice)**	**Range**	**Song Style**
And the world goes 'round, Woman 1(M)	f#-d2	ballad
Yes, company		mod. uptempo
Coffee in a cardboard cup, company		uptempo
The happy time, Man 2 (Bar)	d#-e1	uptempo
Colored lights, Woman 3 (M)	g♭-b1	mod. ballad
Sara Lee, Man 1 (T), Women	d-g1	mod., funny
Arthur in the afternoon, Woman 2 (M)	g♭-d♭2	uptempo, funny
My coloring book, Woman 1	b♭-c2	slow waltz
I don't remember you, Man 2*	b♭-ab1	ballad
Sometimes a day goes by, Man 1*	c-e♭1	mod. ballad
All that jazz, Woman 2, Man 1, company	g#-c2/c#-c#1	mod. fast jazz
Class, Woman 1, 3	both g♭-b1	mod. ballad

Mr. Cellophane, Man 1	b-g1	mod. ragtime
Me and my baby, company		ballad, then fast
There goes the ball game, Women	c1-g2/b-e2/g-e2	uptempo, jazzy
How lucky can you get, Woman 3, Men incidental	e-e♭2	ballad
The rink, company		mod. uptempo
Ring them bells, Woman 3, company	g#-d♭1	uptempo
Kiss of the Spider Woman, Man 2	g#-g#1	hard ballad
Only love, Woman 1†	a-b♭1	ballad
Marry me, Man 1†	e-g♭1	ballad
A quiet thing, Woman 2†	g-e♭1	ballad
Pain, company		uptempo, funny
The grass is always greener, Women 1, 3	g-d2/g-g1	mod. ballad
We can make it, Man 2	A-f1	moving ballad
Maybe this tim,, Woman 1	g♭-b1	driving ballad
Isn't this better?, Woman 3	a♭-b♭1	ballad
Money, money, company		uptempo
Cabaret, company		mod. uptempo
New York, New York, company		uptempo

*These two numbers are then combined together in a quodlibet.
†These three numbers are then combined together in a quodlibet.

A Year with Frog and Toad (2003)

Music by Robert Reale   Lyrics by Willie Reale

Song title, Character (Voice)	Range	Song Style
A year with Frog and Toad, Frog (Bar), Toad (Bar), Birds	both c-f1/SMT	mod. uptempo
Spring, Frog, Toad, Birds	A-a/c#-a	uptempo
Seeds, Toad	A-d1	mod. ballad
The letter no. 1, Snail (T)	e-a1	uptempo
Getta loada Toad, company		mod. uptempo
Alone, Frog	A-b♭	ballad
The letter no. 2, Snail	e-a1	uptempo
Cookies, Frog, Toad, Birds	B-e1/B-d1	uptempo
The kite, Frog, Toad, Birds	B-d#1/A-b	uptempo
Leaves: A year with Frog and Toad, Birds	SMT	mod. ballad
He'll never know, Toad, Frog	c-e♭1/C#-e♭1	soft shoe ballad
Shivers, ensemble		mod. uptempo
The letter no. 3, Snail	e-a1	uptempo
Down the hill, Frog, Toad, Moles	e1-f1/B♭-f1/SMT	uptempo
I'm coming out of my shell, Snail	A-g#1	mod. uptempo
Toad to the rescue, Toad	B-e2	march uptempo
Merry almost Christmas, Toad, Frog, Moles	both B-d1	ballad
A year with Frog and Toad reprise, company		uptempo

Your Own Thing (1968)

Music and Lyrics by Hal Hester and Danny Apolinar

Song title, Character (Voice)	Range	Song Style
No one's perfect, Viola (M), Sebastian (T)	d#1-d2/d#-e1	uptempo
The flowers, Viola	b♭-b♭1	mod. uptempo
I'm me, Danny (T), John (T), Michael (Bar): "The Apocalypse"	all c-f1	uptempo
Baby baby, Viola, Apocalypse	e1-g2/all e-g♭1	rock uptempo
Come away death, Sebastian	B♭-g♭1	ballad
I'm on my way to the top, Sebastian	f-g♭1	uptempo
Well, let it be, Olivia (M)	b♭-c2	mod. uptempo
Be gentle, Viola, Orson (Bar)	f-b1/B♭-e1	ballad
What do I know?, Viola, Apocalypse	g♭-c♭2	mod. ballad
Baby baby reprise, Sebastian, Apocalypse	f-g♭1	mambo rock
The now generation, company		march uptempo
The middle years, Sebastian	A-e1	narrative ballad
Middle years reprise, Olivia	e-c2	mod. ballad
When you're young and in love, Orson, Viola	B♭-e♭1/b♭-c2	uptempo waltz
Hunca munca, company		mambo rock
Don't leave me, Olivia, Sebastian	a-b1/A-f1	ballad
Do your own thing, Apocalypse	c-g1/c-e1/c-c1	mod. uptempo

You're a Good Man, Charlie Brown (1967)

Music and Lyrics by Clark Gesner

Song title, Character (Voice)	Range	Song Style
You're a good man, Charlie Brown, company		march uptempo
Schroeder, Lucy (S)	b#-e2	ballad
Snoopy, Snoopy (T)	G-g1	character ballad
My blanket and me, Linus (Bar)	B-e1	moving ballad
The kite, Charlie Brown (Bar)	B♭-e♭1	uptempo
The doctor is in, Lucy, Charlie	b♭-e♭2/c-f1	slow, funny
The book report, Lucy, Schroeder, Charlie, Linus	STBB	mod. ballad
The baseball game, company		uptempo
Glee club rehearsal, company		mod. ballad
Little known facts, Lucy	c1-c2	mod. uptempo
Suppertime, Snoopy	c-f#1	uptempo, jazzy
Happiness, company		mod. ballad

Zanna, Don't (2003)
Music and Lyrics by Tim Acito
Additional lyrics by Alexander Dinelaris

Song title, Character (Voice)	Range	Song Style
Who's got extra love?, Zanna (M), company	b-e2	uptempo
I think we got love, Mike (Bar), Steve (T)	d-e1/d-g1	uptempo
I ain't got time, Roberta (M), company male	c#1-d#2	uptempo
Ride 'em, Kate (M), Roberta	both b♭-d2	character uptempo
Zanna's song, Zanna	e1-e2	ballad
Be a man, Zanna, company	g1-f#2	uptempo
Don't ask, don't tell, Rita (M), Steve	c#1-a1/c#-b♭	mod. ballad
Fast, Buck (Bar), Tank (Bar), Candi (M)	c-c#1/c-e♭1/c1-a1	uptempo
I could write a book, Mike	c#-c#1	uptempo
Don't you wish you could be in love?, company		mod. uptempo
Whatcha got?, Roberta, others incidental	b-f#2	uptempo
Do you know what it's like?, company		fast ballad
'Tis a far better thing I do, Zanna	c1-c2	mod. ballad
Blow winds, Zanna, company	c1-d2	uptempo
Someday you might love me, Zanna	d♭1-d♭2	ballad
Straight to heaven, Tank, company	f1-e2	uptempo
Straight to heaven reprise, company		uptempo
Sometime do you think we could fall in love?, Tank	f#-e1	moving ballad
Finale, company		uptempo

Note: Not annotated from final score; some changes may exist in final version.

Zorba (1968)
Music by John Kander   Lyrics by Fred Ebb

Song title, Character (Voice)	Range	Song Style
Life, Leader (Bar), chorus	B♭-b♭	mod. ballad
First time, Zorba (Bar)	d-e1 (much spoken)	mod. uptempo
Top of the hill, Leader, chorus	G-b♭	ballad
No boom boom, Hortense (M), four admirals	g#-c#2	uptempo
Vive la difference, four admirals	unison c#-e1	uptempo
The butterfly, Nikos (T), Widow (M)	d-f1/d1-f2	mod. ballad
Goodbye Canavaro, Zorba, Hortense	G#-c#1/a#-a1	uptempo
Khania, Leader	B♭-d♭1	uptempo
I used to have a grandmama, Zorba	A-c#1	uptempo
Only love, Hortense	g♭-b♭1	ballad
Bend of the road, Leader, chorus incidental	G#-c1	mod. uptempo

Y'assou, company		uptempo
Woman, Zorba	E♭-c1	ballad
That's a beginning, Widow, Nikos	a-d♭2/d-f#1	ballad
The crow, Leader, chorus	c-a	uptempo
Happy birthday, Hortense, chorus	g#-a1	uptempo
I am free, Zorba	F-c1	alt. slow/fast

Indexes

Index to Songs for Solo Voices

Soprano Songs

BALLADS

CHARACTER SONGS

Mezzo-Soprano Songs

You don't have to do it for me, 115
You don't tell me, 127
You made me think you were in love,
    167
You should see yourself, 180
You're a loveable lunatic, 159
You're just in love, 28
Young people, 118

BALLADS

After midnight dies, 196
Ain't nothin' up, 151
Alice blue gown, 86
All at once you love him, 142
All for him, 135
All I wanted was the dream, 24
Allez-vous-en, 29
Always you, 30
And I was beautiful, 45
And the world goes 'round, 201
Angels, punks and raging queens, 52
Angry man, 147
Another suitcase in another hall, 53
Anthem, 34
Anyone can whistle, 9
Anytime, 6
As if we never said goodbye, 178
As long as he needs me, 130
As we stumble along, 50
At the glen, 46
Back in baby's arms, 6
Back on base, 39
Back to before, 147
Bali ha'i, 169
Barbara's song, 185
Be happy, 116
Be Italian, 126
Be on your own, 126
Beautiful, 109
Beautiful people of Denver, 190
Beauty and the Beast, 17
Believe, 162
Best night of my life, The, 10
Best thing for you, The, 28
Bewitched, 136
Black is a moocher, 196
Bonjour amour, 74
Boom boom, 50

Bowler hat, A, 135
Boy like you, A, 174
Boy next door, The, 113
Boy of my dreams, 166
Boy! What love has done for me, 70
Brimstone and treacle, 111
Bring my Nettie back, 39
Broadway baby, 62
Buddie, beware, 10
Build a bridge, 122
Bus from Amarillo, The, 18
But not for me, 42, 70
Button up with Edmond, 68
Cake I had, The, 75
Can you find it in your heart?, 63
Carrie, 31
Chain store daisy, 141
Change, 124
Change in me, A, 17
Chanson, 15
Children and art, 177
Children of the heavenly king, 122
Climb every mountain, 169
Coffee, 158
Color purple, The, 39
Colored lights, 150, 201
Come out of the dumpster, 193
Come to your senses, 186
Compliments, 161
Cornet man, 67
Could I leave you, 63
Cow song, The, 170
Crossing, The, 20
Daddy, 52
Dancing all the time, 19
Day by day, 71
Day is gone, The, 148
Days of plenty, 103
Dear God, 39
Dear God—Shug, 39
Dear Lord, 31
Dear Tom, 84
Diamonds are a girl's best friend, 68
Disneyland, 166
Do I hear a waltz?, 48
Do it alone, 137
Do you ever dream of Vienna?, 101
Doatsey Mae, 18
Dulcinea, 107

CHARACTER SONGS

I love a cop, 57
I married seven brothers, 160
I'm an Indian, too, 8
I'm gonna wash that man right out-a
    my hair, 169
I'm just nuts about you, 141
I've an inkling, 61
In Izzen Schnooken, 101
It's better with a union man, 141
Johnny One Note, 14
Josephine, 165
Keokuk social club, The, 117
Ladies who lunch, The, 40
Lady is a tramp, The, 14
Last week, Americans, 48
Little brains, a little talent, A, 44
Little girls, 7
Little things, 40
Look at me, I'm Sandra Dee, 74
Mabel's prayer, 54
Me and my town, 9
Memory, 45
Mene, mene, tekel, 141
Miss Byrd, 38
Moon song, The, 106
My mother's wedding day, 26
Oklahoma, 47
Old fashioned love story, An, 197

One feather tail of Ms. Gertrude
    McFuzz, The, 159
Ooh! My feet, 117
Oom-pah-pah, 130
Prickle pear and lilybud, 151
Plant you now, dig you later, 136
Private Schwartz, 67
Queenie's ballyhoo, 163
Right finger of my left hand, The, 148
So what, 26
Surabaya Santa, 168
Tact, 61
This week, Americans, 48
Throw it out, 124
Totem tom-tom, 154
Touch of the Irish, The, 113
Twiggy, 165
Typische deutsche, 174
Whatever Lola wants, Lola gets, 44
When I leave town, 60
When you've got it, flaunt it, 145
Who'll buy?, 104
Worst pies in London, The, 179
You can't get a man with a gun, 8
Zubbediya, 93

SCENE
Good times, 94

Tenor Songs

UPTEMPO SONGS
Addressing of cats, The, 33
Alas for you, 71
Alive, 89
All about the queen, 193
All I need is the girl, 76
All our friends, 69
Always leave them laughing, 69
Amazing journey, 187
Ambition, 49
And the money kept rolling in, 52
At the Club Elysium, 181
At the fountain, 180
At the Grand Hotel, 73

Baby, baby, 203
Baby, I love you, 166
Banjo, The, 113
Barrett's song, 186
Before too long, 196
Begat, The, 57
Being alive, 40
Better, 38
Bhangra, 22
Big, 19
Big black giant, The, 112
Big dog, 39
Board of governors, 88
Body, mind, and soul, 5

Bass/Baritone Songs

UPTEMPO SONGS

Index to Duets

Duets for Two Women

Take him (MM), 137
Take me or leave me (MM), 149
Teacher's argument, The (MM), 54
Ten petticoats (MM), 46
Thank goodness (MM), 195
This can't be love (SS), 25
This is as good as it gets (SM), 73
We share everything (MM), 164
We'll always be bosom buddies (MM),
   89
Welcome to the 60s (MM), 78
What is this feeling? (MM), 195
What? What? (MM), 58
Wizard and I, The (MM), 195
Wrong note rag (SM), 201

BALLADS
Almost a quarter to nine (MM), 65
Angel mom (SM), 155
Angel of music (SM), 140
Baby, dream your dream (MM), 180
Beauty within (MM), 172
Better if I died (MM), 46
Biggest ain't the best, The (SM), 128
Bosom buddies (MM), 106
Boy like that/One heart (SM), 193
Brimstone and treacle (SM), 111
Buddy kissed me (MM), 164
Can't help lovin' that man (SM), 163
Carnegie Hall pavane (MM), 131
Carrie (MM), 32
Chiquita (MM), 105
Class (MM), 201
Daisy, can you hear what I'm thinking?
   (MM), 165
Dancing on my tippy-tippy toes (MM),
   197
Every day a little death (SM), 102
Feed the birds (SM), 111
Feelings you have got to hide (MM),
   164
For good (MM), 195
Girl who has everything, The (SM), 75
Go home (MM), 97
Grass is always greener, The (MM),
   200, 202
Graveyard, The (SM), 87
Helen's death (MM), 87

Hero (SM), 23
Hey, look me over! (MM), 197
Hysteria/Lullabye (SS), 98
I do miracles (MM), 94
I don't know his name (SM), 162
I know him so well (MM), 34
I still believe (MM), 116
I want to be like everyone else (MM),
   164
I will never leave you (MM), 165
I've just seen him (MM), 4
If you don't mind my saying so (SM),
   119
In Algiers (SM), 58
In his eye (MM), 89
Indian maiden's lament (SS), 132
Just a coupl'a sisters (MM), 128
Kindred spirits (SM), 7
Kiss her now (MM), 90
Kisses and hugs (SS), 155
Ladies (MM), 46
Learning to be silent (MM), 63
Like everyone else (MM), 164
Little Mary Sunshine (SS), 100
Little me (MM), 101
Locker room scene (MM), 31
Love makes the world go round (MM),
   128
Love's never easy (SM), 22
Lucky (MM), 62
Lullabye (SM), 175
Milkmaid's song (SM), 152
My child (MM), 22
Nellie Kelly (MM), 69
Nights on Broadway (MM), 156
Nowadays (MM), 35
Ohio (SM), 200
One boy (SM), 26
One more kiss (SS), 62
Open your heart (MM), 31
Perfect nanny (SS), 111
Perfect strangers (SM), 121
Piano lesson (SM), 119
Private investigation, A (MM), 121
Quiet (SM), 30
Sixteen going on seventeen (SS), 169
Some things are meant to be (SM), 103
Someone wonderful I missed (MM), 83
Something bad is happening (MM), 54

Duets for Two Men

SCENES

Duets for a Man and a Woman

UPTEMPO DUETS

BALLADS

Try not to be afraid (MT), 194
Twin soliloquies (MB), 169
Twisted every way (SB), 140
Two little bluebirds (MT), 178
Two lost souls (MT), 44
Two of a kind (MB), 197
Two of us, The (MB), 200
Two sleepy nights (MB), 4
Unusual way (MB), 126
Unworthy of your love (MT), 12
Ven I valse (MB), 124
Violets and silver bells (MB), 163
Voice in my heart (SB), 100
Waiting for you (ST), 127
Wanting you (SB), 125
Wasn't it fun? (MB), 113
We do not belong together (MT), 177
We kiss in a shadow (ST), 92
We're gonna be fine (MT), 19
We're gonna go to Chicago (MB), 109
What do I do now? (ST), 166
What does a lover pack? (MB), 189
What is a man? (MB), 136
What is it about her? (MT), 197
What you want wid Bess? (ST), 144
What's new at the zoo? (SB), 49
Wheels of a dream, The (MT), 146
When I look at you (MT), 157
When the children are asleep (ST), 31
When there was me and you (MT), 80
When we are on the stage (MB), 61
Where are the snows? (MB), 83
Where did the night go? (ST), 198
Whistle down the wind (MT), 194
Who could ever have dreamed up you
    (SB), 139
Who is Sylvia? (MT), 190
Who taught her everything? (MT), 67
Why am I me? (SB), 163
Why do I love you? (ST), 163
Why shouldn't we? (MB), 154
With every breath I take (MB), 37
With so little to be sure of (MB), 9
With you (MB), 15

Without you (MB), 149
Word of your body, The (MT), 171
Written in the stars (MT), 3
Yesterday I loved you (ST), 134
You and I (MT), 34
You are beautiful (MT), 61
You are love (ST), 163
You are music (ST), 139
You are my home (MT), 156; (MB),
    157
You are my own (ST), 140
You are woman, I am man (MB), 67
You have cast your shadow on the sea
    (ST), 25
You made me love you (MB), 86
You must meet my wife (MB), 102
You remind me of you (MT), 116
You say you care (MT), 68
You should be loved (MT), 164
You want to lose your only friend
    (MT), 34
You were dead you know (ST), 29
You will not touch him (MT), 116
You would if you could (SB), 113
You'll never get away from me (MB),
    76
You'll think of someone (MB), 145
You're gonna love tomorrow (ST), 63
You're just in love (MT), 28
You're not foolin' me (ST), 134
You're timeless to me (MB), 78
Young and foolish (SB), 143
Your majesties (MT), 36
Yours, yours, yours (ST), 161

SCENES
Betty's pitch (MT), 178
Chanson d'enfance (ST), 12
Final scene (MB), 179
Oh daddy (MT), 97
Ok, ok, you got me (MT), 97
Paper dragons (MB), 116
Wedding, The (MT), 89

Index to Trios

Move (you're steppin' on my heart)
    (SMM), 50
Muqin (My mammy) (MBB), 185
My father's a homo (MTB), 108
New life coming, A (SMB), 173
Night they invented champagne, The
    (MMB), 70
No understand (SMT), 48
No way to stop it (MTB), 169
Nobody's ever gonna love you (MMB),
    118
Normandy (STT), 133
Not anymore (MMB), 147
Off to the races (TBB), 121
Oh happy day (BBB), 98
One step (SMB), 173
Only a kiss (MTB), 154
Pearl, you've been honoured (MMT),
    171
Pegasus (MTT), 122
Perpetual anticipation (SSM), 102
Pinball wizard (TTT), 187
Please come to our house (MTB), 108
Pleased with myself (SMB), 173
Poor, unsuccessful and fat (TTB), 124
Pop! (SMM), 192
Posh! (SSB), 35
Prayer (MTB), 158
Prince Edward Island (SMB), 7
Push ka pi she pie (TBB), 59
Put in a package (MMM), 84
Racquetball (TTT), 54
Rain in Spain, The (SBB), 120
Real American folksong, The (TBB),
    42
Reckoning, The (TBB), 48
Reform trio (SSM), 184
Riddle, The (MTB), 157
Ruthless (SMM), 155
Santa Fe (TTB), 149
Scarlet Pimpernel transition (SMT),
    157
She loves me not (STB), 38
Sing for your supper (SSS), 25
Sixty cents (TTB), 155
Skip to my Lou (MTB), 113
Starting here, starting now (SMB), 173
Sunshine girl (TTB), 124
Super trooper (MMM), 105

Tait song (TBB), 72
Tea party trio (MMM), 45
That's your funeral (MTB), 130
There ain't no flies on me (BBB), 124
There goes the ball game (MMM), 202
There'll be trouble (SSB), 174
There's gotta be something better
    (MMM), 180
They like Ike (TTT), 28
Three "B"s, The (MMM), 18
Three friends (SMT), 39
Tide pool, The (STT), 141
To be a performer (MTT), 101
Today you are a man (TTB), 193
Too good to be bad (MMM), 73
Travel (SMB), 173
Truly scrumptious (SSM), 35
Two-a-day for Keith (MBB), 132
Ugly garage (MMB), 45
Uptown (TTB), 196
We certainly requested a boy (SMB), 6
When a peer makes love (STB), 152
When an interesting person (MMT), 61
When you had left our pirate fold
    (MTB), 143
With a little bit of luck (TBB), 119
You are you (MMT), 60
You boys are gonna get me in such
    trouble (MBB), 124
You could drive a person crazy
    (SMM), 40
You will be mine (TTB), 110

BALLADS

All at once you love her (MTT), 141
All that I love (MTB), 110
And would you lie (SMM), 109
Anything for him (MTB), 94
At the ballet (SMM), 36
Beautiful (SMB), 173
Been a long day (MTB), 81
Best years of his life, The (MTB), 96
Bidin' my time (TBB), 42
Big ass rock (TTB), 66
Black and white (SMT), 16
Canceling the bar mitzvah (STT), 54
Children of God (SMT), 87
Class act (MTB), 183

SCENES

Index to
Quartets and Small Ensembles

BALLADS

Index to
Choruses and Company Numbers

Women's Choruses

Children's Choruses

Men's Choruses

Mixed Voices

Ladies, choice!, 114
Ladies of the evening, 25
Lady's maid, 187
Last dance, The, 21
Last part of every party, The, 86
Lazy moon, 72
Lemonade, 14
Let it go, 67
Let peacocks and monkeys in purple
    adornings, 93
Let the sun shine in, 77
Let's go flying, 198
Let's have lunch, 178
Letter sequence, The, 155
Life in the morning, 21
Life is like a bubble in our glasses, 191
Life is like a train, 132
Light at the end of the tunnel, 172
Light fantastic, 198
Light of the world, 70
Lioness chant, 99
Little old New York, 184
Little suffering, A, 179
Locomotion, 172
Long overdue for a miracle, 194
Look what happened to Mabel, 105
Look what you've done, 147
Lookin' good but feelin' bad, 3
Lopsided bus, 142
Loud as the hell you want, 13
Love motif, 55
Loveland, 63
Lovers of New Orleans, 123
Lucky in love, 72
Lullaby of Broadway, 66
Ma-cha-cha, 17
Make it through tonight, 156
Make our garden grow, 30
Make someone happy, 49
Make way—Canon, 11
Mama mia!, 106
Mama who bore me, 170
Man of no importance, A, 107
March of the Trollgers, 167
March of time, The, 38
Marry me now/Without you, 198
Marvin hits Trina, 108
Marvin's giddy seizures, 85
Mary, Mary, quite contrary, 14

Masquerade, 140
May the best man win, 126
May the god of fortune attend you, 181
Me and my girl/Lambeth walk, 113
Meek shall inherit the earth, The, 103
Meet me in St. Louis, 113
Megamix, 80
Merchandiser's song, 34
Merrily we roll along, 114
Message from a nightingale, 51
Midas touch, The, 17
Minnie's boys, 116
Mob song, The, 17
Money changes hands, The, 184
Money, money, 202
Monmart, 29
More than a woman, 156
Morning of the dragon, 116
Movin', 135
Mrs. Sally Adams, 28
Muddy water, 20
Murder in Parkland, 104
Murder, murder, 89
Musical comedy, 69
Musketeer sketch, 120
Muto, Il, 140
My body, 97
My city, 159
My darling, my darling, 194
My heart is so full of you, 118
My Miss May, 184
Mysterious ways, 39
Nag, nag, nag, 174
Name's LaGuardia, The, 57
Natural high, 84
Nerves, 166
Nest, egg, and tree, 160
Never mind, Bo Peep, 14
Never, never be an artist, 29
Never too late to Mendelssohn, 129
New Africa, 39
New Ashmolean marching society,
    The, 194
New deal for Christmas, A, 8
New girl in town, The, 77
New world, The, 168
New Year's Day, 164
New York, New York, 131, 202
Newt Lee's testimony, 137

SLOWER CHORUSES

Index to
Composers and Lyricists

Appendix

Publishers' Addresses and Websites

Music Theatre International
421 W. 54th St.
New York, NY 10019
www.mtishows.com

Rodgers and Hammerstein Theatre Library
229 W. 28th St., 11th Floor
New York, NY 10001
www.rnh.com

Samuel French, Inc.
45 W. 25th St.
New York, NY 10010
www.samuelfrench.com

Tams-Witmark Music Library
560 Lexington Ave.
New York, NY 10022
www.tams-witmark.com

About the Author

David P. DeVenney is professor of music and director of choral activities at West Chester University of Pennsylvania, where he directs the select Concert Choir and the Men's Chorus and teaches courses in conducting and music literature in addition to guiding the graduate program in choral studies. Dr. DeVenney is the author of numerous books on topics as varied as American choral music, opera, Broadway musicals, and American cultural studies, in addition to nearly sixty articles, a conducting textbook series, and many musical editions and compositions.